Personal Salvation
The Way to Peace and Eternal Life

James Malm

ISBN: **978-1-7753510-3-0**
Copyright 2018
All Rights Reserved

Dedication

This work is dedicated to the Great God whose house is eternity; the Father and Sovereign of all that exists and the sum of all Truth, Wisdom, Love, Justice and Mercy.
May God's house be filled with children whose chief joy is to be like Him!

Visit Our Website
theshininglight.info

Table of Contents

Introduction 5
Does God Exist? 7
Humanity Needs an Ultimate Moral Authority 14
The Test in the Garden 19
The Covenants 25
Law and Grace 45
True Godly Love 62
Colossians 2: The Ordinances Against Us 76
The Letter and the Spirit of the Law 81
Discerning Between the Holy and the Profane 88
The Way to Peace and Eternal Life 107
God's Calling 111
Belief and Faith 121
Repentance 126
Baptism and Commitment 132
The Lamb of God Sacrificed for Humanity 157
Perseverance and Overcoming 187
The Resurrection 206
The Holy Spirit 213

Introduction

Everything written in the scriptures from Genesis to Revelation was written for our instruction to teach us the way to eternal life in peace with God and humanity.

Romans 15:4 For whatsoever things were written aforetime were written for our learning, that we through patience and comfort of the scriptures might have hope.

2 Timothy 3:16 All scripture is given by inspiration of God, and is profitable for doctrine, for reproof, for correction, for instruction in righteousness: 3:17 That the man of God may be perfect, throughly furnished unto all good works

1 Corinthians 10:1 Moreover, brethren, I would not that ye should be ignorant, how that all our fathers were under the cloud, and all passed through the sea; **10:2** And were all baptized unto Moses in the cloud and in the sea; **10:3** And did all eat the same spiritual meat; **10:4** And did all drink the same spiritual drink: for they drank of that spiritual Rock that followed them: and **that Rock was Christ**. **10:5** But with many of them God was not well pleased: for they were overthrown in the wilderness.

10:6 Now **these things were our examples**, to the intent we should not lust after evil things, as they also lusted.

10:7 Neither be ye idolaters, as were some of them; as it is written, The people sat down to eat and drink, and rose up to play. **10:8** Neither let us commit fornication, as some of them committed, and fell in one day three and twenty thousand.

10:9 Neither let us tempt Christ, as some of them also tempted, and were destroyed of serpents. **10:10** Neither murmur ye, as some of them also murmured, and were destroyed of the destroyer.

10:11 Now **all these things happened unto them for ensamples: and they are written for our admonition, upon whom the ends of the world are come.** **10:12** Wherefore let him that thinketh he standeth take heed lest he fall.

All of recorded scripture from Genesis to Revelation is the complete Word of God and is intended as instruction for humanity, to teach us to loath wickedness and to love and embrace the righteousness of godliness, which brings us the peace and secure prosperity that mankind longs for.

Jesus [Hebrew: Yeshua] taught that men are to live by every Word of God

Matthew 4:3 And when the tempter [Satan] came to him, he said, If thou be the Son of God, command that these stones be made bread. **4:4** But he answered and said, It is written, **Man shall not live by bread alone, but by every word that proceedeth out of the mouth of God.**

Which God did Jesus know and refer to? The very King of the universe, God the Father in heaven!

4:5 Then the devil taketh him up into the holy city, and setteth him on a pinnacle of the temple, **4:6** And saith unto him, If thou be the Son of God, cast thyself down: for it is written, He shall give his angels charge concerning thee: and in their hands they shall bear thee up, lest at any time thou dash thy foot against a stone. **4:7** Jesus said unto him, It is written again, **Thou shalt not tempt the Lord thy God.**

4:8 Again, the devil taketh him up into an exceeding high mountain, and sheweth him all the kingdoms of the world, and the glory of them; **4:9** And saith unto him, All these things will I give thee, if thou wilt fall down and worship me. **4:10** Then saith Jesus unto him, **Get thee hence, Satan: for it is written, Thou shalt worship the Lord thy God, and him only shalt thou serve.**

Does God Exist?

Aristotle, Philosophy and Logic

Alexander the great conquered the Middle East from Greece to India from 336 to 323 B.C.

Alexander was tutored by Aristotle who in turn had been taught by Plato, and as he conquered, Alexander spread the concepts of Plato and Aristotle's logic far and wide. Since that time the logic of Plato and Aristotle took deep root in the Western World and over time both the Rabbins and the professing Christians in Rome applied the logic of Aristotle to the Holy Scriptures, interpreting the scriptures through human reasoning in place of taking the Holy Scriptures literally.

When examining an argument ALWAYS first address the basic premise on which the logic is based.

All logic whether good or bad is based on a foundational premise: If the premise is true and the logic is faultless then the conclusions will be true, however if the premise is false even the most perfect logic will be wrong.

An example of this is the claim by the proponents of evolution that "the natural selection of the peppered moth is an evolutionary instance of color variation in the moth population as a consequence of the Industrial Revolution. The concept refers to an increase in the number of dark-colored moths due to industrial pollution, and a reciprocal decrease in the population in a clean environment."

During the industrial revolution in Britain because of soot darkening the vegetation the dark colored peppered moths began to dominate as the white moths began to die out.

If this is truly an example of evolution, the white moths would have had to evolve darker to cope with the environment. Did this happen or did BOTH the light and dark colored moths already exist at the beginning of that period?

In fact both the light colored and dark colored moths already existed and because the light colored ones began to stand out on the darker vegetation while the darker ones were well hidden, predators concentrated on the lighter colored moths. There was absolutely NO evolution at all!

Instead of evolving, the lighter colored moths died out; which does not prove evolution but to the contrary tends to prove that evolution is not true at all.

This spurious argument is an example of twisting a fact, to falsely appear to support the preconceived premise.

Another example of assumptions is the Coelacanth, a fish previously declared to have become extinct some 65,000,000 years ago. It is said that fossils of this fish have been found which are claimed to be 400,000,000 years old. Since that unsupported claim, these fish have been found ALIVE, near Indonesia and Australia. Evolutionists call this fish "a living fossil" sure proof of evolution. In this they are clearly showing their bias and predisposition to believe what they want.

Today's fish is completely identical to its fossils; there is absolutely NO DIFFERENCE between this fish and it's fossils: Where is the evolution? There has been NO evolution whatsoever over the claimed 400,000,000 years! Yet they falsely claim that this is proof of evolution!

By starting with the assumed premise that evolution is true, they reach a false conclusion.

In the search for truth one must put all the facts together, without twisting the facts to appear to support a preconceived premise; when in reality they actually disprove that preconceived premise.

Evolution is faith based fantasy which depends on deception as in the above examples

I Exist Therefore God Exists

René Descartes (1596-1650 A.D.) is today considered the father of modern philosophy, but he was himself a champion of the logic of Aristotle and Plato. Lecturers in philosophy courses are fond of quoting Descartes "I think therefore I exist" statement as a starting point for their Aristotelian logic.

This premise is sound, but then they use the logic of Aristotle to focus on humanity while ignoring this premise in relation to the existence of God. If Descartes premise that "I think therefore I exist" is sound; then the premise that "I exist therefore God exists" is also sound!

The existence of thought itself, the existence of man and the existence of all things; is proof of the existence of God! Let us put our premise and logic to the test.

Where Did You Come From?

We all have a biological father and mother; because two fully functional persons coming together; are necessary to make a new human being. **Genesis 1:27** . . . male and female created he them. All the higher animals were created male and female and one fully functional and fertile example of each sex must meet together with the same idea to produce offspring.

That is reality my friends, the female cannot exist without the male, and the male cannot exist without the female, because the species cannot be reproduced without BOTH being present.

Why do you think that evolutionists have spent generations brainwashing our children that it is impossible to answer the question "which came first the chicken or the egg" when the answer is so glaringly obvious; The chicken came first because it takes TWO, a male and a female [a rooster and a hen] to produce a fertile egg! The same is true of an elephant, or a buffalo or a human being.

Evolution is impossible, because reproduction and the continuation of species is impossible. Without both sexes being fully formed, fully functional and present together in the same place at the same time.

When Did Life Begin?

Many have said that life begins with the first drawn breath, while others claim that life begins at a certain number of weeks after egg fertilization; when does life really begin.

Through history there have been many childless women because either the husband of the wife is infertile or the wife is infertile. To procreate it is not enough to have a male and a female come together; they must both be fertile.

One may bathe all the eggs one wants in dead sperm and none of them will be fertilized and produce a child; on the other side one may bathe a dead egg in trillions of live sperm and that egg will never be fertilized to produce a child. What does this mean?

It means that both the sperm from the male and the egg from the female must already have life in them. It means that humanity had life given to both men and women at some point and they have passed on that already existing life in themselves to their offspring!

Life does not begin at birth or at conception, human life began with the first man, and has been passed on by the first man and woman down from generation to generation ever since!

The egg has the life of the woman when it is produced by the woman, and the sperm has the life of the man when it is produces by the man; and then when a sperm fertilizes an egg the life of both the woman and the man are joined together to form a new human being.

The eggs or sperm which do not join together are discarded as cells of the owner as one discards clipped hair or nails, but once combined they form a completely new human being who will never again be duplicated precisely [except for a certain type of twins formed from the same egg and sperm].

Mankind and all higher animals were created male and female, both sexes being created complete, fully formed, fully fertile and fully functional at the same time; and then life was placed in them: which same life has continued from generation to generation from the very beginning of their creation.

The existence of humanity proves the existence of God.

Evolution

The hypothesis of evolution requires vast eons of time to make it appear credible, so vast ages are assigned to various fossils and to the earth itself. There is NO scientific way to measure such vast ages of time! Carbon 14 is based on assumptions and when assumptions enter, true science leaves.

The assumption that the amount of radiation striking the earth to form carbon 14 is a constant, is well known to be false. The amount of radiation striking the earth is strongly influenced by solar activity, the distance to the sun and the strength of the earth's magnetic field. After three half-lives of about 15,000 total years, there is not enough carbon 14 to even be measured! How can you get millions of years from that? You can't!

Other dating methods like potassium argon are even LESS reliable. Material from Hawaii known to be 200 years old was dated as many millions of years old by this method. In addition to the assumptions on dating, evolution breaks every known applicable law of science, including the law of Biogenesis which I went into when discussing male and female.

The difference between an ape skull and a human skull. An ape skull has a brow ridge across the face just above the eyes, a human skull does not. If a skull has a brow ridge it is an ape and if it does not it is human.

No intermediate species has ever been found for any creature, if evolution were true there would have to be more intermediate species fossils for earth's many millions of creatures than there are atoms in the universe, NONE have ever been found.

Many people do not know that evolution is a very ancient philosophy espoused by the Epicureans of ancient Greece and put forward by Epictetus if not much earlier. In thousands of years, not enough evidence has been found to even justify giving this hypothesis, the dignity of the title, theory!

Evolution is an error which along with atheism and all false religions will soon be discarded on the trash heap of history!

The Evil of Religion

Many have looked at this world seeing that many of its horrors are perpetrated in the name of a God or religion, and they see the incredible evils that religion has brought and make the mistake of blaming God for those evils.

In reality, God's Word and ways bring peace, prosperity and life, if only people would live by them; while the obvious evils perpetrated in the name of God are not godly at all and are a departure from the Word of God.

Many religions of man do not accept the Word of God and instead rely directly on the philosophies and traditions of men, many of them very well meaning men. In a similar way most of today's Rabbins and professing Christians hold to the false premise that the Holy Scriptures are to be interpreted by the logic and traditions of men and are not meant to be literal. Then using human logic they replace the truth of God - which brings peace and life - with the traditions of men, causing much suffering because man simply does not know the way to peace apart from the wisdom of God.

Men pay lip-service to God but make the Word of God of no effect through their reasoning's, as to why God's Word does not mean what it says.

Matthew 15:8 This people draweth nigh unto me with their mouth, and honoureth me with their lips; but their heart is far from me. **15:9** But in vain they do worship me, teaching for doctrines the commandments of men.

These men professing to be godly misuse Isaiah's "here a little, there a little" instruction to search for scriptures appearing to support their preconceived conclusions instead of putting ALL the scriptures on a given subject together as Isaiah had intended.

One can make any book mean anything, if one takes lines or words out of their proper context and selects only those words that appear to support a preconceived idea, it is only by putting all scriptures together on a particular subject that a truth can be found and understood.

In truth it is those religions which do not adhere to every Word of God and attempt to interpret the Word of God according to the false traditions and reasoning's of men that have brought such sorrow on this world.

When men do things their own way and not God's way, even well intentioned men; the end of the matter is much sorrow and death, because man just does not have the wisdom of God.

Yes, God exists and we can rejoice in that truth, because it brings hope!

Many intelligent people when they age and the pleasures of self-indulgent youth fade, ask themselves "Is this all there is." When the vigor of youth and self-gratification has run its course and we get older, finally realizing that our life is almost over, the only meaningful question is "Is this all there is?"

Those who live by every Word of God will avoid many of the sorrows of sin in this life and they can stand on the sure promises of God. They have HOPE in God and His promises that God will raise his faithful up from death to eternal life in a far, far, better world.

Humanity Needs an Ultimate Moral Authority

Since the beginning of recorded history the annals of humanity have been written in blood.

Since the day that Cain slew Abel people have striven against each other and as nations arose, nation has striven against nation. The strong have dominated and pillaged the weak and the oppressed have attempted to rise up and throw off their yoke, while the strong saw the possession of the weak as their right and fought one another to maintain their "possessions".

Violence has not been limited to nations and every society on the earth has been filled with murders, robbery and the abuse of people by others.

Man has also done great violence to the very earth itself, creating deserts out of lush grasslands and in more recent times poisoning the air, water and soil in the selfish pursuit of perceived immediate personal gain.

North Africa a vast rich grassland and the breadbasket of Europe before the first century, has been devastated and turned into the ever expanding Sahara desert, today growing southward at the rate of miles each year.

Today the world suffers from mainly man created famines and drought, while millions suffer from environmental diseases like cancer and diabetes due to the poisoning of the water and air of the earth, and the greedy production of massively, sugar, salt and chemical laden food and drink.

Humanity is now at the precipice of catastrophe - with the very seas themselves dying - after vast numbers of human beings have died at the hands of their fellow man over the nightmare of past millennia.

Throughout human history various leaders have tried to solve these problems by establishing empires to try and force peace on the nations: for their own advantage of course. One example is the Pax Romana of the Roman Empire which brought a semblance of peace to Europe through Rome.

From the very beginning all attempted empires had to deal with the unhappiness and tendency to rebel of subject peoples.

A subject people will from time to time produce a few who will regard even death as preferable to the situation they are in, and who will rise up in an attempt to throw off their oppressors. This leaves empires rushing from place to place putting out the political fires of resistance.

The solution as Babylon discovered and Rome discovered after her, was religion.

A subject people might not fear physical death, but if they could be made to believe that they were rebelling against a god - who had power over eternity to give eternal joy and pleasure or eternal death or pain - they would be willing to endure anything and would never rise up for fear of eternal death or suffering.

Convincing people to sincerely and deeply believe that rejecting the authority of a man was rejecting God and brought damnation; was REAL POWER indeed!

To gain this supposed authority of a god, from Babel to Paul many emperors simply declared themselves to be gods. This was easy because after all, every nation had many gods and the emperor would be just one more god among many.

Then along came Paul to the Roman world and turned that world upside down, teaching that there was only ONE God and that the emperor was NOT a god at all!

It was many years later that these folks found a way to subvert this teaching about God, by admitting that the emperor was not God, but then claiming that the emperor was God's choice to rule the empire and because he was God's anointed, rebellion against him was the same as rebellion against God; and the Holy Roman Empire began.

This system worked by using a religious leader claiming to be God's representative on earth and "God's decider on the earth in the absence of God's presence in the earth", with Ultimate Moral Authority over the lives of the people and the moral authority behind the emperor. To rebel against the emperor was to rebel against the pope, and to rebel against the pope was to rebel against God.

Today, many religious leaders have also adopted this error by claiming that they are ultimate moral authorities over their various corporate Ekklesia organizations and demanding that they be obeyed as if they were God, by claiming to be the agents of God

The big problem arises when the religious leaders decide right and wrong for themselves and do not live by every Word of God, but exalt themselves to accept or reject parts of God's Word according to their own judgment.

Most will also take small pieces of truth out of their proper context and spin them to appear to mean something far different from what they really meant in their proper context, in an effort to support their own preconceived ideas; this includes taking one scripture and ignoring other scriptures on the same subject.

When the empire or corporate church demands that the human leader be followed without question, claiming that he is an agent of God; that organization may be united in following the man, but they have fallen into idolatry of exalting the man, the system and the organization above the Word of God and they are in rebellion against God.

As long as nations, groups of people or even individuals, do what they decide for themselves is right instead of living by the Word and Way that truly brings peace, the earth will be filled with violence; and eventually humanity and life on this planet is doomed to complete destruction.

> **To have world peace:** Humanity NEEDS a single Ultimate Moral Authority - a Father Figure - a God; who will be universally accepted, looked to and obeyed by all people; and humanity NEEDS a change in the selfish nature of mankind.

However not just any moral authority or god will do: This Ultimate Moral Authority - Father Figure - God; must have a Wisdom surpassing all the wisdom of men, He must have a totally selfless love for ALL people and exercise His power; Honestly, Fairly and Justly for the good of all!

The Creator God made mankind and because the Creator God is the Father of all humanity He has the right to rule all humanity; by right of Creatorship and Fatherhood. God also has the further right to rule as the Ultimate Moral Authority of humanity by virtue of vastly superior experience, knowledge, intellect, power and wisdom.

Genesis 1:1 In the beginning God [Hebrew: Elohim (plural meaning Mighty Ones)] created the heaven and the earth.

We know that before God created the physical universe, God had created the angels composed of spirit; because no man had yet been created at the beginning of the universe and yet the Son's of God shouted for joy at that event.

Job 38:5 Who hath laid the measures thereof, if thou knowest? or who hath stretched the line upon it? **38:6** Whereupon are the foundations thereof fastened? or who laid the corner stone thereof; **38:7 When the morning stars [angels] sang together, and all the sons of God [angels] shouted for joy?**

First, God created spiritual beings and then God directed billions of spirit beings in the creation of the physical universe.

Consider the experience level and wisdom of a God who has lived for countless eons, and the Intellect, Wisdom and Knowledge of a being that could create spirit beings much greater than man and then create the entire physical universe. Consider the Management Skills of a God who could oversee billions of angels.

Consider the wisdom of a being who could make all things as we know them on this planet and in the universe.

Then consider the marvelous wonder that is mankind, with his thinking and creative capacity and the simple fact that the Creator of all these awesome things - which man does not yet understand - is far greater than that which He created.

God the Father as the Executive Creating Authority of the universe and therefore owns the entire universe; God the Father is King of the Universe by right of creation! God the Son, who gave up his God-hood to become

Jesus Christ, was the Implementing Creator of all things, fulfilling the plan and will of God the Father.

God the Father has trillions of years more experience, vastly more knowledge and infinitely more wisdom than any man or all men put together.

While man tries to figure out the universe, Almighty God understood its workings and actually created it.

Can man even take proper care of this earth to dress it and keep it as God commanded us? Can men even get along together? Human history gives us the answer: Which is a resounding NO!

What is the wisdom of man compared to the Wisdom of God? Man needs God as a babe needs its parents!

The Test in the Garden

In Genesis 3 God gave a command to test the man and the woman to see if they would be faithful to their Maker or if they will follow another or decide right and wrong for themselves.

Satan the Adversary of God is allowed to appear on the scene to test the human couple and begins to entice the woman by bringing up the subject of the forbidden fruit.

Notice very carefully here: God did not say that the fruit would kill; he said that the act of eating the fruit would kill; for the wages of sin [living contrary to the way that brings life] is death.

The nature of this fruit had nothing to do with the issue.

Which issue is: Will we live by and keep the Word of God our Father, or will we decide for ourselves what is good or evil, without the knowledge, experience and wisdom of God?

Since that day, mankind has rejected living by the Word of God for millennia. The "wisdom" of man has destroyed the planet and brought endless bloodshed, pain and misery on humanity and all other creatures.

WE NEED GOD! Like any young child needs its parents!

Like a little child we may think that we are able, but we simply lack the experience, the wisdom, and the ability to take care of ourselves and properly care for this good earth which God has given to us.

WE NEED A FATHER to lead and guide us and teach us how to live and how to get along with each other.

Eve and Adam thought that they could decide things for themselves and so rejected their Father Creator.

All history since then has been a bloody and graphic demonstration of how wrong they were. Mankind cannot find the way to peace or life eternal.

We cannot discern between right and wrong on our own, we need HELP, we need someone to show us the way. Only when all peoples realize this and are ready to humble themselves before their Creator will they begin to follow His instructions leading to peace.

Any departure from what God has commanded us is a rejection of the wisdom of God

Eating a fruit that God forbade them to eat, was not simply about the fruit itself; it was about rejecting obedience to God, by not doing what God has said.

In the garden Eve and then Adam turned away from obeying their Creator to decide right and wrong for themselves, rejecting the Word of their Creator!

Ever since that time, the vast majority have rejected the Word of God to remain faithful to their idols of men and their false contrary to scripture traditions! Even those who pay lip-service to the Word of God take lines out of context and twist them to fit their own misguided opinions.

Genesis 3:1 Now the serpent was more subtil than any beast of the field which the LORD God had made. And he said unto the woman, Yea, hath God said, Ye shall not eat of every tree of the garden?

3:2 And the woman said unto the serpent, We may eat of the fruit of the trees of the garden: **3:3** But of the fruit of the tree which is in the midst of the garden, God hath said, Ye shall not eat of it, neither shall ye touch it, lest ye die.

Then Satan told the woman the lie that she would not die if she rejected the Word of God, to decide right and wrong for herself!

3:4 And the serpent said unto the woman, Ye shall not surely die: **3:5** For God doth know that in the day ye eat thereof, then your eyes shall be opened, and ye shall be as gods, knowing good and evil.

God said; listen to me and do what I say, for I made you and love you; and Satan said, decide for yourself and do whatever you want to do.

Deciding for ourselves always looks good to those who have no love for the Word of God. Most love self, more than they love God, and because of this self-love and self-exaltation and pride, we are led away from our zeal to live by every Word of God as Eve was.

Then Eve and Adam chose to reject the instructions of their Creator and to decide right and wrong for themselves.

This issue was a TEST of obedience and had nothing to do with the kind of fruit being referred to.

3:6 And when the woman saw that the tree was good for food, and that it was pleasant to the eyes, and a tree to be desired to make one wise [thinking it was wise to decide the matter for herself instead of obeying God], she took of the fruit thereof, and did eat, and gave also unto her husband with her; and he did eat.

Then instead of running to God in sincere repentance, they tried to cover up for themselves.

The following is literal and is also figurative, for they knew that they were physically and spiritually naked; no longer clothed with the righteousness of obeying God.

Eve and Adam were not ashamed of seeing each other naked; most men and women are comfortable seeing the nakedness of their spouse. They were already one flesh and "knew" one another fully.

This nakedness was not about any shame of being naked in front of one another; it was about being ashamed of themselves and being naked of righteousness before God.

Adam and Eve were afraid of being seen by God, for they knew that they had sinned and disobeyed him. They were moved to try and hide their physical and spiritual nakedness by making clothing and hiding in the bush.

3:7 And the eyes of them both were opened, and they knew that they were naked; and they sewed fig leaves together, and made themselves aprons.

The Creator came to see his creation; and they hid from him, because their sin had separated them from God. They had rebelled and decided for themselves what would be right or wrong in their own eyes; in place of obeying their Creator.

Isaiah 59:1 Behold, the Lord's hand is not shortened, that it cannot save; neither his ear heavy, that it cannot hear: **59:2** But **your iniquities have separated between you and your God, and your sins have hid his face from you, that he will not hear.**

Consider, when we were all little children, didn't most of us at some time do something that we knew our parents had forbidden or taught us was wrong? Were we afraid that our parents would find out and correct us?

Adam and Eve, although fully adult were full of that same fear of correction, because they knew that they had acted against the Word of their Creator.

3:8 And they heard the voice of the LORD God walking in the garden in the cool of the day: and Adam and his wife hid themselves from the presence of the LORD God amongst the trees of the garden.

Adam knew that he was naked of faithfulness to keep the Word of God and did not have on the garments of the righteousness of God. He feared the anger of his Creator because of his sin.

3:9 And the LORD God called unto Adam, and said unto him, Where art thou? **3:10** And he said, I heard thy voice in the garden, and I was afraid, because I was naked; and I hid myself.

Such is human nature. Adam blamed his wife instead of taking responsibility for his own actions.

There are very many out there who will feel safe in justifying themselves with the Nazi excuse that "I was only following orders" or blaming some organization, or religion, or its elders for their own sins, like Eve did in blaming Satan and Adam did in blaming Eve. "I was only following this person" they will say.

Brethren, this Nazi excuse that we were only following others; WILL NOT WORK WITH Almighty God! Each and every human being is completely responsible for their OWN conduct; regardless of what others say or do.

It did not work for Adam, and it will not work for anyone else: We shall each be accepted into or denied entry into the paradise of eternal life based on our OWN personal conduct.

Revelation 20:12 And I saw the dead, small and great, stand before God; and the books were opened: and another book was opened, which is the book of life: and **the dead were judged out of those things which were written in the books, according to their** [own] **works. 20:13** And the sea gave up the dead which were in it; and death and hell delivered up the dead which were in them: and **they were judged every man according to their** [own] **works.**

Adam admitted that he had sinned and disobeyed God and blamed another.

Genesis 3:11 And he said, Who told thee that thou wast naked? Hast thou eaten of the tree, whereof I commanded thee that thou shouldest not eat? **3:12** And the man said, The woman whom thou gavest to be with me, she gave me of the tree, and I did eat.

Eve admitted that she had sinned and disobeyed God and blamed Satan and it is true that Satan tempted her, but she was still responsible to obey God regardless of the temptation. Both the woman and the man were personally responsible for listening to the temptation and deciding for themselves to disobey the Word of God.

So it is with us today, when people fall to the temptation to follow idols of men and turn away from living by every Word of God; they are still personally responsible before God!

3:13 And the LORD God said unto the woman, What is this that thou hast done? And the woman said, The serpent beguiled me, and I did eat.

Every person is responsible for their own conduct, yet there is also a very heavy responsibility of guilt for the original deceiver as well. Because of this Satan was cursed and our elders and leaders who teach people to follow themselves and to turn away from any zeal to live by every Word of God are facing a most severe correction.

Because they use their office to deceive and have not fulfilled their responsibility to teach zeal to live by every Word of God, they will be rejected from being shepherds of God's flock; and they will be rejected from the resurrection to eternal life, unless they quickly repent. (Ezek 34, Jer 25, Isaiah 56:11)

3:14 And the LORD God said unto the serpent, Because thou hast done this, thou art cursed above all cattle, and above every beast of the field; upon thy belly shalt thou go, and dust shalt thou eat all the days of thy life:

The spiritual serpent [dragon] shall bruise a man [Satan would crucify Christ] and then Satan shall be destroyed by the Son of a woman, even Jesus Christ, after the Millennium.

3:15 And I will put enmity between thee and the woman, and between thy seed and her seed; it shall bruise thy head [A son of a woman (Messiah the Christ) shall destroy Satan after the millennium, but first Satan shall temporarily bruise Messiah the woman's seed, by killing Christ who will not remain dead], and thou shalt bruise his heel.

Because of her sin the woman was given the monthly cycle and pain in childbirth which no animal has, and Christ here set the man to rule [to learn to rule responsibly and lovingly] over his wife.

3:16 Unto the woman he said, I will greatly multiply thy sorrow and thy conception; in sorrow thou shalt bring forth children; and **thy desire shall be to thy husband, and he shall rule over thee.**

Adam is judged for letting the woman lead him away from keeping the Word of God; and we shall all be judged for listening to anyone other than our Mighty God!

3:17 And unto Adam he said, Because thou hast hearkened unto the voice of thy wife, and hast eaten of the tree, of which I commanded thee, saying, Thou shalt not eat of it:

Because the man and woman listened to and followed others, rather than the Eternal God, the man and woman were then cast out of paradise and made to struggle against all manner of adversity, that they might learn to keep the whole Word of God.

Adam and his descendants are being forced to learn the difference between godliness, which brings peace and life: and deciding for themselves what is right and wrong, which self-will brings all manner of adversity, suffering, decay and finally death.

Satan lied saying that man could become God, simply by deciding right and wrong for himself.

The Covenants

When we marry, the bride commits to obey her husband and the husband commits to care for, provide for and love his wife; that is the marriage covenant.

There is no list of the husband's wishes in the Marriage Covenant; exactly what the husband wants is not part of the actual Marriage Covenant.

Physical Israel committed to obey God at Sinai first, which was the Mosaic marriage Covenant; later God as the Husband laid out what he expected from Israel his bride.

The covenant of obedience is that we must live by every Word of God, the laws that God gave through Moses were not part of that Covenant, they were the things that God wanted done; while the Covenant itself was a commitment to do anything and everything that God wanted done.

The sacrificial system was instituted as soon as Adam sinned in the garden, and later Cain slew Abel over his own unacceptable sacrifice for his sins.

The Sabbath was established at creation and Israel was told to REMEMBER the Sabbath which had been forgotten in Egypt. The law of clean and unclean was known from creation since only clean animals may be sacrificed and later God commanded Noah to take seven pairs of clean animals and only one pair of each unclean animal aboard the ark (Gen 7:2) showing that the concept of clean and unclean was well understood long before Moses.

All people on the earth except eight souls were destroyed for sin, and since if the law did not exist no sin could be imputed to those people; the law did indeed exist because the people were destroyed for their sins!

The same thing can be said about Sodom, they were destroyed for their sin, the existence of the sin being proof of the existence of the law: Long BEFORE Moses and Sinai.

God kept Abimelech king of Gerar (Genesis 20) from doing what? From sinning by taking Sarah! God kept Joseph from sinning with Potiphar's wife. The existence of the sin proves the existence of a law against those deeds: Long BEFORE Sinai and Moses!

God's law was not some new thing instituted at Sinai, God's Law existed from creation and was first broken in the flesh by Adam and Eve.

The law defines both sin and righteousness [which is the keeping of the whole Word of God]:

The law and sin existed from Adam until Moses. We know this because Noah, Abraham, Able and others obeyed God BEFORE Moses!

At Sinai Physical Israel committed to obey and to live by every Word of God; then God gave the same law that had always existed to his bride; with certain additions to help them to keep his law; like further details of the Sacrificial System, an organized physical priest hood to instruct the people and the annual Festivals to come before God and be reminded of God's law.

Marriage as an allegory of the relationship God wants with mankind

In the garden God gave authority over the family to the man - the husband - and commanded the woman to submit to her husband:

Genesis 3:16 Unto the woman he said, I will greatly multiply thy sorrow and thy conception; in sorrow thou shalt bring forth children; and **thy desire shall be to thy husband, and he shall rule over thee.**

This was not done on some whim by God, but was to be a physical instructional allegory of the spiritual relationship God desired with humanity. Long after mankind was expelled from the garden; God called physical Israel out of bondage in Egypt and established a Marriage Covenant with Israel at Sinai.

The Marriage Covenant

When a man and woman marry, they agree that he will take care of and love her and that she will love and obey him. We call this our marriage vows. At the marriage, we do not spell out everything that we desire, because the agreement to love, care for and obey covers all else.

Even so, the marriage covenant between Christ and Israel was about the obedience of Israel and the blessings of God. The law of God was the expression of God's will, His expectations of His new wife.

What He expected of His wife in the past, God will also expect of His wife in future, for, I change not, saith the Eternal (Mal 3:6). If we desire to be a part of His collective bride; we must fulfill our obligations as a wife and seek to please and obey our spiritual Husband; Doing His will and living by His Word!

The covenant, whether old or new, is not a detailed list of things that we agree to do. It is an agreement to do EVERYTHING that our Lord may require. It is a marriage agreement to obey our husband in ALL things.

The law is the list of the things that our Lord requires of us. Since the Eternal does NOT CHANGE (Mal 3:6), and Jesus Christ is the same yesterday, today and forever (Heb 13:8), He will expect and require of us, the same things that He has ALWAYS required of His people.

When Christ died, it was the Marriage Agreement, that the Eternal would be their God and that physical Israel would be His people, which ended; but God's law did not end because it had existed before the marriage and continues to exist after the marriage.

The desire of God for a faithful, obedient, loving, caring wife, did not end. God's nature, as revealed in His Word did not end. God's will, as expressed by His Word, did not end. NOTHING about God changed, only His relationship with physical Israel changed!

NOTHING about God's commandments changed. NOTHING was done away. Even the sacrificial system was not done away! It was FULFILLED BY CHRIST! He was the perfect and complete sacrifice, ALL other sacrifices were merely prophetic shadows of His TRIUMPH. Being perfect and complete, he need never die again. Yet, we weak persons still sin, so that perfect sacrifice needs to be constantly re applied.

Christ's sacrifice, only applies to sins committed before our sincere repentance, it could never be applied in advance, for this would be a true license to sin. His sacrifice could only be applied to PAST sins sincerely repented of and cannot be applied to anticipated future sin. However each time sin is committed and sincerely repented of (Acts 2:38, Luk 3:3) Christ applies His sacrifice, atoning for us.

If the law of sacrifice were done away, there would no longer be a legal framework, for the atonement of today's sins; for the application of the sacrifice of Christ sacrifice today!! Christ's sacrifice has fulfilled the entire law of sacrifice and it is that law that allows for atonement for ALL REPENTANT SINNERS. That is why the law of sacrifice is hated and despised by Satan and his world!

This Mosaic Covenant between Israel and God - which was mediated by Moses - was a Marriage Covenant, in which God as the Husband promised to protect, provide for and bless Israel his bride; as long as the bride was faithful to live by every Word of Her Husband.

Speaking to Judah God said: Jeremiah 3:14 Turn, O backsliding children, saith the Lord; for **I am married unto you**: and I will take you one of a city, and two of a family, and I will bring you to Zion:

Later speaking of the Mosaic Covenant of marriage which Israel did not keep, God told the prophet: **Jeremiah 31:32** Not according to the covenant that I made with their fathers in the day that I took them by the hand to bring them out of the land of Egypt; which my covenant they brake, **although I was an husband unto them,** saith the Lord:

Throughout the history of Israel and Judah they are referred to as an adulterous wife whenever they went astray after other gods; and those who were faithful to God are likened to a faithful virgin.

In the Mosaic Covenant Israel was married to God, as an example that the New Covenant faithful will also become married to God; and a wife is commanded by God to obey her husband [in the LORD, always putting God first].

The Mosaic Covenant was a marriage agreement between God and the descendants of Jacob (Jer 3:14, Isaiah 54:5).

The Mosaic Covenant was a marriage covenant: **Isaiah 54:5:** For **thy Maker** [The Creator] **is thine husband**; the LORD of hosts is his name;

and thy Redeemer the Holy One of Israel; The God of the whole earth shall he be called.

Like all marriages, this Marriage Covenant would remain only until the death of one of the parties (Rom 7:2-3).

The Being who became Jesus Christ was the God Family personage who married Israel (1 Cor 10:4). All things were created by Jesus Christ (Eph 3:9). He was later made flesh and dwelt among men (Joh 1:14), giving up the glory that He had with God the Father before the world began (Joh 17:5).

THEN HE DIED, thus ending the marriage covenant with Israel!

Today the Mosaic Marriage Covenant has been annulled by the death of one of the parties. It no longer exists. Neither Israel nor Judah are in a Mosaic Covenant of marriage with God any longer; because the Mosaic Marriage Covenant ended with the death of the Husband!

The Mosaic Marriage Covenant

The Mosaic Marriage Covenant between physical Israel and God was an instructional example that a spiritual New Covenant of Marriage was still to come

On the fifteenth day of the third month after the spring New Year and the exodus from Egypt, Israel arrived at Sinai and was married to God.

Exodus 19:1 In the **third month,** when the children of Israel were gone forth out of the land of Egypt, **the same day** came they into the wilderness of Sinai. **19:2** For they were departed from Rephidim, and were come to the desert of Sinai, and had pitched in the wilderness; and there Israel camped before the mount [Sinai].

There the Marriage Covenant took place between Israel and the Eternal; with God and physical Israel; binding themselves together in a Marriage Covenant.

19:3 And Moses went up unto God, and the LORD called unto him out of the mountain, saying, **Thus shalt thou say to the house of Jacob, and tell the children of Israel; 19:4** Ye have seen what I did unto the Egyptians, and how I bare you on eagles' wings, and brought you unto myself. **19:5** Now therefore, **if ye will obey my voice indeed, and keep my covenant, then ye shall be a peculiar treasure unto me above all people: for all the earth is mine: 19:6 And ye shall be unto me a kingdom of priests, and an holy nation.**

God commanded Moses to speak all these words to Israel, and Moses did so as an official might recite certain words at any marriage ceremony. In doing this Moses was the Marriage Intermediary [like today's presiding official in any marriage] arranging the marriage between God and Israel.

. . . These are the words which thou shalt speak unto the children of Israel. **19:7 And Moses came and called for the elders of the people, and laid before their faces all these words which the LORD commanded him.**

Then Israel responded to the words of the Creator and Deliverer, and entered into a Marriage Covenant with him.

All marriages are the same agreement; the husband vows to care for and love his wife, and the wife vows to love and obey her husband in all things, as God had commanded in Eden.

Spiritually this is precisely the same agreement that we make by being baptized today!

We agree to love God and to live by every Word of God, doing all that our espoused Husband says, and He agrees to fulfill the duties of a husband; and if we continue and are faithful in our spiritual espousal we will fully married at the resurrection.

When we compromise with the Word of God and pollute his Sabbaths; or idolize any man or organization above our love for our espoused Husband: Then we have BROKEN our baptismal marriage vows! We have become spiritual adulterers!

19:8 And all the people answered together, and said, All that the LORD hath spoken we will do. And Moses returned the words of the people unto the LORD.

Then after Israel agreed to enter the Mosaic Marriage Covenant with God, the Husband of Israel, to whom Israel had pledged obedience, THUNDERED his basic will from the mount to his collective bride!

The Eternal is the God who brought physical Israel out of bondage in Egypt, as an example that he would bring people out of spiritual bondage to Satan and sin; by giving up his God-hood and then giving up his very life for us as the Lamb of God!

Exodus 20:1 And God spake all these words, saying, 20:2 I am the LORD thy God, which have brought thee out of the land of Egypt, out of the house of bondage.

We are not to allow anything to come between us and God the Father and our Husband [who later gave up his Godhood to become flesh as Jesus Christ]; no, not even family members, or church organizations, or elders, or friends; nor money, nor any temptation to do any sin, nor are we to fear any threat against us!

We are to exalt God our Father above ALL others and we are to obey Him above ALL others!

We are never to follow any person contrary to the Word of God; we are to test every word of men by the Word of God and to obey God and not follow any man contrary to the Word of God (Mat 4:4, 1 Thess 5:21, Acts 17:10-11, Rev 2:2)

Deuteronomy 4:39 Know therefore this day, and consider it in thine heart, that the Lord he is God in heaven above, and upon the earth beneath: there is none else.

4:40 Thou shalt keep therefore his statutes, and his commandments, which I command thee this day, that it may go well with thee, and with thy children after thee, and that thou mayest prolong thy days upon the earth, which the Lord thy God giveth thee, for ever.

God as the Husband was to be obeyed by His wife, physical Israel: as an example for the coming New Covenant Spiritual Israel, that they are to obey God their Husband in all things!

Exodus 20:3 Thou shalt have no other gods before me.

To follow anyone other than our LORD would be spiritual ADULTERY against God our Husband

The Eternal is God and there is NO other God like HIM! We are to follow every Word of God and we are NOT to follow any man who strays from any part of the Word of God.

Jeremiah 10:6 Forasmuch as there is none like unto thee, O LORD; thou art great, and thy name is great in might. **10:7** Who would not fear thee, O King of nations? for to thee doth it appertain: forasmuch as among all the wise men of the nations, and in all their kingdoms, there is none like unto thee.

There is ONE Elohim [Family of Mighty Ones], Who is Mighty to Save; even Jesus Christ the Creator, and God the Father in heaven.

Jeremiah 10:10 But the LORD is the true God, he is the living God, and an everlasting king: at his wrath the earth shall tremble, and the nations shall not be able to abide his indignation.

Why will we not be zealous for the Awesome Creator who made all things, to whom we have committed ourselves in a baptism of espousal to follow ONLY him and God the Father? Why will we idolize men and follow them away from zeal for our Mighty One?

Jeremiah 10:12 He hath made the earth by his power, he hath established the world by his wisdom, and hath stretched out the heavens by his discretion. 10:13 When he uttereth his voice, there is a multitude of waters in the heavens, and he causeth the vapours to ascend from the ends of the earth; he maketh lightnings with rain, and bringeth forth the wind out of his treasures.

Why will we stand on our own ways, when we are as dumb beasts in comparison to him?

10:14 Every man is brutish in his knowledge:

Exodus 20:4 Thou shalt not make unto thee any graven image, or any likeness of any thing that is in heaven above, or that is in the earth beneath, or that is in the water under the earth. **20:5** Thou shalt not bow down thyself to them, nor serve them: for I the LORD thy God am a jealous God, visiting the iniquity of the fathers upon the children unto the third and fourth generation of them that hate me; **20:6** And shewing mercy unto thousands of them that love me, and keep my commandments.

Idolatry is not just bowing to statues and pictures, it is allowing anything to come between us and God, it is exalting anything above the Word of God, it is following any teaching contrary to the Word of God, it is following and obeying anyone other than our Husband!

The true spiritual Ekklesia are those who follow the Lamb of God and live by EVERY WORD of GOD (Mat 4:4), never turning to follow any other contrary to the Word of God.

God the Husband then continues to list what he requires from his wife:

20:7 Thou shalt not take the name of the LORD thy God in vain; for the LORD will not hold him guiltless that taketh his name in vain.

God says that a wife should love, stand by and respect him; not badmouth him!

20:8 Remember the sabbath day, to keep it holy. **20:9** Six days shalt thou labour, and do all thy work: **20:10** But the seventh day is the sabbath of the LORD thy God: **in it thou shalt not do any work, thou, nor thy son, nor thy daughter, thy manservant, nor thy maidservant, nor thy cattle, nor thy stranger that** [anyone that you are responsible for] **is within thy gates: 20:11** For in six days the LORD made heaven and earth, the sea, and all that in them is, and rested the seventh day: wherefore the LORD blessed the sabbath day, and hallowed it.

First and foremost we are to honour God our Father in heaven by enthusiastically learning and living by his every Word (Mat 4:4). We are to honour our physical parents [and the same is true of elders and church organizations] ONLY as they honour God our Father in heaven! Our spiritual Father is God the Father in heaven; and our spiritual mother is the heavenly New Jerusalem from which flows the Word of God and the Holy Spirit (Gal 4:26).

20:12 Honour thy father and thy mother: that thy days may be long upon the land which the LORD thy God giveth thee.

The word kill refers to murder, the shedding of innocent blood. Our authorities and governments are commanded to kill the wicked.

20:13 Thou shalt not kill.

Physical adultery is becoming one flesh with anyone other than our spouse, emotional adultery is loving any one other more than our spouse; and spiritual adultery against our God and spiritual Husband is following or obeying anyone contrary to the Word of God.

20:14 Thou shalt not commit adultery.

We are to take nothing which belongs to others and which we have no right to take; including the brethren the spouse of God, by seeking to make them followers of ourselves and our own ways.

20:15 Thou shalt not steal.

False witnessing can be outright lies, or it can be taking points out of context to make them seem to mean anything different or even the opposite of what they were intended to mean. It can be subtle twists of the truth to deceive. False witness means to be deceitful, to deceive about anything.

20:16 Thou shalt not bear false witness against thy neighbour.

Covet means to unlawfully desire. If you want something belonging to another then offer to buy it lawfully and if the answer is no, then give it up and do not dwell on your desire which has become unlawful.

Spiritually this refers to desiring to do anything contrary to the Word of God.

20:17 Thou shalt not covet thy neighbour's house, thou shalt not covet thy neighbour's wife, nor his manservant, nor his maidservant, nor his ox, nor his ass, nor any thing that is thy neighbour's.

Then the people saw the awesomeness of God and greatly feared.

Spiritually we are to love God and to respect Him so that we fear to offend Him by doing anything contrary to His Word.

20:18 And all the people saw the thunderings, and the lightnings, and the noise of the trumpet, and the mountain smoking: and when the people saw it, they removed, and stood afar off.

Then the people asked Moses to be a intercessor or mediator between them and God.

20:19 And they said unto Moses, Speak thou with us, and we will hear: but let not God speak with us, lest we die. **20:20** And Moses said unto the people, Fear not: for God is come to prove you, and that his fear may be before your faces, that ye [be impressed and obey God and] sin not.

An idol is ANYTHING that comes between us and God

Today this world is full of idols and the Ekklesia [brethren] is filled with idolizing men and corporate entities; which the brethren exalt above the Word of God!

Exodus 20:22 And the LORD said unto Moses, Thus thou shalt say unto the children of Israel, Ye have seen that I have talked with you from heaven. **20:23** Ye shall not make with me gods of silver, neither shall ye make unto you gods of gold.

The laws, statutes, precepts, ordinances and judgments of God, further explain how these ten commandments are to be kept.

God's judgments and statutes, many of which [such as divorce] were for a physical unconverted people, to maintain peace and order among a hardhearted people; fulfill the foundational principles of the ten commandments on which successful societies can be built.

The Ten Commandments represent the whole law gelled down to the very basic principles of the nature of God. The Statutes define the commandments a little further, by explaining how we should keep the commandments under various circumstances. The Statutes are also principles by which we may make other judgments; for example the issue of " if an ox gore a person" is directly applicable to us if our dog or any other [owned] animal attacks a person.

The foundations of a successful society are:

1. Security of our person from harm and security of our lives,
2. Security of our families,
3. Security of our property, and
4. Security of our livelihood, or ability to make a living.

All of which are preserved and defended by the commandments, statutes, precepts, ordinances and judgments contained in the Word of God

The Promise of a NEW COVENANT

Since physical Israel the bride could not obey God her Husband and kept wondering astray into the adultery of following others contrary to the Word of God; God promises to make a New Covenant with Israel, as it is written:

Jeremiah 31:31 Behold, the days come, saith the Lord, that **I will make a new covenant with the house of Israel, and with the house of Judah:**

31:32 Not according to the covenant that I made with their fathers in the day that I took them by the hand to bring them out of the land of Egypt; which my covenant they brake, although I was an husband unto them, saith the Lord:

31:33 But this shall be the covenant that I will make with the house of Israel; **After those days, saith the Lord, I will put my law in their inward parts, and write it in their hearts; and will be their God, and they shall be my people.**

31:34 And they shall teach no more every man his neighbour, and every man his brother, saying, Know the Lord: for they shall all know me, from the least of them unto the greatest of them, saith the Lord: for I will forgive their iniquity, and I will remember their sin no more.

In this New Covenant, sin may be repented of and a true efficacious atonement can come through the application of the sacrifice made by the Lamb of God, who was the very Creator God.

This sincere repentance and redemption by the sacrifice of the Lamb of God brings the enabling gift of the Holy Spirit to the sincerely repentant who commit to "go and sin no more"; which will empower us to be a faithful bride living by every Word of God our Husband.

Reconciling man with God

If we are sincerely repentant of all PAST sins and commit to sin no more, the sacrifice of Jesus Christ will be applied to us and then God the Father will then provide his Holy Spirit; and through that Spirit, write the laws and commandments - the Word of God - which reveals the very nature of God, on the hearts and in the minds of all sincerely repentant people; **empowering them to keep all of God's laws and commandments and empowering all sincerely repentant people to live by every Word of God; if they are willing to use God's Spirit and follow God.**

As physical Israel was the Mosaic Covenant People, the New Covenant people are a kind of spiritual Israel; therefore any faithful keeper of the New Covenant has been spiritually grafted into Israel and is an Israelite in spirit: If not in the racial sense; then most certainly in the spiritual sense.

For it is written that any stranger may be grafted into Israel by repentance and by accepting the covenant:

Exodus 12:48: And when a stranger shall sojourn with thee, and will keep the Passover [representative of the sacrifice of the spiritual Lamb of God] to the LORD, let all his males be circumcised [a token of repentance and sensitivity to obey God like baptism], and then let him come near and keep it; and he shall be as one that is born in the land: for no uncircumcised person shall eat thereof.

Circumcision of the flesh is an instructional allegory that we must become circumcised in heart in a New Covenant, to receive the promises of the New Covenant:

Deuteronomy 10: 16 Circumcise therefore the foreskin of your heart, and be no more stiff necked [stubborn and self-willed].

Therefore this New Covenant which was promised to Israel; is a covenant to spiritually empower Israel and all those spiritually grafted into

Israel, to KEEP ALL the COMMANDMENTS OF GOD and enable them to live by every Word of God.

When physical Israel enters the New Covenant she shall have a New marriage Covenant and be a widow no more.

Isaiah 54:4 Fear not; for thou shalt not be ashamed: neither be thou confounded; for thou shalt not be put to shame: for **thou shalt forget the shame of thy youth, and shalt not remember the reproach of thy widowhood any more**.

All physical Israel will yet enter into a spiritual New Covenant and all of humanity will then be grafted into that spiritual Israel: A New Covenant which has a truly efficacious atonement for sin, reconciling the sincerely repentant to God the Father; and providing the power of God's Holy Spirit, empowering us to OBEY GOD.

The Mosaic Covenant was an agreement to obey God, which the people broke and could not keep.

The New Covenant is an agreement to obey God; which men will be empowered to do; through an efficacious atonement for past sins repented of; and the indwelling of the Holy Spirit, the very nature of God.

At this time only a few have become the spiritual children of Abraham (Gal 3:7) receiving the Holy Spirit, but on a future Feast of Pentecost at the coming of Christ; God's Spirit will be poured out in ALL flesh (Joel 2:28), and ALL humanity will be grafted into a New Covenant spiritual Israel; and ALL Israel shall be saved (Rom 11:26).

Obedience to God was required before the Covenants

The sacrificial system was instituted as soon as Adam sinned in the garden and Cain slew Abel over his own unacceptable sacrifice.

The Sabbath was established at creation and Israel was told to REMEMBER the Sabbath which had been forgotten in Egypt; the law of clean and unclean was known from creation and was kept by Noah taking seven pairs of clean animals and only one pair of each unclean animal aboard the ark (Gen 7:2).

The Marriage Covenant:

BOTH the Mosaic and the New Covenant are agreements to live by every Word of God: period!

AFTER the Mosaic Marriage Covenant was made at Sinai; God repeated the law which had already existed from the very beginning, as the way to live for His people!

God our Husband requires us to live by His every Word, which includes, but is NOT LIMITED TO, the laws which have ALWAYS existed!

For example: God told the people to go in and inherit the land and they refused (Numbers 14). That was a sin against the Covenant because they would not obey God.

The Covenant is a marriage agreement to do: ALL THAT THE HUSBAND [God] SAYS.

This means keeping ALL the laws and Commandments, living by every Word of God; and it means going further and doing whatever else God might want done.

Israel broke the Covenant by rebelling and disobeying time after time; refusing to be a faithful wife unto their God. Finally their God [Jesus Christ] was made flesh and dwelt among them. He was then killed, dying to atone for the sins of His creation; should those sins be sincerely repented of.

The death of the Husband ended the Mosaic Covenant marriage. It is for this reason that Israel is called a WIDOW by Almighty God, who spoke of the New Covenant [also a Marriage Covenant] as removing the reproach of widowhood:

Isaiah 54:4 Fear not; for thou shalt not be ashamed: neither be thou confounded; for thou shalt not be put to shame: for thou shalt forget the shame of thy youth, and shalt not remember **the reproach of thy widowhood any more**.

The New Covenant

I will put my laws into their minds and write them in their hearts: and I will be to them a God, and they shall be to me a people (Jer 31:33, Heb 8:9-10). I will put my laws into their hearts, and in their minds will I write them (Heb 10:16). Behold the days come, saith the Lord, that I will make a new covenant (Jer 31:31 and Jer 32:37-41).

For the past six thousand years, from Abel to Noah, Moses, Elijah, John Baptist and many others have been called into espousal towards this New Covenant marriage. They have lived their physical lives learning to live by every Word of God.

At the resurrection and the marriage of the Lamb, these people will be raised to spirit and eternal life and be finally fully married to God, the Husband to which they have been called. See "The Biblical Spring Festivals" book for a detailed explanation.

The New Covenant, like the Mosaic Covenant, is a Marriage Covenant. During our physical lives, we are in a period of engagement, where our fitness to marry the Great King is being assessed (1 Pet 4:17). At the resurrection, when the Bridegroom comes to take His Bride, the wedding will take place and the New Covenant will fully begin with the marriage of the Lamb (Mat 25:1-13).

Like all marriages, this New Covenant bestows certain obligations upon it's participants. The bride must fulfill all the duties of a wife; to submit, obey, love and please her husband in every way. While the husband undertakes to; love, care for, protect, provide for and nurture his bride.

The presence of God's Spirit within the collective bride will enable us to fulfill our obligations to God.

Those who seek to live and to be united with God for all eternity, must prepare themselves NOW, by learning FAITHFUL SUBMISSION and LOYALTY to their LORD.

Just as a man or woman does not want a disloyal spouse, God is not willing to enter into marriage with a person He cannot TRUST, who may at some future time rebel, causing immense damage and suffering, therefore a trial and learning period in this life is necessary.

A marriage covenant is an agreement between two parties, to be kept as long as they shall live. Physical marriage is a reflection of the spiritual relationship between Christ and His people (Eph 5:21-33, especially verse 32).

Because of this, Satan does all he can to pervert and damage physical marriage, in order to obscure the spiritual reality of God's intentions.

Right now, some humans are being given a token amount of God's Spirit so that they can prepare for that spiritual union at the resurrection of the dead, being tested and judged now, to determine their worthiness for this honour.

The wedding and wedding feast will take place immediately after the resurrection. Shortly after this, God's Spirit will be poured out upon all flesh (Joel 2:28), making a New Covenant of espousal with ALL MANKIND, ushering in a millennium of peace, a Sabbath of rest, with all men living in the presence of their CREATOR (Rev 20:2 and 4). For it is written; I will make a NEW COVENANT with the HOUSE OF ISRAEL (Heb 8:8-10), writing my laws upon their hearts, that is, giving them the HOLY SPIRIT!

At that time a New Covenant of espousal between God and physical Israel will be established and ALL MANKIND will be grafted into the natural olive tree, the New Covenant family of Israel, (Romans 11).

YES, the NEW COVENANT WILL ultimately be established with the whole house of Israel, and all those who agree to live by every Word of God will be grafted into a spiritual Israel to create a new Spiritual Israel.

For it is written that any stranger who agrees to be circumcised, in the flesh and to keep the commandments and the Passover, shall be considered as an Israelite (Ex 12:48). since this be true of the Mosaic Covenant, it is also true of the New Covenant to be made with a spiritual Israel. Any stranger who agrees to keep the commandments of God and the Passover [accepting the sacrifice of the Lamb of God] and is circumcised in the SPIRIT [having the veil of sins removed] shall be counted as an Israelite, a participant in the New Covenant! A part of SPIRITUAL ISRAEL!

The New Covenant IS the writing of God's laws upon the hearts and in the minds of people. God IS going to do this with ALL FLESH. HE SAID SO!

He WILL do this at the return of Christ to establish the Kingdom of God!

As a token of the Holy Spirit was given to the called out ones throughout history, God demonstrated at Pentecost, that the same token shall be given to all flesh at the Return of Christ, on the same day of Pentecost (see "The

Biblical Spring Festivals" book), as all flesh are then called into His kingdom.

When the called out of sin of this age have been chosen and changed from flesh to spirit, they shall then fully enter this New Covenant of Marriage with Christ.

Even so, when God's Kingdom is established on this world, this opportunity to be espoused to God will be extended to all persons living at that time, for God's Spirit will be poured out upon ALL FLESH (Joel 2:28) and at their final choosing and change into spirit, they shall also enter into the fullness of the New Covenant of Marriage with Christ.

Later, He WILL perform the same process with all of the main harvest, after their resurrection to flesh, during the Ingathering of All Nations [see "The Biblical Fall Festivals" book]!

The Law was not the law of Moses, nor is the law of God a part of the Mosaic Covenant; it is God's law, which has existed since before creation!

When we marry, the bride agrees to honour and obey her husband; that is the marriage covenant; later the husband may decide that they will do a certain thing. Is that thing the marriage itself? No, The marriage is to obey whatever the husband wanted.

The Old or Mosaic Covenant was simply an agreement to obey the Husband in return for certain blessings.

The law was a list of the desires and expectations that the Husband required from his wife and the wife had pledged to obey the Husband in ALL things. The law of God had existed from before Adam and was not a new thing as part of the Mosaic Covenant.

The law of God existed before, and it exists after; the Mosaic Covenant.

Since sin is the transgression of the law (I John 3:4) and the sins of Adam and Eve made their expulsion from the Garden of Eden a necessity; it then follows that the laws of God which defined sin also had to be in effect since the Garden of Eden, because "without the law there is no sin" (Rom 5:12-14).

When a man and woman marry, they agree that he will take care of and love her and that she will love and obey him. We call this, our marriage vows.

At our marriage, we do not spell out everything that we desire, because the agreement to love, care for and obey covers all else.

Even so, the Marriage Covenant between God and Israel was about the obedience of Israel and the blessings of God. The law which existed since before Adam was re-given at Sinai when the people covenanted to marry their Creator.

Then God re-gave his law through Moses, and that law of God [Christ] was the expression of the Husband's will, His expectations of His wife.

What He expected of His wife in the Mosaic Covenant, He will also expect of His NEW wife of the New Covenant, For, I change not, saith the Eternal (Mal 3:6). If we desire to be part of His New Covenant bride, His collective bride; we must fulfill our obligations as a wife and seek to please and obey our espoused Husband. Doing His will and living by every Word of God (Mat 4:3)!

The law existed BEFORE the Mosaic Covenant, therefore the law did not end when the Mosaic marriage ended! That law existed from Adam and was not obeyed by most; God's will [law] existed before and continues to exist after the Mosaic Covenant.

The New Covenant is the same as the old Mosaic Covenant, a marriage agreement to obey God our Husband, but with a BETTER SACRIFICE AND BETTER PROMISES!!

The actual Covenant, whether old or new, is not a detailed list of things that we agree to do. It is an agreement to do EVERYTHING that our Lord may require. It is a marriage agreement to obey our Husband in ALL things.

The law is the list of the things that our Lord has always required of humanity.

Since the Eternal does NOT CHANGE (Mal 3:6), and Jesus Christ the same yesterday, today and forever (Heb 13:8), He will expect and require of us, the same things that He has ALWAYS required of humanity.

When Christ died, it was the agreement, that he would be their God and Israel would be His people, which ended.

The New Covenant is the very same Marriage Covenant, with a larger spiritual context; our Husband now wants us to observe the letter AND the very spirit and intent of the letter of the law!

The desire of God for a faithful, obedient, loving, caring wife, did not end with the end of the first marriage!

God's nature, as reflected by His commandments, did not end. God's will, as expressed by His commandments, did not end.

NOTHING about God changed, only His relationship with physical Israel ended, freeing him to take a New Wife in a New Covenant of marriage!

NOTHING about God's commandments changed. NOTHING was done away.

This law was not only the 10 commandments but also the statutes and civil judgments contained in Exodus 20-23.

Noah was well aware of the laws of clean and unclean as were Abel and Cain as well as being aware of the sacrificial law.

The Mosaic Covenant was an agreement to obey God, which the people broke and could not keep.

The New Covenant is an agreement to obey God, which men will be empowered to do through the true atonement for past sin repented of; and the indwelling of the Holy Spirit, the very nature of God.

The Creator made a Marriage Covenant (Jer 3:14, Isaiah 54:5); with the whole house of Israel. That Marriage Covenant made at Sinai was like any other marriage covenant. The Husband committed to loving, protecting, caring for and blessing his bride. In return the bride committed to loving, obeying, caring for, cooperating with and pleasing her husband in all things.

As a physical couple become one flesh and over time become of like mind; Israel would have become of like mind with their Creator if only they would have kept their side of the bargain. They did not; they utterly failed to keep their side of the bargain to live by every Word of God and the scriptures bear record of their failures.

Israel was a hardhearted, rebellious, stiff necked people who agreed to serve God and then refused to do so in practice.

That Mosaic Marriage Covenant ended with the death of the Husband as all marriages end with the death of one of the party's.

Now the Creator knew that the people could not keep their side of the marriage even before he called them out of Egypt. Yet he went through this process for our example and our instruction.

2 Timothy 3:16 All scripture is given by inspiration of God, and is profitable for doctrine, for reproof, for correction, for instruction in righteousness: **3:17** That the man of God may be perfect, thoroughly furnished unto all good works.

We are to learn from the example set by the Creator and his wife. The Husband was willing to fulfill his promises of national greatness for Israel in every way, yet physical Israel continually rebelled and her sins separated her from her Lord.

Isaiah 59:1 Behold, the LORD's hand is not shortened, that it cannot save; neither his ear heavy, that it cannot hear: **59:2** But your iniquities have separated between you and your God, and your sins have hid his face from you, that he will not hear.

Over and over, both Israel and Judah rebelled against their Husband and their sins separated them from him and his blessings. And because their sins separated them from God; they fell into many trials and much sorrow. And when they were humbled with sorrows, then they returned to their Husband and he forgave them and quickly took them back into his loving arms; comforting and blessing them.

The very same separation can come for those espoused to Christ in the New Covenant!

If we begin to grow lax or lukewarm; if we lose our zeal for our Beloved; if we begin to compromise with God's Word: We cut ourselves off from God and quench his Spirit within us, until our lights begin to flicker and go out.

We do NOT have it made by following the elder, or staying with some group. Christ and his Father are assessing us based on our zeal for THEM! RIGHT NOW!

Almighty God is Sovereign, and we are to live by EVERY WORD of God!

Law and Grace

The Covenants and Commandments are all about our personal relationship with Almighty God; and our Personal Responsibility to Him!

Our eternal salvation depends on our relationship with Almighty God; and NOT on being a part of any Group or Church. Following any man will separate us from God therefore we are to test all things by the Word of God; and follow men, ONLY as they follow God!

Personal Responsibility

At the end of World War Two the victors brought certain German officials to trial for their actions; All of them, [except for Speer] took the defense that they were only following orders; which were lawful in Germany at that time.

At Nuremberg it was decided to base the hearings on "the higher moral laws". This euphemism for the law of God was used to hold these people to the Commandments of God; without actually saying so.

There is no such thing as a natural "higher moral law" in human affairs. Laws demand a Lawgiver. This "Higher Law" is the law of God. Without a God, there would be NO HIGHER LAW than the laws of nations. Without

God and his "higher moral laws" the law of: Might makes right; the law of the jungle, prevails.

Today, the nations are rejecting that "higher law of God" in favour of the law of the jungle; just like the NAZI's did.

How could this be? People make this an excuse for their actions and are ready to do what men tell them because they are afraid to take responsibility for their own actions. They are comfortable obeying orders. They feel that if something is wrong; they have the excuse that they were just: good, loyal, obedient people.

The same thing is true today.

Whatever the various leaders say, most obey the instructions of men without question.

WHY? Because, they have forgotten that it is obedience to Almighty God and His Higher Law; that is required for salvation. They have been misled into obeying men and NOT GOD!

Remember the Holy Scriptures:

1 Thessalonians 5: 21 Prove all things; hold fast that which is good.

Yes, test the words of ALL men against the Word of God, and

1 Thessalonians 5: 22: Abstain from all [even the] appearance of evil.

True religion is not a game of follow some human leader! True religion is to love God and to do God's will; to live by every Word of God.

YES: Esteem those who are your teachers! Just Esteem God MORE!

Don't become so focused on your teachers, that you lose sight of God! Test all things against the standard of the Word of God, that to avoid being deceived. (Luk 21:8).

Many will come claiming to be the servants of Jesus Christ and will deceive many even within the brotherhood (Mat 24).

The job of godly teachers is to focus people on God and NOT on themselves.

How can we discern God's servants?

A servant: SERVES his Master. A servant DOES his master's WILL. A servant keeps his master's COMMANDMENTS. A servant's word is CONSISTENT with the word of his Master. A servant will ACCEPT CORRECTION from his Master.

Romans 6:16 Know ye not, that to whom ye yield yourselves servants to obey, his servants ye are to whom ye obey; whether [a servant] of sin unto death, or of obedience unto righteousness [which is living by every Word of God]?

A servant of God will be serving God through living by every Word of God and will be teaching others to do so; he will be exalting God above all else!

If any man says that he is a servant of God and then thinks that he can do anything he wants; he has made himself master and made God his subject, because he has set himself up as the decider of whatever HE wants, and he insists that God must back him up, he is NOT a servant of God! Such a person is not obeying God; he is doing quite the opposite and is setting himself up above God.

And how do we know if a man is doing this? By studying the Master's Word ourselves; and then comparing what we are being taught, with the Master's Word!

Test, test, test; check, check, check what ALL men say; judge their words by the standard of God's Word. Paul tells us to follow him or any man ONLY as they follow Christ;

1 Corinthians 11:1 Be ye followers of me, even as I also am of Christ.

Paul teaches that the head of Christ is God the Father and the head of every godly man is Christ.

1 Corinthians 11:3 But I would have you know, that **the head of every man is Christ**; and the head of the woman is the man; and t**he head of Christ is God**.

We are to follow men only as they follow Christ and Christ commanded us to:

Matthew 4:4 But he answered and said, It is written, **Man shall not live by bread alone, but by every word that proceedeth out of the mouth of God.**

The entire Bible was recorded and preserved for our instruction

2 Timothy 3:16 All scripture is given by inspiration of God, and is profitable for doctrine, for reproof, for correction, for instruction in righteousness:

1 Thessalonians 5:21 Prove all things [by the scriptures] ; hold fast that which is good.

Jesus commends those who test men by the Word of God and reject false teachers who have departed from God's Word.

Revelation 2:2 I know thy works, and thy labour, and thy patience, and how thou canst not bear them which are evil: and **thou hast tried them which say they are apostles, and are not, and hast found them liars**:

Paul commends the Bereans for testing all things by the Word of God

Acts 17:11 These were more noble than those in Thessalonica, in that they received the word with all readiness of mind, and searched the scriptures daily, whether those things were so.

When we stand before our God on judgment day: Will we be judged by God's Word, or by what some man said? Will the very King of the Universe accept the plea that "we were just following the orders of some man"?

Brethren: We are all completely PERSONALLY RESPONSIBLE for our conduct before God.

There will be NO excuses. When you declare: I was following what this person said: the Great God will ask you: WHY WERE YOU NOT DOING WHAT I SAID?

The Law of God and Eternal life

Sin, Salvation and the Law of God

Thousands of years ago Satan told Eve in the garden:

Genesis 3:4 And the serpent said unto the woman, Ye shall not surely die: **3:5** For God doth know that in the day ye eat thereof, then your eyes shall be opened, and ye shall be as gods, knowing [deciding] good and evil [for yourself].

Satan was telling the woman: if you decide for yourself what is right and what is wrong, you shall be like God; who is now the decider for you. You shall exalt yourself and become equal with God. You can become a God through your own efforts.

This same lie has been repeated continually, ever since. Most religions say trust and believe God. They then go on to say that "we are God's spokesmen and you MUST OBEY US". They then proceed to substitute their own ideas, traditions and philosophies for the Word of God.

Where in the Bible does it say that Sunday should be observed as the weekly Sabbath?
Where does God say that; "YOU SHALL NOT DIE", that you have an eternal spirit?

It does say:

Ezekiel 18: 20 The soul that sinneth, it shall die. And, **Romans 6: 23** For the wages of sin is death; but the gift of God is eternal life through Jesus Christ our Lord.

Yes, the gift of God is eternal life. And the way to eternal life is revealed by the Word of God. God's law shows us every way that leads to life and reveals the ways that lead to death.

The ultimate consequence of breaking these laws and principles of life is death. Sin brings death by its very nature. This being the case, the avoidance of sin, leads to eternal life. God's Law shows the way to life eternal.

What is sin?

1 John 3: 4 Whosoever committeth sin transgresseth also the law: for **sin is the transgression of the law.**

Therefore since sin results in death and keeping the Law of God results in eternal life. The law of God is Holy and Good.

Romans 7: 12: Wherefore **the law is holy, and the commandment holy, and just, and good.**

God's commandments are GOOD

James 1: 25 But whoso looketh into the perfect law of liberty, and continueth therein, he being not a forgetful hearer, **but a doer of the work** [a diligent keeper of the Law and Word of God], this man shall be blessed in his deed [blessed for his actions of obeying the Word of God, with the gift of God which is eternal life].

All those who live by every Word of God will have a place in eternity.

Revelation 22: 14 Blessed are they that do his commandments that they may have **a right to the tree of life**, and may enter in through the gates into the city [the New Jerusalem the city of eternal life] .

Those who ultimately refuse to live by every Word of God shall be thrown into the fire and destroyed.

Revelation 20: 13 And the sea gave up the dead which were in it; and death and hell [the grave] delivered up the dead which were in them: and they were judged every man according to their works [according to whether they keep God's Word and Law, the way to life]. **20:14** And death and hell were cast into the lake of fire. This is the second death. **20:15** And whosoever was not found written in the book of life was cast into the lake of fire.

Who is Sovereign, God or Men?

There is a false teaching going around that "we do not keep the commandments because we have to; we keep the commandments because we want to,"

Let us examine this concept carefully before swallowing it whole.

"We do not keep the commandments because we have to; we keep the commandments because WE want to".

Now of course we should want to obey God, so this part of the statement is good; however this positive point is then used to subtly slip in the lie that we do not really have to obey our Father in heaven and that whether we obey God or not is up to us!

This is the very lie that Satan told Eve in the garden! We do not really have to obey God, we can decide what we want to do for ourselves!

What does that accomplish? It exalts the will of men ABOVE the Word of God! It makes man the decider and removes the sovereignty of Almighty God as the decider of what is right and what is wrong!

It insists that men can decide right and wrong for themselves and that men can decide to do what they want and are under no salvational moral obligation to obey God!

The underlying foundational false doctrine behind this very subtle false teaching is that Grace trumps the Law and that all you need is an emotional kind of ersatz love: Making living by every Word of God OUR choice; since our sins have already been paid for in advance.

The Biblical Doctrine of Law and Grace is very simple; if we sincerely repent of all PAST breaking of the Word of God and commit to STOP breaking God's Word, fully committing to go forward to live by EVERY WORD of GOD and sin no more in the future; then the grace [pardon, forgiveness] of God will be granted through the application of the sacrifice of the Lamb of God, Jesus Christ; and we will be reconciled to God the Father.

The grace or free pardon through sincere repentance and the application of Christ's sacrifice, reconciles us to God the Father, and living by every Word of God in future, KEEPS us reconciled to God the Father. It is that simple.

At baptism we are committing ourselves to learning and living by every Word of God, FOREVER; without turning to the right or to the left from God the Father and Jesus Christ and every Word of God. We are NOT joining a corporate church; we are espousing ourselves to an Awesome Husband, Jesus Christ; and we are to be totally loyal to HIM and HIS FATHER in ALL things and at ALL times!

Romans 2:13 (For not the hearers of the law are just before God, but the doers of the law shall be justified.

We are saved by grace through faith; **but faith saves, ONLY if it is married to the works of faith; which is obedience to every Word of God**

James 2:14 What doth it profit, my brethren, though a man say he hath faith, and have not works? Can faith save him? **2:15** If a brother or sister be naked, and destitute of daily food, **2:16** and one of you say unto them, Depart in peace, be ye warmed and filled; notwithstanding ye give them not those things which are needful to the body, what doth it profit?

2:17 Even so **faith, if it hath not works, is dead, being alone. 2:18** Yea, a man may say, You hast faith, and I have works. **Show me thy faith without thy works, and I will show thee my faith by my works. 2:19** Thou believest that there is one God; thou doest well: the devils also believe, and tremble.

Yet the demons will not obey God's Word, therefore their belief brings them nothing but the sure knowledge of their coming judgment.

2:20 But wilt thou know, O vain man, that **faith without works is dead**?

2:21 Was not Abraham our father justified [by his deeds] by works when he [obeyed God] had offered Isaac his son upon the altar? **2:22** Seest thou how faith wrought [worked with] with his works and by works was faith made perfect? **2:23** And the scripture was fulfilled which saith, Abraham believed God, and it was imputed unto him for righteousness: and he was called the Friend of God.

2:24 Ye see then how that by works a man is justified, and not by faith only. **2:25** Likewise also was not Rehab the harlot justified by works, when she had received the messengers, and had sent them out another way? **2:26** For **as the body without the spirit is dead, so faith without works is dead.**

Faith without works cannot stand on its own. If we have faith, if we believe God, then we will do what God says; which is our works.

We cannot do what God says if we do not believe [have faith] in Him!

Faith is inseparable from the works of faith. If we have faith and no works, our faith is meaningless, it is a waste of time, it has absolutely no value since it produces nothing in us!

Believing without acting on that belief is a waste of time; it won't get you anywhere.

The false view is that; yes we are to keep the Commandments, but God is love and will overlook our transgressions and wink at them in future as long as we also tolerate sin in the name of love, because Christ has died to cover them.

In other words they forget the lessons of scripture that God will utterly destroy all unrepentant sinners; which is the lessons of the Noah flood, Sodom, the Canaanites and the captivities of straying Israel and Judah. In forgetting that God will destroy all unrepentant self-justifying sinners they make the sacrifice of Christ a license to continue in sin; and thereby make a mockery of Christ's sacrifice.

Scripture tells us that we must first repent [STOP sinning], and them make a baptismal New Covenant commitment to live by every Word of God; only then can we be cleansed of PAST sin and forgiven and receive the gift of the Holy Spirit.

Acts 2:38 Then Peter said unto them, **Repent, and be baptized** every one of you in the name of Jesus Christ for the remission of sins, and ye shall receive the gift of the Holy Ghost.

The Holy Spirit is given ONLY to those who live by every Word of God.

Acts 5:32 And we are his witnesses of these things; and so is also the Holy Ghost, **whom God hath given to them that obey him.**

Paul tells us that if we sin willfully, and sin is breaking the Word of God; there is NO more forgiveness until we learn our lesson and sincerely repent.

Hebrews 10:26 For if we sin wilfully after that we have received the knowledge of the truth, there remaineth no more sacrifice for sins,

Failure to condemn sin is actually hate, and not love at all; since by not rebuking sin, the brethren are allowed to go to their destruction without a warning (Ezek 33). This is the same foolishness as: supposedly out of love, not rebuking our children for running into traffic.

In order to follow God the Father and Jesus Christ as our Head: We must do what Christ taught, and Jesus Christ taught all people to live by every Word of God the Father (Mat 4:4)!

John 14:31 But that the world may know that **I** [Jesus Christ] **love the Father; and as the Father gave me commandment, even so I do**. Arise, let us go hence.

What did Jesus Christ Command?

Matthew 19:17 If you will enter into life, KEEP THE COMMANDMENTS

John 15:10 If ye keep my commandments, ye shall abide in my love

Revelation 12:7 Which keep the commandments of God, and have the testimony of Jesus Christ

Revelation 14:12 Here is the patience of the saints: here are they that keep the commandments of God, and the faith of Jesus

Revelation 22:14 Blessed are they that do His commandments, that they may have right to the tree of life

Matthew 5:17 Think not that I am come to destroy the law, or the prophets: I am not come to destroy, but to fulfil.

Christ came to keep and complete the Word of God by revealing the spirit and intent of God's Word, making it complete by making it binding in the letter and in the spirit!

Jesus Christ did NOT come to destroy God the Father's commandments, but to reveal their spiritual intent: and to set an example that we are to follow; zealously keeping the Whole Word of God in the letter and in the spirit and in its full intent!

5:18 For verily I say unto you, Till heaven and earth pass, one jot or one tittle shall in no wise pass from the law, till all be fulfilled [the Word and Law of God will be fulfilled (that is KEPT) forever!].

No part of God the Father's Word will ever pass away, and ultimately all living men will be passionately keeping those commandments in BOTH the letter and the spirit. Then the law will be written on our hearts and not on tables of stone (Jeremiah 31).

5:19 Whosoever therefore shall break one of these least commandments, and shall teach men so, he shall be called the least in the kingdom of heaven: but whosoever shall do and teach them, the same shall be called great in the kingdom of heaven.

If anyone says that this or that is just physical, or only a "little thing"; consider these words. To break the law in one point, is to break the whole law, therefore such a person will not even be in God's Kingdom unless he repents, and even then he will be the least.

Many, who think they are great now, may not even be chosen, or will be accounted least in the Kingdom of God.

5:20 For I say unto you, That except your righteousness shall exceed the righteousness of the scribes and Pharisees [who made God's Word of no effect by their false traditions of men], ye shall in no case enter into the kingdom of heaven.

To be a Pharisee is to make the law of God of no effect by following our idols of men and our own false traditions; to be zealous for our own ways and not for God's ways; to exalt men and the traditions of men and organizations instead of being totally faithful to God and his law; to have a pretense of godliness without the power [the true spirit] of godliness; and to serve with the lips and not with deeds; to be filled with guile, deceit and hypocrisy.

Those who would be pillars must be zealous for God and must be doers of his Word no matter what the cost, or they shall NOT be in the resurrection of the called out first fruits to eternal life.

God wants to save those he calls to himself and reward them with eternal life and a resurrection to spirit, but Satan wants to prevent that and will seek to persecute and destroy those faithful to Almighty God and his Word.

We are told to pray to our Heavenly Father, "thy will be done" (Mat 6:10). Will you express this sentiment and then refuse to do His will yourself, by defying His Word?

I have kept my Fathers commandments (John 15:10). Since sin is the transgression of the law (1 John 3:4) and Christ had no sin (Heb 4:15); Jesus kept the commandments of God the Father as our example that we should do likewise.

How can we as weak mortals live by every Word of God?

Our Lord said that He would send us a comforter (Joh 14:16, 14:26): The spirit of power, and of love and of a sound mind (2 Tim 1:7) is the The Holy Spirit of God and of Jesus Christ (Ph'p 1:19-20 and 1 Cor 2:10).

In this way, Christ can dwell within you. Hereby know ye the spirit of God, Every spirit that confesseth that Jesus Christ is come in the [that Jesus Christ dwells in our flesh through the Holy Spirit] flesh is of God (1 Joh 4:2).

Every person who says that he is of Christ must follow the example of Christ and live as Christ lived; and Jesus Christ lived by every Word of God the Father!

1 John 2:6 He that saith he abideth in him [Christ] ought himself also so to walk [conduct himself or live], even as he [Jesus Christ] walked [lived].

Jesus Christ is consistent. He is the same yesterday, today and forever (Heb 13:8). Therefore He will be doing the same things today that He did in the past, He will be keeping His Fathers commandments and living by every Word of God! It is the Spirit of Christ in you that empowers you, to keep the Fathers Word!

The only way to reconciliation and peace with God and people is for ALL people to;

- Believe God,
- Repent turning away from the PAST breaking of any part of God's Word,
- Commit at baptism to keep all God's commandments and to live by every Word of God in future,
- Have the atoning sacrifice of Christ applied to himself, thus having all sins paid for and forgiven,
- He is then reconciled to God the Father in heaven, gaining access to Him, with the right to call Him Father (Rom 8:14-16 and Gal 4:6).
- He must then remain godly by continue to live by EVERY WORD of GOD, and to work diligently to internalize the very nature of God the Father and the Son into himself; becoming LIKE Christ and like God the Father in every way.

The New Covenant is about committing oneself to live by EVERY WORD of GOD.

Matthew 4:4 But he [Christ] answered and said, It is written, **Man shall not live by bread alone, but by every word that proceedeth out of the mouth of God.**

True Godliness and true Christianity is about taking personal responsibility for our own conduct before God. We are each responsible for everything that we do and we will each be personally judged by every Word of God.

Revelation 20:13 And I saw the dead, small and great, stand before God; and the books were opened: and another book was opened, which is the book of life: and the dead **were judged out of those things which were written in the books, according to their works.**

Matthew 11:12 The Kingdom of God is taken by violence [must be achieved by struggle against sin].

Acts 14:22 It is through much tribulation [struggle against Satan and sin] that we may enter the Kingdom of God

John 16:33 In this world you shall have much tribulation [struggle against sin] .

Be comforted for Christ has overcome the world, nevertheless be prepared to be rejected by those you love, to be denied the best things this world has to offer and to suffer the ridicule, hate and contempt of society.

This world loves its own, if you are not of this society it will NOT love you (Joh 15:19).

If you embrace the New Covenant, be prepared and expect many trials with eventual persecution and martyrdom (Mat 10:21-36, Joh 12:25). This is a LIFELONG COMMITMENT to live by every Word of God, with an expectation of much trial. It is NOT to be entered lightly.

Once one has sincerely repented of living contrary to the Word of God and has made a commitment to live by every Word of God and to go and sin no more [John 5:14), the next step is baptism. The word baptize means, to immerse. This immersion is symbolic of a death and burial of the old sinful self and the resurrection to a new life in godliness.

To simply sprinkle a few drops of water on someone does NOT reflect this concept and the baptizing of children before they are mature enough to make such a personal commitment is a gross misunderstanding of the purpose and meaning of baptism. Baptism also symbolizes the washing away of sincerely repented sin through the application of the sacrifice of Jesus Christ, the Lamb of God (1 Cor 5:7, Joh 1:29).

New Covenant baptism is the seal of sincere repentance, destroying the existing sinful person so that a new person can rise up in godliness to live by every Word of God. Baptism represents the making of an agreement to come into full unity of mind and actions with God the Father, and entering into a free will espousal to marry [come into complete unity with] the Son of God.

Baptism is a marriage espousal agreement between us and Jesus Christ, committing us to do the will of, and to live by every Word of God. Such an agreement must be made by mature and informed persons, who know what they are doing and know what they are getting into.

Marriage is NOT for children. To sprinkle a child and pronounce him baptized is an act of forcing an uninformed, innocent and helpless person into a situation over which he has no choice. Children are unable to make such commitments. To make a baptismal commitment, one must be mature, informed and able to act out of free will.

When we choose to make this commitment we should be baptized (immersed in water) into God the Father, the Son and the Holy Spirit (Mat 28:19).

Since this is done at the direct command of Jesus Christ, it is done in His name, that is, by His authority.

When this commitment has been made, we may then ask that the Holy Spirit of God be given to us. This is the gift of God and Christ and enables us to keep our commitments to live by every Word of God.

As only those who are physically circumcised and commit to keep all the commandments of God were allowed to take part in the Passover of the Mosaic Covenant, only those who have been circumcised in their hearts through sincere repentance and the commitment of baptism, having the veil of sin removed from their hearts, may partake of the Christian Passover (Deu 10:16, Rom 2:29).

Also let it be understood that all baptized persons are obligated to partake of the Lord's Passover, following the example of our Lord Jesus Christ (Mat 26, Mark 14, Luk 22, Joh 12-17 and 1 Cor 11:19-34).

This completes the beginning of the process of conversion toward God.

From here we must go forward in learning and growing and overcoming and living by every Word of God until the day our physical lives end. We must continually work to purge out the leaven of sin and to take into ourselves the Bread of Life of the very nature of Jesus Christ an the Father (1 Cor 5:6-8).

Grace

According to Strong's Concordance Greek Dictionary; GRACE #5485 means a benefit, favour or gift.

Grace simply means, that Jesus Christ has paid the penalty for our past sins, on our behalf, through the gift of His sacrifice.

Since the penalty for our past sins has been paid as a free gift, we are no longer required to pay that penalty for ourselves.

There is one small requirement: WE MUST REPENT and STOP doing those things that required such a tremendous sacrifice (Acts 2:38), before that gift will be given.

To REPENT means to CHANGE, to be sorry enough to STOP sinning!

What is sin? **1 John 3:4** Sin is the transgression of the law,

To stop sinning, we must STOP TRANSGRESSING THE WORD OF GOD!!

Grace or a pardon, covers Sincerely Repented sins!

Grace does not justify continuing in sin (Rom 6:1-2 and Romans 6:15-16). Also read the entire book of James, as well as 1, 2 and 3 John.

We MUST stop sinning and become like Christ, who had no sin.

If you are pardoned by a judge for some crime, does that then give you the right to go out and repeat the crime at will? Of course not! Why try to use such ridiculous reasoning to try and avoid doing God's will?

God's will is; that we keep His commandments. The commandments of God are an expression of what God wants us to do. The commandments are an expression of His will. They are His instructions, concerning what He expects of us, and how He wants us to behave.

How is it, that some people dare to pray to the Father, Your will be done; and then REFUSE TO DO HIS WILL THEMSELVES? To do this is to MOCK GOD!

It is written that, sin is the transgression of the law (1 Joh 3:4). If we break God's law, if we transgress His commandments, we have sinned. Now Paul tells us that if we sin willfully after we have received the knowledge of the truth, there remains NO MORE SACRIFICE FOR SINS (Heb 10:26-31).

There is no grace, no forgiveness, no sacrifice for sin without: Sincere REPENTANCE!

REPENTANCE means to be SORRY enough to CHANGE YOUR BEHAVIOR

When you correct your child and he is sorry and resolves not to repeat his error, do you not forgive him? But if that person claims to repent and then repeats his folly again and again, and says sorry without any intention of stopping his bad behavior, he is just mouthing words and is not really sorry. In fact, he is a liar for claiming to be sorry when he is not.

That kind of behavior reflects a complete lack of respect for the parent, and his judgment.

We are called to become the children of God, He will not respect such behaviour any more than we would.

God will NOT BE MOCKED!

Galatians 6:7 Be not deceived; God is not mocked: for whatsoever a man soweth, that shall he also reap.

6:8 For he that soweth to his flesh shall of the flesh reap corruption; but he that soweth to the Spirit shall of the Spirit reap life everlasting.

6:9 And let us not be weary in well doing: for in due season we shall reap, if we faint not.

Why? Because He loves us. God is love, His Word is love and His commandments are love. God loves all of us and His commandments reveal how to love Him and how to love one another. They reveal how to avoid harming ourselves or one another. For the Law is Just and Holy and Good (Rom 7:12).

Yes, we are saved by grace which is the free gift that has been given by Jesus Christ, who gave Himself to die in our place, making possible the forgiveness of God the Father.

No, we are not saved by works, since no works can make right those things that we have done wrong in the PAST.

Grace is the forgiveness of those things that we have done wrong in the past, the forgiveness of our past sins. Such grace, such forgiveness, is made possible because Jesus Christ paid the penalty for our sins in our place.

Nevertheless we make a MOCKERY of GRACE if we continue to do those things that required such a terrible bloody sacrifice.

Indeed, if we use the forgiveness of God as an excuse to continue in sin, we make a MOCKERY of the sacrifice of JESUS CHRIST! Who gave His life for us, so that we could be freed from the bondage of sin and the penalty of death. (Rom 6:1-2 and Rom 6:15-16).

Jesus Christ was nailed to the stake, He was made sin for us (2 Cor 5:21), paying the penalty that WE owed for our wickedness.

The list of the commandments that we had broken, our indictment, was nailed to the stake with Him, blotting out the list of our past crimes against God, the list of our sincerely repented sins (Col 2:14).

His sinless life and his death, paid for every sin on that list. If we then continue to break those laws, we make a mockery of what he did for us; and the list of our sins is renewed!

We must STOP doing the things that required such a terrible penalty

If we do not STOP sinning, there is no longer a sacrifice remaining for us (Heb 10:26); and we are doomed to pay the penalty of death that we have so richly earned.

What then was done away, by Christ's sacrifice? Only those PAST sins that we have Sincerely REPENTED of and resolved with the help of God, never to do again.

The Mosaic Covenant was ended by the death of one of the parties to that Covenant, Jesus Christ; who was the God of the Mosaic Covenant before He gave up his God-hood to become flesh (John 1).

At the death of the Lamb of God, the Levitical Priesthood ended and at the resurrection of Christ, he was restored to the Eternal Priesthood of the Melchizedek order, the whole book of Hebrews.

The WILL OF GOD REMAINS. GOD DOES NOT CHANGE (Mal 3:6). Therefore His will, His desire for us to live by every Word of God DOES NOT CHANGE!

The idea, that because a penalty has been paid for past lawbreaking, it somehow justifies continuing to break the Word of God, is simply a rather pathetic attempt at self-justification.

There is NO REMOVAL OF SIN EXCEPT BY DEATH (Heb 9:22), for: the wages of sin is death (Rom 6:23).

Either we STOP our commandment breaking, which is sin; and accept the sacrifice of Jesus Christ to ATONE for our PAST sins and then STOP sinning, or we must die for our own sins.

The penalty MUST BE PAID and we MUST STOP doing those things that require such a penalty in future!

Those who do not stop will be destroyed (Rev 20:15); for ONLY those who keep ALL THE COMMANDMENTS OF GOD and live by EVERY WORD of GOD, shall be given access to ETERNAL LIFE (Rev 22:14).

> "Cheap grace is the theology that expects the benefits of grace without the sacrifice of obedience." [Dietrich Bonhoeffer]

True Godly Love

When we truly love someone; we seek to please them, to make them happy, to do them good. If we loved Jesus Christ; we would be trying to please Him, we would be doing what He said.

What did Jesus Christ command us to do?

He told us to pray to the Father in Heaven in Christ's name, and to ask that God the Father's will be done (Mat 6:10).

Who's will? God the Father's will.

If we are trying to please Christ we would be obeying Christ, and therefore we would be doing the Father's will (Mat 4:4).

Matthew 5:16 Let your light so shine before men, that they may see your good works, and glorify your Father which is in heaven

In doing this, your light will so shine that men will glorify who? Jesus Christ? Yes; but also your Father in Heaven.

How are we to let our light shine? By doing the will of God the Father and His Son, through living by EVERY WORD of God the Father with enthusiastic zeal!

How do we know what the will of God our Father is? We need to study His Word, for in His Word, He has revealed His will.

What is God's will?

Why God's will is that we listen to Him, that we DO what He says to us; and through doing his will, that we become like him, internalizing his very nature.

And how did Jesus Christ say we ought to love Him? He said; If you love me KEEP MY COMMANDMENTS, (Joh 14:15, Joh 14:21).

It is NOT enough to sing; Oh how I love Jesus, or to repeatedly exclaim how much we love Him. We must keep His sayings! (Joh 14:21-23).

No matter how much we claim to love Him, or claim to have God's love, we are deceiving ourselves if we are not willing to do what God says.

John writes that;

1 John 5:2 By this, we know that we love the children of God, when we love God and KEEP HIS COMMANDMENTS. **5:3** For this is the love of God, that we KEEP HIS COMMANDMENTS, and His commandments are not grievous,

Whose commandments is John referring to? Why God the Father's commandments, the whole Word of God the Father in Heaven.

2 John 6 "this is love, that we walk [live by] after His commandments". To please God and His Christ we must keep all of their commandments.

For Jesus said that "I and my Father are one" (Joh 10:30, Joh 14:7-11):

1 John 2:3 And hereby we do know that we know him, if we keep his commandments. **2:4** He that saith, I know him, and keepeth not his commandments, is a liar, and the truth is not in him. **2:5** But whoso keepeth his word, in him verily is the love of God perfected: hereby know we that we are in him. **2:6** He that saith that he abideth in Him ought himself also so to walk [live], even as He walked [lives]",

Jesus said "I have kept my Father's commandments" **John 15:10**.

We are to live just like Jesus lived; therefore we must also live by every Word of God the Father, just like Jesus Christ did!

When we turn away from sin, which is the transgression of the law of God, (1 Joh 3:4), we have the sacrifice of Jesus Christ applied to us, atoning for our past sins. This allows us to be espoused as part of the collective bride of Christ and to be adopted as children of God the Father (Rom 8:14-16).

Did Jesus not COMMAND us to honor God our Father? (Mat 19:17-19). Those who say that we should only obey Christ now and need not obey the

Father's Word, condemn themselves for Christ COMMANDED us to honor God our Father, and our Father is the ETERNAL GOD OF HEAVEN AND EARTH; the Head of Jesus Christ (1 Cor 11:3)!

Again Jesus said that "MY FATHER IS GREATER THAN I" **John 14:28** Boldly declaring that He could do NOTHING without the Father (Joh 5:19 and Joh 5:30).

Jesus said "if you had known me, ye should have known my Father also" **John 8:19**. Therefore; if you love Christ, you would love God the Father, for Christ loved His Father and commanded that we Honor and Do the Will of God the Father.

If we do not love the Father, we do NOT love Christ. If we do not keep the Father's Word, we will NOT obey Christ either, for Jesus Christ commanded us to keep the Father's Word and to do the Father's will.

Jesus Christ said that the GREATEST commandment is to: "love the Lord thy God (the Father in heaven) with all thy heart, and with all thy soul, and with all thy mind" **Matthew 22:37**. That we, must love to keep God the Father's commandments 2 John 6.

The second great commandment is to "love thy neighbour as thyself" **Matthew 22:39-40**. How do we do this? We do not steal from him. We do not lie to him. We do not take his wife. We honour our physical parents. We do not covet his property. We FORGIVE him when he trespasses against us. All these things are a part of the Father's GREAT LAW which is HOLY JUST AND GOOD (Rom 7:12).

Was the law of God part of the Mosaic Covenant?

The Mosaic Covenant was a marriage covenant. Like any marriage, it ended with the death of one of the parties: In this case with the death of the husband, Jesus Christ.

Wasn't the law, just a part of the Mosaic Covenant and did it not end with the end of that Covenant?

Paul writes that sin is not imputed when there is no law (Rom 5:13). Yet God imputed sin to Abimelek when he thought to take Abraham's wife (Gen 20:1-9). Joseph spoke of sin to his master's wife (Gen 39:9). Sin was imputed to Sodom (Gen 13:13).

For what reason were Adam and Eve put out of the garden for eating the forbidden fruit, if that was not sin? The lesson of the forbidden fruit is clear; deciding right and wrong for ourselves and not living by every Word of God is transgression of God's Word and is sin.

Why was the world destroyed by water in the days of Noah, if not for the wickedness of sin? Therefore the law existed in those days and existed since the very creation!

Sin is the transgression of the law (1 John 3:4). Where there is no law to transgress, there can be no sin in breaking a non existent law.

What is the law and the commandments, but the whole Word and Will of God; for God is our Father and we are to honor our Father in heaven foremost above all and are to live by his every Word.

Clearly the law existed and was in effect throughout history, from the very creation. For Adam and Eve were rejected for their sin; and Cain and Abel knew of the Sacrificial Law and of the Law of Clean and Unclean, necessary for sacrifices (Gen 4:7).

The Sabbath Law was made at creation (Gen 2:2-3).

The Law of the Clean and Unclean was obeyed by Noah (Gen 7:2).

The Law concerning Adultery was clearly known as shown above. God destroyed most of mankind in Noah's day and then later destroyed Sodom because of their transgressions.

Was not Cain judged for breaking the Law that said THOU SHALT NOT SHED INNOCENT BLOOD? All this demonstrating that the Law of God was known since the day of creation.

The law of God is an expression of God's will and has been in existence since creation.

The Word of God did not end with the Mosaic Covenant, because it was never exclusive to the Mosaic Covenant. The Mosaic Covenant was extended to Israel so that they could be an example of godliness to ALL nations; and the Mosaic Covenant was an allegory of the New Covenant

The WILL OF GOD is defined by His law! The law of God existed from the beginning and remains in existence today.

SIN IS THE TRANSGRESSION OF THE LAW (**1 John 3:4**)

Sin has existed in MAN since Eve disobeyed her Creator Father and took of the forbidden fruit.

Therefore the commandment to honor father and mother must have been in effect at that time, or no sin could have been imputed to her (Rom 5:13).

In conclusion we may say that we honor our Heavenly Father and His Christ by obeying them and through living by every Word of God.

This is how we can please them, this is how we can show our love for them.

The LAW was given for our GOOD: To show us how to get along with God and with one another, and to protect the innocent and to guarantee the right of all peoples to peace and security.

There is NOTHING in the law that is harmful to any innocent person.

The law prevents us from hurting one another and points us toward respecting the greater wisdom of God our Father. The law prevents anarchy, confusion and violent chaos. It is a defender of the weak and the innocent and a destroyer of those who would destroy others.

The Sacrificial Law provides a legal framework for an ATONEMENT for SIN. It provides the means by which the Creator gave Himself as the Passover Lamb of God, in ultimate love, for His creation and save them from the consequences of their rebellion and sin.

No wonder; Paul writes that the LAW IS HOLY AND JUST AND GOOD!

The Law and Word of God is the MOST WONDERFUL GIFT that mankind could be given, as wonderful as life itself.

For it shows the way to LIFE and the PEACE AND HARMONY that all men seek.

People cannot find peace in this world, because they reject the only WAY TO PEACE! May God's will be done, may everything that breathes live by EVERY WORD of GOD!!

God's commandments are the ONLY way to peace, for GOD IS LOVE (1 Joh 4:7-8), therefore His Law could be nothing else, but for our GOOD!

The God of Heaven truly knows how to give GOOD GIFTS (Mat 7:9-11) for He IS A LOVING FATHER INDEED!

Obey What Commandments?

The Gospel is about the Kingdom of God; its constitution, laws, history and the way to enter that kingdom, to become citizens of the Kingdom.

The Gospel of Christ is about repentance from breaking the laws of that Kingdom; and a commitment to keeping those laws in future with the same zeal with which Christ kept them.

The gospel is about LOYALTY to the Great King of the universe and about loving him enough to DO what he says; to diligently seek to become LIKE HIM, by doing all that he says and by seeking to please him with all our hearts.

Jesus Christ preached the Gospel of **REPENTANCE** and said:

Matthew 19:17 . . . if thou wilt enter into life, keep the commandments.

That brings us to the question: Which commandments are to be obeyed under the New Covenant?

The New Covenant is a replica of the Mosaic Covenant, with an added spiritual component; and the SAME commandments are to be obeyed; now in the spirit and intent, as well as the letter of the law.

Jesus said: "if thou wilt enter into life, keep the commandments." At that time he was referring to all the commandments that he had given through Moses!

We all know about the basic Ten Commandments; and the foundational Two Great Commandments, but what about all the other laws, statutes and judgments?

They are ALL in effect and to be obeyed because they are the Word and Will of God our Father in heaven and the commandment requires us to honor our father and mother.

> Spiritually our father is God the Father in heaven and our mother is the heavenly Jerusalem the city of God from which flows the Word of God!
>
> **Matthew 15:4** For God commanded, saying, Honour thy father and mother: and, He that curseth [disrespects or refuses to obey] father or mother, let him die the death.
>
> **Galatians 4:26** But Jerusalem which is above is free [obeying the Word of God from the heavenly Jerusalem frees us from bondage to sin], which is the mother of us all.

If one is walking in his yard, he need not be concerned about the road speed limit; it simply does not apply to the situation.

We are to obey all the commandments that apply in our particular situation.

God is TESTING people as to whether we will put him first, and obey him; or whether we will decide for ourselves what is right or wrong. God is testing to see if we will follow him and become Godly righteous; or whether we will decide for ourselves and be self-righteous.

Adam and Eve failed their TEST; and since that time most of humanity has failed as well. People will not obey God; they insist on doing things their own way. Our own self-righteous arrogance and pride is the cause of our wars and troubles on this world. Only when mankind [including church people] is humbled enough to listen to and obey God, will we find the answers to our sorrows.

God is now TESTING all peoples. The TEST is simple: Will we obey him; or will we do what we think is right?

If we deliberately sin or deliberately find pleasure in the sins of others by deliberately exposing ourselves to sinful conduct; if we vicariously sin through the sins of others, by loving to watch the sins of others; if we mentally participate in the sins of others; or if we actually participate in the sins of others: God will not tolerate physical or spiritual uncleanness, and if we tolerate such sin: **God's Spirit WILL BE QUENCHED within us**.

We are to follow that Spirit as it guides us into all truth. We are to become a spiritual people, understanding the spirit and intent of the law. We are NOT to quench God's Spirit by tolerating evil!

A physical commandment: **Leviticus 11:8:** Of their flesh shall ye not eat, and their carcase **shall ye not touch**

The spiritual meaning of this law is: Touch not the physically or spiritually unclean thing.

2 Corinthians 6:17 touch not the unclean thing [avoid all sin]; and I will receive you.

What is the spiritually unclean thing? The spiritually unclean thing is anything that separates us from our God; it is breaking or compromising with any part of the Word of God!

2 Corinthians 6:16 And what agreement hath the temple of God with idols? For ye are the temple of the living God; as God hath said, I will dwell in them, and walk in them; and I will be their God, and they shall be my people. **6:17** Wherefore come out from among them, and be ye separate, saith the Lord, and **touch not the unclean thing;** and I will receive you.

Brethren we are also forbidden to partake of, or to participate in the sins of others.

1 Timothy 5:22 . . . neither be partaker of other men's sins: keep thyself pure.

I have heard it said over and over, that we may go out and buy food on the Sabbath because these people will work anyway. Shall we then steal, or commit adultery, or lie; because others will do these things anyway: Or are we to live a better way and set a godly example?

1 Thessalonians 5:22 Abstain from all appearance of evil.

Brethren; we are to abhor and avoid the spiritually unclean thing just as zealously as the physically unclean thing! The whole point of establishing a law of the physically unclean was to teach us about spiritual things.

The law is clear: you shall not work on the Sabbath Day [Friday sunset to Saturday sunset] and you shall not require others to serve you.

To commit a sin because others are doing it; is to join them in their sin, and to sin ourselves. It is to partake and participate in the sins of others; it is to touch and associate with the spiritually unclean thing. It is to set an evil example instead of letting our light shine. It is to fail the TEST concerning the Sabbath day.

In the various religious organizations it is the common practice to exalt men and their institutions above God by equating loyalty to them with loyalty to God. This is idolatry, it is making an idol out of men or their corporate churches, to do this is SIN!

This present crisis is a great TEST for God's people. God wants to know: Who will turn from this evil and put him first.

Matthew 24:48: But and if that evil servant shall say in his heart, My lord delayeth his coming; **24:19** And shall begin to smite *his* fellow servants, and to eat and drink with the drunken;

This evil MUST come so that the servants of God may be made known.

1 Corinthians 11:19 For there must be also heresies among you, that they which are approved may be made manifest among you.

It is God's purpose to separate out those who will repent of the idolatry of exalting men and corporations and turn to him; from those who will not.

Therefore God will allow those he is working with to become totally disillusioned with men and their corporations. In this way, he will bring them to repentance and turn them to **HIM!**

Brethren; we should not buy food or cook on a Sabbath or a Holy Day, We are to use the previous day before the Sabbath or High Day; for preparation days as God has commanded.

Nehemiah 10:31 . . . we would **not buy it** of them **on the Sabbath, or on the holy day**.

This is about us buying; it is not about what the unconverted do: **IT IS ABOUT WHAT WE DO!**

Nor should we participate with those who smite our fellow servants. Instead we are commanded to mark such evil and avoid it.

Yes, we are commanded to mark and avoid those who will do evil and will not accept sound doctrine, who will smite their fellow servants, and who will pollute God's Holy Sabbath Day.

Romans 16:17 Now I beseech you, brethren, mark them which cause divisions and offences contrary **to the doctrine** which ye have learned; and avoid them. **16:18** For they that are such serve not our Lord Jesus Christ, but their own belly; and by good words and **fair speeches deceive the hearts of the simple**.

True Godliness is about *sound doctrine*; it is about what we do and how we live; it is about following God, true godliness is NOT about following men and organizations AWAY from God!

Only the Eternal should be loved and exalted as our ultimate moral authority.

To love and exalt any organization or person, no matter what it calls itself, or claims to be: is spiritual and emotional ADULTERY against our espoused Husband Jesus Christ! It is loving something other than our pledged espoused Husband: IT IS SPIRITUAL ADULTERY and Jesus Christ WILL put us away; he WILL spew us out (Rev 3:16); if we do not quickly repent.

The religious leaders who do these sins and teach others to do such wickedness; will be corrected by our loving Father; Those who justify such evil, instead of condemning it; will also be corrected: for they are an abomination to the Eternal.

Proverbs 17:15 He that justifieth the wicked, and he that condemneth the just, even they both are abomination to the LORD.

Brethren, the day is coming when there will be a clear choice to be made; a choice between following evil seducers in their evil deeds of rejecting God's Word for their own opinions and the false traditions of men just because they are leaders in an organization of men: or whether we will choose to turn to Almighty God with a whole heart rejecting such wickedness.

I would that such uncleanness of men; who smite their brethren and lord it over others, exalting themselves as an ultimate moral authority between men and God, did not exist even in the imaginations of men.

This grotesque abomination DOES exist and abounds; and it needs to be repented of; and those who refuse to repent should be rejected by those brethren filled with the love and Spirit of our ALL WISE FATHER!

Those who are self-righteous deceivers need to repent quickly, lest the Eternal quickly correct you. I speak to ALL peoples.

Wake up and turn to the Eternal with a whole heart!

Remember that we are all but dust in the eyes of God; that we are all just brothers; that we are all in this TOGETHER; and we should be helping each other to focus on the Life Giving Father: not exalting ourselves and making merchandise of our brethren.

The Master Builder is doing a marvelous work in this latter day; he is sifting and separating out those who will repent of exalting men: He is turning the hearts of the children to their Father in heaven!

There is enormous talk about brotherly love and the "Philadelphian Christian" in the assemblies. It is important to have a good understanding of the subject of love and the meaning of godly love.

Regardless of all the hair splitting over the meaning of words like Agape Love, if we seek to be godly we should let God's Word define love for us and then live by that definition. God defines godly love as keeping the commandments of God the Father.

1 John 5:3 For this is the love of God, that we keep his commandments: and his commandments are not grievous.

Anyone who claims to be in Christ must live just as Christ lived and lives.

1 John 2:6 He that saith he abideth in him [Christ] ought himself also so to walk [live], even as he walked [lived and lives].

Jesus Christ lived as an example which we should follow, and taught his people to live by every Word of God.

John 15:10 If ye keep my commandments, ye shall abide in my love; even as **I have kept my Father's commandments, and abide in his love.**

Matthew 4:4 But he answered and said, It is written, Man shall not live by bread alone, but by every word that proceedeth out of the mouth of God.

Deuteronomy 5:32 Ye shall observe to do therefore as the Lord your God hath commanded you: ye shall not turn aside to the right hand or to the left. **5:33** Ye shall walk in all the ways which the Lord your God hath commanded you, that ye may live, and that it may be well with you, and that ye may prolong your days in the land which ye shall possess.

True godly love is to love God enough to seek to please God by doing what God says. The godly pillar is the person who lives by every Word of God out of a passionate love for God and the Truth, and love for other humans is based on the foundation of our love for godliness.

The epistles to the Thessalonians were recorded and preserved for God's faithful pillars who stand unshakable on every Word of God; and encourages them in their patient enduring while giving them key prophetic information.

While the epistles of Paul are addressed to individual congregations; they are likewise preserved as Holy Scripture and recorded for instruction of all those who are called by God.

1 Thessalonians 1:1 Paul, and Silvanus, and Timotheus, unto the church of the Thessalonians which is in God the Father and in the Lord Jesus Christ: Grace be unto you, and peace, from God our Father, and the Lord Jesus Christ.

Just as Colossians was meant as an encouragement to godliness for the Colossians and the latter day Laodiceans, this epistle is especially for the faithful in Thessaloniki and for the faithful pillars throughout history and in these later days.

The Thessalonians were full of faith and the works of faith, and diligent to patiently live by every Word of God, so are the pillars of these last days and of all ages. We are to patiently endure, growing in godliness and overcoming all sin, and in so doing we shall be saved at the resurrection to spirit.

Luke 21:19 In your patience possess ye your souls [attain eternal life].

Colossians was written specifically to Laodicea (Rev 3:14-22) and the epistles to the Thessalonians were (and are) a direct encouragement and instruction for the pillars, called the Philadelphian Ekklesia in Revelation 3.

1 Thessalonians 1:2 We give thanks to God always for you all, making mention of you in our prayers; **1:3** Remembering without ceasing **your work of faith, and labour of love, and patience of hope in our Lord Jesus Christ, in the sight of God and our Father; 1:4** Knowing, brethren beloved, your election [calling] of God.

This letter is addressed to the Thessalonians who are presented as faithful pillars of light.

These messages contain no correction at all, only instructions and encouragement for God's pillars. These folks in Thessalonica had a true Philadelphian attitude of love for and of living by every Word of God; which we would do well to emulate.

1:5 For our gospel came not unto you in word only, but also in power, and in the Holy Ghost, and in much assurance; as ye know what manner of men we were among you for your sake.

The pillars are called out in much affliction and endure very much for God's way, yet they remain solidly grounded on the sound doctrine of the whole Word of God. They follow every Word of God with joy, and through their zeal for all things of God, are full of the Holy Spirit of TRUTH.

1:6 And ye became followers of us, and of the Lord, having received the word in much affliction, with joy of the Holy Ghost.

Paul reminds them that they received the Word through much affliction; meaning that they suffered much for the sake of their love, zeal and faith toward God.

The pillars know that they were sinners and they know that they are weak, and that they are saved by the mercy and power of God. Therefore they stand upon and rely upon their Mighty Deliverer, cleaving to him and continually relying upon their Mighty One; diligently living by every

Word of God and never turning aside to follow idols of men or their own imaginations.

They endure adversity and receive and embrace the truth of God with great joy.

Where has that great joy in discovering and understanding the things of God gone in the Laodicean church of today? Has it not been buried in a misguided zeal for false tradition and idols of men, instead of a Philadelphian love of the TRUTH?

The pillars are a Shining Light of example for their Laodicean brethren who reject them for a time; but will later remember that shining example and likewise turn to the Eternal!

1:7 So that ye were ensamples to all that believe in Macedonia and Achaia.

Today the spiritual Ekklesia has fallen far away from a godly zeal and love for TRUTH and an enthusiastic zeal for all of God's Word, falling into a blind unquestioning faith in idols of men; above our first love and faith in our espoused Husband and his Father.

How did this happen?

We have been deceived by thinking that "Philadelphia" means brotherly love [love for men] while forgetting that the proper foundation of brotherly love is a mutual love for God the Father.

All those who love God the Father and live by every Word of God will be bound together by their mutual love of God and will love one another on that common foundation. That is the definition of a Philadelphian pillar!

True godly love is to love God with all our beings, and if we truly love God we will seek to please him and we will do what God says. Our love of God and our living by every Word of God then becomes the foundation for loving mankind.

Matthew 22:37 Jesus said unto him, Thou shalt love the Lord thy God with all thy heart, and with all thy soul, and with all thy mind. **22: 38 This is the first and great commandment. 22:39** And the second is like unto it, Thou shalt love thy neighbour as thyself.

If God is left out of the equation by paying lip service to God but having no love to live by every Word of God the Father, our love other people becomes idolatry because it exalts love for people above love for God.

Yet today, there are still a few faithful like these Thessalonians, and the scattered Philadelphian pillars are a Shining example of passionate zeal for the truth of God.

1:8 For from you sounded out the word of the Lord not only in Macedonia and Achaia, but also **in every place your faith to God-ward is spread abroad**; so that we need not to speak any thing.

Others will one day point to the example of the faithfulness and zeal of the patiently enduring pillars; and how we turned from idolizing men to serve the Omnipotent God.

1:9 For they themselves [others tell us of your example] shew of us what manner of entering in we had unto you, and how **ye turned to God from idols to serve the living and true God; 1:10** And to wait [to wait patiently for the deliverance of the coming Christ] for his Son from heaven, whom he raised from the dead, even Jesus, which delivered us from the wrath to come.

The Thessalonians and the faithful pillars of today have received the Word of Truth with joy, and have cleaved to the Word of the Eternal God through the strength of his Spirit; which is given to those who love and live by every Word of God.

Who will be chosen to be a part of the Bride in the resurrection to spirit? Those who are full of love for God, all godliness and for living by every Word of God!

Revelation 22:14 Blessed are they that do his commandments, that they may have right to the tree of life [eternal life], and may enter in through the gates into the city [the city of New Jerusalem on the new earth].

Revelation 14:12 Here is the patience of the saints: Here are they that keep the commandments of God, and the faith of Jesus.

Calling oneself a godly Christian and then engaging in egregious idolatry of a man or men, is self-deception and a great lie!

Colossians 2: The Ordinances Against Us

When a criminal is sentenced his indictment - which is a list of the laws he has broken - is read out. This indictment or list of his crimes is the list of ordinances he has broken, the list of the ordinances against him.

Jesus Christ was nailed to a stake and died paying for our list of sins. When he was nailed to the stake and died for our sincerely repented past sins, the list of ours sins was nailed to the stake with him.

Because he was crucified for OUR sins, the list of the ordinances which we had broken, the list of our sins which were paid for by his death was nailed to the stake in the person of Jesus Christ. Thus it is written that the ordinances which were against us were nailed to the cross; simply meaning that Christ died for, paid the penalty for and did away with; the list of our past sins.

This does not mean that the ordinances themselves were naturally bad and against us, it means that we were facing a penalty for having broken those ordinances, which penalty was paid in full by Jesus Christ the Lamb of God.

The ordinances or laws were not done away, it was our sins against those ordinances which was paid for and blotted out by the sacrifice of our LORD.

Colossians 2:14 Blotting out the handwriting of ordinances that was against us [the list of ordinances which we had broken], which was contrary to us [because we faced the death penalty for breaking them], and took it out of the way, nailing it to his cross [paying the penalty for us];

In context this is more easily understood:

Let no one beguile you into sin and compromise with any part of the whole Word of God.

Colossians 2:4 And this I say, lest any man should beguile you with enticing words.

As Paul was absent from Colossae at that time, he is also absent in the flesh today, but we have his written scriptures that we should be always zealous to keep live by every Word and the will of God.

2:5 For though I be absent in the flesh, yet am I with you in the spirit, joying and beholding your order, and the stedfastness of your faith [and the works of faith which is the diligent keeping of every Word of God] in Christ.

If we have sincerely repented and made a baptismal commitment to sin no more; we will receive the gift of the Holy Spirit, and we are to live as Christ lived through the strength of Jesus Christ living in us.

2:6 As ye have therefore received Christ Jesus the Lord, so **walk** [live as he lived] **ye in him**: **2:7 Rooted and built up in him, and stablished in the faith, as ye have been taught, abounding therein with thanksgiving.**

1 John 2:6 He that saith he abideth in him [Christ and God] ought himself also so to walk [live], even as he walked [lived and lives].

Stay fully grounded on the sound doctrine of the whole Word of God and let no person deceive you into compromising with any part of the whole Word of God.

Contend earnestly for the Scriptures as admonished by Jude and never compromise with the Sabbath or any part of the Word of God.

Jesus will not blink at a little willful sin, he will cast the sinner out of God the Father's temple! and we should love God the Father and Christ so much, that any willful sin would be disgustingly repellent to us.

Let no one spoil [plunder and gain control over you] by enticing you to cook, travel or buy food or anything else on God's Biblical Sabbath and

Holy Days, or lead you into minimizing and compromising with any part of the Word of God.

Let no man entice you to tolerate any sin; and do prove all things by the scripture. Beware of those who use the name of Christ to teach us to tolerate sin, saying that Christ died for us and we need no longer be zealous to keep the whole Word of God.

Colossians 2:8 Beware lest any man spoil [make plunder of you, and overcome you] **you through philosophy and vain deceit** [deceitful arguments], **after the tradition of men, after the rudiments of the world, and not after Christ.**

2:9 For in him [Jesus Christ] dwelleth all the fulness of the Godhead bodily.

For we are spiritually circumcised with the removal of our PAST sins and the old sinful man was destroyed in the watery grave of baptism; that we should rise up as new people in Christ being passionate to live by every Word of God in Christ-like zeal.

Then, IF we are diligent to learn, to grow and to overcome through the power of Christ dwelling in us by the Holy Spirit, we shall be raised up from the grave incorruptible as Jesus Christ was raised up incorruptible.

2:10 And ye are complete in him, **which is the head** of all principality and power: **2:11** In whom also **ye are circumcised with the circumcision made without hands, in putting off the body of the sins of the flesh by the circumcision of Christ: 2:12 Buried with him in baptism, wherein also ye are risen with him through the faith of the operation of God, who hath raised him from the dead.**

We the wicked, have been reconciled to God the Father and cleansed of our PAST sins by sincere repentance and the application of the atoning sacrifice of Jesus Christ, if we commit ourselves to go forward and sin no more.

2:13 And you, being dead in your sins and the uncircumcision of your flesh, hath he [the Father] quickened [made spiritually alive] together with him [Christ], having forgiven you all trespasses [by removing the veil of sin from our hearts in a spiritual circumcision through the application of the sacrifice of Christ];

God the Father erased the indictment against us, the list of our past sins; accepting our sincere repentance and the application of the sacrifice of Christ.

2:14 Blotting out the handwriting of ordinances that was against us, which was contrary to us, and took it out of the way, nailing it to his cross;

Jesus Christ through his perfect sinless life and his willingness to obey God the Father to the death, was worthy to be given all power in the universe [under God the Father]

2:15 And having spoiled principalities and powers, he made a shew of them openly, triumphing over them in it.

Remember this is a letter to the Gentiles at Colossae who had never previously abstained from unclean things and who had never before observed the Biblical Sabbath, Holy Days and New Moons. They being newly converted were just beginning to do these things and were being subjected to condemnation by other Gentiles for beginning to keep these things and Paul was encouraging them to faithfully live by every Word of God.

2:16 Let no man therefore judge [condemn us] you in meat, or in drink, or in respect of an holyday, or of the new moon, or of the sabbath days: 2:17 Which are a shadow of things to come; but the body [the complete scriptures, including these things; define the nature of Jesus Christ and God the Father] is of Christ.

Therefore we are to keep God's Sabbaths, New Moons and Holy Days, and we may eat scripturally clean meats although we must be diligent to avoid the unclean meats; which teaches us to put a difference between the holy and the profane.

We are to live by all things which are in the Word of God, and we are not to permit any person to criticize us and turn us away from living by every Word of God.

The reference to abstaining from meat or drink [wine] is a direct reference to the asceticism, vegetarianism and teetotaler teachings of the Stoics, as the traditions of men which might appear humble but are really self-willed.

True humility is faithfulness to submit to and live by every Word of God in deeds [the works of faith] and not mere appearances.

These things are commanded to be kept and they are prophetic of God's plan; and without keeping them as God commanded them to be kept, we cannot understand prophetic things.

This is why there is so little understanding, because we do not put a difference between the clean and unclean, between the holy and the profane; and because we do not keep the Biblical Sabbath, Holy Days and New Moons on the dates proscribed by the Word of God, and we do not keep them in the way that God's Word commands.

The Letter and the Spirit of the Law

Beware of false teachers who claim that the "spirit" of the Word of God does away with the letter of the law of God! There are those who claim that it is Pharisaic to be zealous for keeping the law of God in its physical letter, such men try to substitute what they regard as "spiritual" things for God's law.

What did Jesus teach? Jesus taught that we are to be zealous to live by BOTH the letter of the law in its physical application and the spirit of the law.

Matthew 23:23 Woe unto you, scribes and Pharisees, hypocrites! for ye pay tithe of mint and anise and cummin, and have omitted the weightier matters of the law, judgment, mercy, and faith: these ought ye to have done, and **not to leave the other undone**.

Technically we can keep the letter of the law without keeping the spirit of the law, but it is impossible to keep the spirit of the law without also keeping the letter of the law, because the letter of the law is the foundation of the spirit and intent of the law.

The letter of a law is the foundation of any possible intent of a law! How can there be a spirit and intent of a law when that law does not exist in the letter?

Yes, keeping only the letter of the law engenders death; for we can keep the letter and still break the spirit and intent of God's Word.

Nevertheless keeping both the law in the letter AND the spirit, gives life eternal; provided we sincerely repent of PAST law breaking and go forward to "sin [break the law in both letter and spirit] no more". This is evident in the resurrected Christ who kept both the letter and the spirit of the law and taught us to do likewise.

In Fact, one cannot even keep the letter of the law by one's own strength without God's Holy Spirit! The history of Israel reveals that one cannot even keep the letter of the law under the Mosaic Covenant, because that Covenant contained no promise of the Holy Spirit without which it is impossible to obey God in either letter or spirit.

Romans 8:7 Because the carnal mind is enmity against God: for it is not subject to the law of God, neither indeed can be.

2 Corinthians 3:7 But if the ministration of death [because there was no sacrifice for breaking the spirit of the law], written and engraven in stones [at Mount Sinai], was glorious, so that the children of Israel could not stedfastly behold the face of Moses for the glory of his countenance; which glory **was to be done away** [the Mosaic Covenant was to end and a New Covenant was to come, Jeremiah 31:31]:

3:8 How shall not the ministration of the [the spiritual New Covenant which brings life eternal] spirit be rather glorious?

The spiritual New Covenant of Jeremiah 31:31, is much more glorious than the merely physical Mosaic Covenant; because the physical Mosaic Covenant ended with the death of the Husband of Israel, but the spiritual New Covenant is eternal: IF we keep it, obeying our LORD.

3:9 For if the ministration of condemnation [The Mosaic Covenant condemns us because we are not able to keep it, lacking the Spirit of God; and because there is no propitiation for breaking the spirit (intent) of the law.] be glory, much more doth the ministration of righteousness exceed in glory.

The Mosaic Covenant was a physical covenant with sacrifices for physical sin. Those who sinned could be reconciled to that Mosaic Covenant by the physical sacrifices, but there was no SPIRITUAL sacrifice for breaking the intent, purpose and spirit of the law.

That Mosaic Covenant which had no promise of eternal life, is surpassed by the spiritual New Covenant, that does promise and will produce eternal life for its adherents. The Mosaic Covenant was temporary; the spiritual New Covenant is eternal (Jer 31:31).

The New Covenant is a SPIRITUAL Covenant, which imparts SPIRITUAL knowledge and understanding of the purpose and intent, the spirit of the law. The New Covenant also provides an effectual sacrifice for the breaking of the intent, purpose and spirit of the law, and enables us to keep that spirit of the law, by placing a new spirit and attitude within us; the Spirit of God!

Remember, that one cannot keep the spirit of a nonexistent law: Therefore the law remains; and we are to keep all of God's Word in BOTH the letter and the spirit of the law.

Jeremiah 31:33 But this shall be the covenant that I will make with the house of Israel; After those days, saith the Lord, **I will put my law in their inward parts, and write it in their hearts; and will be their God, and they shall be my people.**

The New Covenant is that God will write His law upon our very hearts and in our minds so that God's law and the whole Word of God becomes our very nature. As we grow in understanding we keep the Word of God more and more perfectly in the letter and the purpose, intent and spirit, becoming holy as God is holy!

By keeping and internalizing every Word of God, we ARE internalizing Jesus Christ and God the Father, and becoming like them! For the law defines the very nature of God!

2 Corinthians 3:10 For even that which was made glorious [the Mosaic Covenant] had no glory in this respect [lacking the Holy Spirit and the promise of eternal life], by reason of the glory that excelleth [which is the eternal spiritual New Covenant].

3:11 For if **that which is done away** was glorious [Paul knew the Mosaic Covenant was ended by the death of Christ the Husband], much more that which remaineth [the eternal New Covenant] is glorious.

3:12 Seeing then that we have such hope, we use great plainness [boldness to speak openly] of speech: **3:13** And not as Moses, which put a vail over his face, that the children of Israel could not stedfastly look to the end [upon the glory of that which was to end] **of that which is abolished** [Paul clearly tells us that the Mosaic Covenant was abolished in his day and we know that a Marriage Covenant ends with the death of the Husband]: **3:14** But their minds [spirits] were blinded: for until this day remaineth the same vail [of sin] untaken away in the reading of the old testament [Mosaic Covenant]; which vail [of sin can only be removed by the application of the sacrifice of Christ] is done away in Christ.

This veil represents the sin of breaking the purpose and intent of the law; which the Mosaic Covenant had no real atonement for. The sacrifices of the Mosaic Covenant could not atone for sin against the spirit of the law; they only atoned for breaking the physical Mosaic Covenant and pictured the need for a spiritual atonement by the ultimate sacrifice of our Creator and the entering in of a New Covenant through the atonement of Jesus Christ.

3:15 But even unto this day, when Moses is read, the veil [the veil of sin separating us from God and the spirit of the law; remains without the sacrifice of Christ; because the Mosaic Covenant had no effective propitiation to atone for spiritual sin] is upon their heart.

Brethren, the Mosaic Covenant did not provide the Holy Spirit to teach us that we CANNOT keep even the physical letter of the law by our own will and strength. The New Covenant provides the holy Spirit to all sincerely repentant persons which Spirit enables us to live by every Word of God in both the letter and in its spirit and intent.

- BEWARE, those false teachers who try to claim that we must live by the letter of the law but that we need not go beyond the letter to keep God's Word in its spirit and intent.

- BEWARE those false teachers who say that we need only keep the spirit of the law and Word of God and say that we need not keep the letter of the law as well. In teaching this they lead people away from living by the Word of God, into following their own false traditions and are true Pharisees indeed!

Faith and the Works of Faith

James 2:14 What doth it profit, my brethren, though a man say he hath faith, and have not works? Can faith save him? **2:5** If a brother or sister be naked, and destitute of daily food, **2:16** and one of you say unto them, Depart in peace, be ye warmed and filled; notwithstanding ye give them not those things which are needful to the body, what doth it profit?

2:17 Even so **faith, if it hath not works, is dead, being alone. 2:18** Yea, a man may say, You hast faith, and I have works. **Show me thy faith without thy works, and I will show thee my faith by my works. 2:19** Thou believest that there is one God; thou doest well: the devils also believe, and tremble [Yet the demons will not obey God's Word, therefore their belief brings them nothing but the sure knowledge of their coming therefore their belief brings them nothing but the sure knowledge of their coming judgment]. **2:20** But wilt thou know, O vain man, that **faith without works is dead**?

2:21 Was not Abraham our father justified [by his deeds] by works when he [obeyed God] had offered Isaac his son upon the altar? **2:22** Seest thou how faith wrought [worked with] with his works and by works was faith made perfect? **2:23** And the scripture was fulfilled which saith, Abraham believed God, and it was imputed unto him for righteousness: and he was called the Friend of God.

2:24 Ye see then how that by works a man is justified, and not by faith only. **2:25** Likewise also was not Rehab the harlot justified by works, when she had received the messengers, and had sent them out another way? **2:26** For **as the body without the spirit is dead, so faith without works is dead.**

What then are the works of faith? the works of godly faith are to live by every Word of God in BOTH the letter and the spirit! When Jesus was tempted to satisfy his hunger by turning a stone into bred, did he rationalize that stone and bread are only physical?

NO! He said that we must live by every Word of God

Luke 4:2 Being forty days tempted of the devil. And in those days he did eat nothing: and when they were ended, he afterward hungered.

4:3 And the devil said unto him, If thou be the Son of God, command this stone that it be made bread.

4:4 And Jesus answered him, saying, "It is written, **That man shall not live by bread alone, but by every word of God**".

Brethren we CANNOT keep the spirit of the law without keeping the letter of the law, because the letter is the very foundation of the laws spirit and intent. Jesus taught us this when he declared:

Matthew 15: 3 But he answered and said unto them, Why do ye also transgress the commandment of God by your tradition?

15:4 For God commanded, saying, Honour thy father and mother: and, He that curseth father or mother, let him die the death.

15:5 But ye say, Whosoever shall say to his father or his mother, It is a gift [an offering], by whatsoever thou mightest be profited by me; **15:6** And honour not his father or his mother, he shall be free. Thus have ye made the commandment of God of none effect by your tradition.

15:7 Ye hypocrites, well did Esaias prophesy of you, saying, **15:8** This people draweth nigh unto me with their mouth, and honoureth me with their lips; but their heart is far from me. **15:9** But in vain they do worship me, teaching for doctrines the commandments of men.

In saying this Jesus clearly taught that we are to keep the letter of the law in order to fulfil the spirit of the law!

We are to live by the letter and the intent and spirit of the law, in passionate enthusiastic Christ-like zeal!

True godly love is to live by every Word of God, which means keeping the letter of the law as the foundation of the spiritual intent of that law. Without the letter of the law there can be no spirit or intent of a non-existent law!

1 John 2:5 But whoso keepeth his word, in him verily is the love of God perfected: hereby know we that we are in him. **2:6** He that saith he abideth in him ought himself also so to walk, even as he walked.

1 John 5:2 By this we know that we love the children of God, when we love God, and keep his commandments. **5:3** For this is the love of God, that we keep his commandments: and his commandments are not grievous.

One cannot even keep the letter of the law by one's own strength of self will! The history of Israel reveals that one cannot even keep the letter of the law under the Mosaic Covenant, because that Covenant contained no promise of the Holy Spirit without which it is impossible to obey God in either letter or spirit.

Romans 8:7 Because the carnal mind is enmity against God: for it is not subject to the law of God, neither indeed can be.

Folks start off with the assumption that the Pharisees were zealous for God's law; and conclude that since Christ condemned the Pharisees, they think that Christ also objected to zealously living by God's Word and law.

The first rule of logic: BEWARE of a possible foundational false premise in any argument!

The Pharisees were NOT zealous for God's law! They made God's law of no effect because they were zealous for and exalted their own false traditions ABOVE the Word and law of God! UCG has swallowed this false premise and used it as the basis to replace their zeal for living by God's Word with a false emotional feel good "love" and organizational loyalty.

Discerning Between the Holy and the Profane

In this confusing world, how are we to know who is a true servant of the Living God and who is not?

The answer to this question is given to us in Matthew 7, Deuteronomy 13 and Deuteronomy 18:20-22. While the term prophets is used, this instruction is equally applicable to anyone who claims to be a man of God.

1 Corinthians 11:3 But I would have you know, that the head of every man is Christ; and the head of the woman is the man; and the head of Christ is God.

The ONLY ecclesiastical authority which exists is the authority of the TRUTH itself and God's Word is Truth. Therefore the whole Word of God is the ultimate moral authority and the authority by which all people will be judged by God.

All people will be judged by Almighty God; either to life eternal for those who live by every Word of God, or to damnation for those who refuse to live by every Word of God.

Since we will all be judged by our fidelity to every Word of God; it is imperative that we make absolutely sure that any teachings of men which we accept and follow must be consistent with every Word of God. Therefore we must "prove all things" by the Word of God and "hold fast that which is good" by God's Word (1 Thess 5:21)

Not every person who claims to be godly, is godly. There are many false teachers desiring to have personal followings. Such people may be seeking wealth and the adulation of men, or they may be genuinely sincere but sincerely wrong; and so claiming to be of God they USE the term "God" to pass on their own ideas.

They may claim to love and follow God the Father or Jesus Christ, they may even be well meaning but deceived themselves and teaching wrongly, not understanding.

Mark 7:7 Howbeit in vain do they worship me, teaching for doctrines the commandments of men.

How do we understand the truth and how do we discern who is teaching the truth? The key is really very simple, we are the servants of those that we obey, as Jesus asked:

Luke 6:46 And why call ye me, Lord, Lord, and do not the things which I say?

Some teach error out of sincerity and some are so wicked that they think and teach that they can do anything they want and God will back them up, but the scriptures say:

Romans 6:16 Know ye not, that to whom ye yield yourselves servants to obey, his servants ye are to whom ye obey; whether of sin unto death, or of obedience unto righteousness?

If we were God's servants we would be living by every Word of God and doing what God says; Almighty God and His Word would always be sovereign over our lives and deeds and we would always be subject to God and the Word of God!

If we decide we can do whatever we want and think that God will back us up, even if our decisions are contrary to God's Word; then we have exalted ourselves to be sovereign above God and the Word of God, and we have made God and the Word of God subject to our own personal decisions! We are not obeying the Word of God, we are requiring that God follow us!

If we obey the Word of God, then we are God's servants indeed; but if we do what WE decide, we are NOT the servants of God but the servants of our own devices.

The godly man lives by EVERY WORD of GOD (Mat 4:4); while the wicked man claims that he has the right to bind and loose God's Word and to decide for himself what is right and what is wrong for himself.

How then do we tell the difference between those who serve God and those who do not serve God; the difference between the true man of God and the false teacher; the difference between the holy and the profane?

A godly person lives by every Word of God and teaches all people to do likewise, and if he should slip it will be a rare situation and not the norm; and he will acknowledge his fault ad quickly repent. He will also be eagerly seeking to grow continually in knowledge and understanding of godliness and will be quick to discard past errors and false traditions of men as he learns the truth.

The wicked person will stand on his own - or his organizations - false traditions, and will do everything he can to avoid accepting or living by every Word of God.

The things a godly person says; MUST be true according to every Word of God; and all godly people will teach all men to live by every Word of God. In other words EVERYTHING that they say MUST be consistent with every Word spoken by God (Mat 4:4).

It is vital that we be able to discern between Godly people and ungodly people, between God's Spirit and deceitful false spirits, between good and evil. Here are a few keys to spiritual discernment between God's Holy Spirit and the many counterfeit spirits trying to deceive us and lead us astray.

Satan presents himself as an angel of light, counterfeiting the gifts and fruits of God's Spirit.

2 Corinthians 11:14 And no marvel; for Satan himself is [presents himself] transformed into an angel of light. **11:15** Therefore it is no great thing if his ministers also [present themselves as] be transformed as the ministers of righteousness; whose end shall be according to their works.

2 John 1:7 For many deceivers are entered into the world, who confess not that Jesus Christ is come [those who reject that Jesus Christ will dwell in our flesh, through his spirit empowering us to live as Christ lives] in the flesh. This is a deceiver and an antichrist.

Any person or spirit that says that Jesus Christ will not come to dwell in us and enable us to live by every Word of God as Jesus did and does; is an antichrist!

How can we discern between the Holy Spirit of God and the counterfeits presented by Satan to deceive us away from God?

The Spirit of God is truth and leads those who follow it, into all truth. The Word of God is truth, therefore the Spirit of God and the Word of God are always consistent.

John 17:17 Sanctify them through thy truth: thy word is truth.

The first key;

God's Spirit is the Spirit of Christ, for God the father and Jesus Christ are in full unity with one another, and those in whom Christ dwells will do the same thing that Jesus did, and will keep the whole Word of God as Jesus did.

The Holy Spirit will lead us to keep the whole Word of God without any hint of compromise.

God is not divided against himself and God's Spirit would NEVER lead us to compromise with any sin; it would never lead us to set aside sections of scripture to enable us to try to justify our sins; instead it would lead us into all truth and into a zealous keeping of the whole Word, the truth of God; as Christ did and does.

John 14:15   If ye love me, keep my commandments. **14:16** And I will pray the Father, and he shall give you another Comforter, that he may abide with you for ever; **14:17** Even **the Spirit of truth;** whom the world cannot receive, because it seeth him not, neither knoweth him: but ye know him; for he dwelleth with you, and shall be in you.

God's Spirit is not available to the worldly; because the worldly, the carnally minded, are not subject to God and cannot be. God's Holy Spirit is given ONLY to those who keep God's Word.

Acts 5:32 And we are his witnesses of these things; and so is also **the Holy Ghost, whom God hath given to them that obey him**.

John 14:23 Jesus answered and said unto him, **If a man love me, he will keep my words:** and my Father will love him, and we will come unto him, and make our abode with him. **14:24 He that loveth me not keepeth not my sayings**: and the word which ye hear is not mine, but the Father's which sent me. **14:25** These things have I spoken unto you, being yet present with you. **14:26** But the Comforter, which is the Holy Ghost, whom the Father will send in my name, **he shall teach you all things, and bring all things to your remembrance, whatsoever I have said unto you.**

Romans 8:9 But ye are not in the flesh, but in the Spirit, if so be that the Spirit of God dwell in you. Now if any man have not **the Spirit of Christ,** he is none of his. **8:10** And if Christ be in you, the body is [the flesh will die, but the spirit will be resurrected] dead because of sin; but the Spirit is life because of righteousness.[empowering us to live as Christ lived, keeping the whole Word of God]

What did Jesus teach?

Matthew 19:17 And he said unto him, Why callest thou me good? there is none good but one, that is, God: but **if thou wilt enter into life, keep the commandments.**

God's Spirit is the Spirit of truth and is the very nature of God the Father and Jesus Christ; that nature is a Gift from God the Father to dwell within all those who have sincerely repented and committed themselves to living by every Word of God.

The Holy Spirit is ONLY given to those who obey all the teachings [doctrines] and live by every Word of God the Father and Jesus Christ; for the Holy Spirit is the very nature of God; and is not, and cannot, be divided against God.

The Holy Spirit is ONE in complete UNITY with Jesus Christ and with God the Father; and if it is dwelling is us, it will lead us into complete wholehearted UNITY with God the Father and with Jesus Christ.

Those who have not sincerely repented of breaking or compromising with the Word of God, and who have not committed to STOP sinning and to START learning of God and living by every Word of God with passionate zeal: Will NOT be given the GIFT of the Holy Spirit! and if they did have it and have gotten lax for God's Word; they are quenching that Spirit!

John 15:26 But when the Comforter is come, whom I will send unto you from the Father, even **the Spirit of truth**, which proceedeth from the Father, he shall testify of me:

God is spirit (John 4:24); the Holy Spirit of God is the Spirit of truth (John 14:17, 1 John 5:6, John 14:18-28).

What is truth? God's Word is truth: (John 17:17)

Ephesians 5:8 For ye were sometimes darkness, but now are ye light in the Lord: [therefore] walk [live] as children of light: **5:9** (For the fruit of the Spirit is in all goodness and righteousness and truth;)

The Spirit of God leads us into all truth and we are to prove out what is true by comparing all things to the Word of God

5:10 Proving what is acceptable unto the Lord [by the Word of God].

We are to have nothing to do with false doctrine or willful sin; and we are commanded NOT to tolerate, but to reprove all false doctrine and sin

5:11 And have no fellowship with the unfruitful works of darkness, but rather reprove them.

James 1:22 But **be ye doers of the word**, and not hearers only, deceiving your own selves. **1:23** For if any be a hearer of the word, and not a doer, he is like unto a man beholding his natural face in a glass: **1:24** For he beholdeth himself, and goeth his way, and straightway forgetteth what manner of man he was **1:25** But whoso looketh into the perfect law of liberty [from sin], and continueth therein, he being not a forgetful hearer, but a doer of the work, this man shall be blessed in his deed.

Therefore, in **John 16:7** Christ said: Nevertheless I tell you the truth; It is expedient for you that I go away: for if I go not away, the Comforter will not come unto you; but if I depart, I will send him unto you.

Jesus Christ had to fulfill his mission and die for the sins of the world so that those who are called of God the Father, to come to Christ and believe on him; who are called to repent of disobedience to the Word of God; those who commit themselves to live by every Word of God at baptism, washing away the sins of the past and becoming alive to Christ and dead to sin; might then receive the GIFT of God's Spirit.

God's Spirit is a gift given ONLY to those who obey all the commandments of God without compromise.

Acts 5:32 And we are his witnesses of these things; and so is also **the Holy Ghost, whom God hath given to them that obey him.**

It is time to be absolutely clear: God is NOT divided against himself; God the Father and the Son are ONE in complete unity; and their Spirit is ONE (John 10:30, 17:11, 17:21) in complete unity: The Holy Spirit is the nature of God the Father and the nature of the Son; and is NOT divided against them!

The Holy Spirit will lead and empower us to live by every Word of God; and will NEVER lead us to compromise with that Word or to reject parts of it, or to countenance and tolerate anything false or any willful sin.

Therefore any spirit which teaches tolerance for doctrinal diversity, or teaches that doctrine - the teachings of the Word of God - is not important; and any spirit that teaches that a little willful sin is all right because Jesus will understand and forgive: and any spirit that rejects sections of scripture [like on the Sabbath or Calendar or Holy Days] to justify false teachings and sin: IS the false spirit of antichrist, it is a satanic spirit attempting to counterfeit God's Spirit and lead us astray from Almighty God!

Look at the various groups of the spiritual Ekklesia and think about what they are doing! By rejecting truth they are rejecting the Holy Spirit of truth for false demonic spirits of deceit and sin! They are quenching God's Holy Spirit by rebellion against any zeal to live by every Word of God; and because they have rejected any zeal to keep the Word of God, Jesus Christ is going to reject them and spue them out of his body (Rev 3:16).

This is serious! This is a salvational matter!

Therefore God in his mercy and willing to try to save us; will cast us into great tribulation that through the affliction of the flesh the spirit might be brought to sincere repentance and be saved. But we are forewarned and we can TEST and PROVE the spirits: whether they are of God or of the Wicked One.

How do we discern the spirits whether they be holy or evil?

We are commanded to test and prove out all things by the whole Word of God.

1 John 4:1 Beloved, **believe not every spirit, but try the spirits whether they are of God:** because many false prophets are gone out into the world.

2 Timothy 3:16 All scripture is given by inspiration of God, and is **profitable for doctrine, for reproof, for correction, for instruction in righteousness: 3:17** That the man of God may be perfect, thoroughly furnished unto all good works.

2 Timothy 2:15 Study to shew thyself approved unto God, a workman that needeth not to be ashamed, rightly dividing the word of truth.

1 Thessalonians 5:21 Prove all things; hold fast that which is good. 5:22 Abstain from all appearance of evil.

That is the reason for the scattering of the Ekklesia today: We have apostatized and blindly followed idols of men, not proving all things by the Word of God as to whether they be true, like the Bereans and Ephesians did; and we have refused to be zealous to live by every Word of God: We have quenched the Holy Spirit of God!

The Holy Spirit is the GIFT of God to those who have sincerely repented of following the false traditions of men, and who have committed themselves to love and cherish God and every Word of God.

By leaving our first love to turn back into the spiritual Egypt of slavery to the false traditions of men; we have been deceived into rejecting much of God's Word, and because we have rejected him: He will also reject us until we repent!

Ezekiel 34 the entire chapter is about those shepherds in BOTH physical and spiritual Israel who are wolves and feed themselves with all the good things of the flock while neglecting to feed the flock with the truth of the sound doctrine of God's Word in due season.

Ezekiel 34:1 And the word of the LORD came unto me, saying **34:2** Son of man, prophesy against the shepherds of Israel, prophesy, and say unto them, Thus saith the Lord GOD unto the shepherds; Woe be to the shepherds of Israel that do feed themselves! should not the shepherds feed the flocks?

The Vine and Branches

This is a powerful; explanation of the meaning of the command to cut branches and bring them into the temple at the Feast of Tabernacles. Bringing in the branches with great rejoicing represents bringing in of the harvest of humanity into the Family of God.

Jesus teaches that he is the vine [or trunk] of the tree of life; and that the called out to him are the branches. As a branch receives its nourishment from the vine and trunk of the tree; so we receive our spiritual nourishment from the Bread of Life, the true VINE; Jesus Christ!

To have eternal life; we MUST be in FULL UNITY with Christ; and if we turn away from living by every Word of God the Father in the letter and in the spirit and intent of the law; we will be rejected by Christ and by God the Father, because we have already rejected their Word.

If we remain faithfully loyal to Jesus Christ and God the Father by diligently studying and zealously KEEPING and living by every Word of God; we will still be tried, tested and given experiences bad and good, to increase our spiritual growth and development into FULL UNITY with Christ.

John 15:1 I am the true vine [trunk of the tree, the Logos the whole Word of God], and my Father is the husbandman. **15:2 Every branch in me that beareth not fruit** [is NOT faithful and zealous to live by every Word of God as Christ does] **he** taketh **away: and every branch that** beareth **fruit** [which comes through living by EVERY WORD of GOD]**, he** purgeth [trims and trains] **it, that it may bring forth more fruit**.

If we abide in the Word of God, doing those things that please Jesus Christ and God the Father; they will abide in us through the Spirit of God. If we are NOT zealous to KEEP the Word of God; WE ARE NONE OF HIS!

Remember that when you are asked by your elder to pollute the Sabbath or to take Passover and observe High Days on the wrong dates, or in the wrong ways; or are told that you need not eat Unleavened Bread every day of the Feast of Unleavened Bread as God has commanded.

After washing the disciple's feet; they were all clean except one. That one being the person who did not spiritually abide in Christ the true VINE

15:3 Now ye are clean through the word which I have spoken unto you. **15:4** Abide in me, and I in you. **As the branch cannot bear fruit of itself, except it abide in the vine; no more can ye, except ye abide in me.**

Beware false Christ's who tolerate sin and are not filled with Christ-like zeal to live by every Word of God; Because without a firm close FULL UNITY with the true Christ who lives by every Word of God; our religion is vain and meaningless, and falls to the status of a human social club.

15:5 I am the vine, ye are the branches: He that abideth in me, and I in him, the same bringeth **forth much fruit: for without me ye can do nothing.**

To be grafted into the true vine of Christ; we MUST be called of God the Father; believe, repent and be baptized, for the remission of sins to be granted. And IF we remain abiding in God; with him dwelling us; IF we follow the Holy Spirit's lead into all truth diligently keeping God's Word, then we shall bear much fruit!

15:6 If a man abide not in me [living in Christ-like zeal to live by EVERY WORD of GOD], **he is cast forth as a branch, and is withered; and men gather them, and cast them into the fire, and they are burned.**

Those who compromise with any part of the whole Word of God , which Christ loves; and who tolerate sin, which Christ hates; will be rejected and cast into the furnace of affliction; and if they still do not repent they will be cast into the fire of ultimate destruction.

15:7 If ye abide in me, and my words abide in you, ye shall ask what ye will, and it shall be done unto you. 15:8 Herein is my Father glorified, that ye bear much fruit; so shall ye be my disciples. 15:9 As the Father hath loved me, so have I loved you: continue ye in my love.

"Continue in my love" means that Christ wants our loving relationship with HIM to continue, through our learning and keeping the Word which he has preached; which is to do God the Father's will and to live by every Word of God, internalizing the very nature of God the Father.

Watch Out! Many will teach to keep the commandments, but by commandments they mean their own false traditions and not the whole Word of God.

15:10 If ye keep my commandments, ye shall abide in my love; even as I have kept my Father's commandments, and abide in his love.

What did Christ command us? He kept the whole Word of God fully and we are to do likewise, living as he lived and as he will live in us.

Jesus Christ lived a life of perfect obedience to his beloved Father, and he will live a life of perfect obedience to God the Father in us!

Matthew 19:17 . . .but if thou wilt enter into life, keep the commandments

John 15:11 These things have I spoken unto you, that my joy might remain in you, and that your joy might be full.

15:12 This is my commandment, That ye love one another, as I have loved you [true godly love is defined by the Word of God]. **15:13** Greater love hath no man than this, that a man lay down his life for his friends.

We are to be willing to lay down our lives for God the Father and Jesus Christ; as Christ laid down his life for us! How long will we squabble over who gets to lead; and over who gets what?

How has the love of God disappeared from us? Where has our zeal to live by every Word of God gone? Where is our unity with God?

15:14 Ye are my friends, if ye do whatsoever I command you.

Amos 3:3 Can two walk together, except they be agreed?

The fruits of a spirit, or a man; are the results of their thoughts and actions, and these fruits sum up the character of the person or spirit, whether it is godly or evil.

Discerning Between Men of God and False Teachers

Jesus Christ instructed us:

Matthew 7:15 Beware of false prophets, which come to you in sheep's clothing, but inwardly they are ravening wolves.

A wolf feeds himself and ravages the flock.

Matthew 7:16 Ye shall know them by their fruits. Do men gather grapes of thorns, or figs of thistles? **7:17** Even so every good tree bringeth forth good fruit; but a corrupt tree bringeth forth evil fruit.

Those who are political and seek the chief seats, who seek self-aggrandizement and personal advantage; are the wolves hiding among the sheep. Today there are very many wolves who do not feed the sheep the true Gospel of: warning, repentance, and diligent faithful obedience to God which brings eternal salvation.

If any man teaches tolerance for sin out of a phony false love; if any elder tolerates sin [the breaking of God's commandments, not the breaking of some organizational edict] without rebuke; if any organization does not preach a message of warning and repentance to the world; They are corrupt branches that will be pruned off at the judgment!

The True Good Shepherd feeds the flock with the words of truth; with the teachings that lead to salvation; strongly rebuking all sin. We are to follow that true Good Shepherd with the diligent KEEPING of the whole Word of God, so that the whole flock internalizes God the Father and the Son; growing into a full spiritual unity with God!

Matthew 7:18 A good tree cannot bring forth evil fruit, neither can a corrupt tree bring forth good fruit. **7:19** Every tree that bringeth not forth good fruit is hewn down, and cast into the fire.

The good tree is that Good Shepherd [Jesus Christ] who is working to bring the whole flock into a fullness of unity with God the Father! We are to follow that Good Shepherd who gave his all, his very life for God the Father's flock and did not seek his own.

We are to follow that example that was set for us, and faithfully serve God the Father by feeding his flock with the very Word of God, the very nature of God; without fear or compromise; regardless of what men think or do.

There are some good elders among you even now, who teach the true way of salvation and are alert watchmen discerning the signs of the times. They may be kept down, ridiculed and even persecuted by others, yet God the Father will reward them.

Luke 12:42 And the Lord said, Who then is that faithful and wise steward, whom his lord shall make ruler over his household, to give them their portion of meat in due season? **12:43** Blessed is that servant, whom his lord when he cometh shall find so doing **12:44** Of a truth I say unto you, that he will make him ruler over all that he hath.

Matthew 7:19 Every tree that bringeth not forth good fruit is hewn down, and cast into the fire.

The evil servant

Luke 12:45 But and if that servant say in his heart, My lord delayeth his coming; and shall begin to beat the menservants and maidens, and to eat and drink, and to be drunken;

Those who abuse others and seek their own pleasures will be taken by surprise and sternly corrected

Luke 12:46 The lord of that servant will come in a day when he looketh not for him, and at an hour when he is not aware, and will cut him in sunder, and will appoint him his portion with the unbelievers. **12:47 And that servant, which knew his lord's will, and prepared not himself, neither did according to his will, shall be beaten with many stripes.**

The unconverted who did not know the will of God, shall have much less correction than the converted who grow lax, lukewarm, complacent and self-willed.

12:48 But he that knew not, and did commit things worthy of stripes, shall be beaten with few stripes. For unto whomsoever much is given, of him shall be much required

Matthew 7:20 Wherefore by their fruits ye shall know them.

We will know the good shepherds by their love of God and their diligent keeping and teaching of every Word of God and by their diligence to do the will of HIM who called them.

Matthew 23:11 But he that is greatest among you shall be your servant. **23:12** And whosoever shall exalt himself shall be abased; and he that shall humble himself shall be exalted.

Matthew 7:21 Not every one that saith unto me, Lord, Lord, shall enter into the kingdom of heaven; *but he that doeth the will of my Father which is in heaven.*

7:22 Many will say to me in that day, Lord, Lord, have we not prophesied in thy name? and in thy name have cast out devils? and in thy name done many wonderful works? **7:23** And then will I profess unto them, I never knew you: depart from me, ye that work iniquity.

7:24 Therefore whosoever heareth these sayings of mine, *and doeth them,* I will liken him unto a wise man, which built his house upon a rock: **7:25** And the rain descended, and the floods came, and the winds blew, and beat upon that house; and it fell not: for it was founded upon a rock.

Those who internalize the nature of God the Father and Jesus Christ; who become one with them in total spiritual unity, through a deep love for God and all the things of God, those who love the passionate keeping of all of their commandments and who set a good example of godliness and FEED THE FLOCK with the good pasture of the Word, watering them with the Spirit of Godliness; are building on the foundation of the Word of God which shall NEVER be moved.

Ephesians 2:20 And are built upon the foundation of the apostles and prophets, Jesus Christ himself being the chief corner stone;

Matthew 7:26 And every one that heareth these sayings of mine, **and doeth them not,** shall be likened unto a foolish man, which built his house upon the sand: **7:27** And the rain descended, and the floods came, and the winds blew, and beat upon that house; and it fell: and great was the fall of it.

The Word of God is not plainly taught today, because it is NOT KEPT! It is because the Word of God exposes the many false shepherds among us! It is because the Word of God cuts sharply into the very heart and spirit of our organizations and convicts us of our sins and egocentric complacency; and our lack of God centeredness; exposing our almost total lack of Christ-like zeal for God the Father's will and ways!

Jesus Christ [Hebrew: Yeshua] stands at the door of each of those called to him; knocking (Rev 3:14-22), calling us to repent of our self-righteous idolizing of our own ways; calling us to a diligent dedicated passionate obedience to every Word of God; calling us to a zeal for the keeping of God's Word and instructions; calling us to sincerely repent of our self-seeking embracing of worldliness.

It is only by studying and doing the Word of God, that we begin to learn to discern between the holy and the profane; between the wolves and the true shepherds and sheep; for truly the wolves do disguise themselves diligently, and can only be discerned through a proving of all things by the scriptures.

Matthew 7:28 And it came to pass, when Jesus had ended these sayings, the people were astonished at his doctrine: **7:29** For he taught them as one having authority, and not as the scribes.

Jesus Christ had the authority of the Word of God, because he taught, stood on and lived that Word!

Any person who teaches the very Word of God, has the authority of the Word of truth which he teaches.

Christ taught us to live by every Word of God the Father! Christ's authority was from God the Father, because he stood on and taught what God the Father had commanded him!

As long as he taught what the Father had commanded; Christ was speaking in the Name Of, and by the Authority Of: The very King of the Universe!

John 12:49 For I have not spoken of myself; but the Father which sent me, he gave me a commandment, what I should say, and what I should speak.

It is the Word of God which is authoritative and no man has any NO authority whatsoever, regardless of whether they are ordained or not; and regardless of what office they claim! Yet, if what a man teaches is the truth, then it has the inherent authority of that truth! Therefore judge the words of ALL men by the whole Word of Almighty God!

We are to test all men and spirits by the scriptures and we are to discern between the righteous and the wicked, by their fruits [deeds].

If the spirit we are following were godly, it would lead us towards a deeper unity with God through the diligent and enthusiastic keeping of the whole Word of God. Instead many are doing the exact opposite and departing further and further from any zeal to live by every Word of God.

God's Spirit will always be totally consistent with the truth of the whole Word of God, and a false spirit will decry any zeal for the Word of God and try to get you to live contrary to the Word of God!

There is NO authority in any man; all authority is in the Word of God, and any man who teaches contrary to God's Word; is NOT of God and has absolutely NO moral authority!

Working miracles, healings, or the ability to speak many languages is no indicator of the presence of the Holy Spirit of God.

Matthew 7:21 Not every one that saith unto me, Lord, Lord, shall enter into the kingdom of heaven; **but he that doeth the will of my Father which is in heaven. 7:22 Many will say to me in that day, Lord, Lord, have we not prophesied in thy name? and in thy name have cast out devils? and in thy name done many wonderful works? 7:23 And then will I profess unto them, I never knew you: depart from me, ye that work iniquity.**

2 Timothy 1:7 For God hath not given us the spirit of fear; **but of power, and of love, and of** a **sound mind**.

God's Spirit is the Spirit of a sound mind and power; it is the Spirit of self-control. God's Spirit is not the spirit of the loss of self-control or of extreme emotional ecstasy. The Holy Spirit is a Spirit of self-control that strengthens us to calmly and wisely decide to do right and refuse to do wrong; empowering us to live by every Word of God.

God's Spirit is love and what is love? Love is defined by God's Word as:

2 John 1:6 And this is love, that we walk after [live by] **his commandments.**

1 John 2:5 But whoso keepeth his word, in him verily is the love of God perfected: hereby know we that we are in him. 2:6 He that saith he abideth in him ought himself also so to walk [live], **even as he walked** [lived and lives].

There are those who claim that they live by every Word of God and then claim that all but the Ten Commandments are done away in God's Word: LIE! The New Covenant is the Mosaic Covenant with the addition of the

Holy Spirit to empower us to live by every Word of God just as Jesus Christ perfectly kept the entirety of the Holy Scriptures, not just the Ten Commandments!

If we had God's Spirit we would understand that to break any part of the whole Word of God is to break the Ten Commandments as well; for disobedience to God is dishonouring our Father!

John 14:21 **He that hath my commandments, and keepeth them, he it is that loveth me:** and he that loveth me shall be loved of my Father, and I will love him, and will manifest myself to him **14:22** Judas saith unto him, not Iscariot, Lord, how is it that thou wilt manifest thyself unto us, and not unto the world? **13:23** Jesus answered and said unto him, **If a man love me, he will keep my words**: and my Father will love him, and we will come unto him, and make our abode with him; **14:24 He that loveth me not keepeth not my sayings:** and the word which ye hear is not mine, but the Father's which sent me.

Let us prove all things by the Word of God, and in doing that and living by every Word of God; we show that we love God the Father and Jesus Christ: and if we do not do that, we do not love God the Father of Jesus Christ no matter what we claim.

Romans 2:13 (For not the hearers of the law are just before God, but **the doers of the law shall be justified.**

James 1:22 But **be ye doers of the word, and not hearers only,** deceiving your own selves

Godly teachers will teach all people the difference between the holy and the profane, and teaching the difference between sin and living by every Word of God

Ezekiel 44:23 And **they shall teach my people the difference between the holy and profane, and cause them to discern between the unclean and the clean**. Study the scriptures and learn to discern between good and evil.

Hebrews 5:14 But strong meat belongeth to them that are of full age, even those who by reason of use have their senses exercised to **discern** both good and evil.

Prove all things, spirits and men by the whole Word of God, and hold fast that which is good and consistent with the whole Word of God.

Proverbs 3:5 Trust in the Lord with all thine heart; and lean not unto thine own understanding. **3:6** In all thy ways acknowledge him, and he shall direct thy paths.

God gave this instruction anciently to Moses:

Deuteronomy 13:1 If there arise among you a prophet, or a dreamer of dreams, and giveth thee a sign or a wonder **13:2** And the sign or the wonder come to pass, whereof he spake unto thee, saying, **Let us go after other gods** [do anything contrary to the Word of God]**, which thou hast not known, and let us serve** [obey] **them;**

Regardless of appearances [for Satan and his ministers present themselves as angels of light], we are to prove all things by the scriptures; we are to follow only the whole Word of God and not idols of men

13:3 Thou shalt not hearken unto the words of that prophet, or that dreamer of dreams: **for the LORD your God proveth you, to know whether ye love the LORD your God with all your heart and with all your soul.**

God Tests His People!

God wants to know just how much we really love HIM! Do we truly love God enough to do what God says? or will we be turned aside by every person who claims to be of God?

13:4 Ye shall walk after the LORD your God, and fear him, and keep his commandments, and obey his voice, and ye shall serve him, and cleave unto him.

Those who seek to dominate the brethren to cause people to follow themselves and their false traditions in place of the Word of Almighty God will be destroyed by the Eternal if they do not repent.

Brethren that means that nearly every church of God leader and elder is facing rejection by Jesus Christ (Rev 3:14-22), and stern correction in the soon coming great tribulation.

13:5 And that prophet, or that dreamer of dreams, **shall be put to death; because he hath spoken to turn you away from the LORD your God,** which brought you out of the land of Egypt, and redeemed you out of the house of bondage, to thrust thee out of the way which the LORD thy God commanded thee to walk in. So shalt thou put the evil away from the midst of thee.

Miracles and fulfilled prophecy are not proof of whether a man is of God or not: the proof that a person is godly is their zeal and faithfulness to live by and teach others to live by every Word of God.

Anyone who water's down or diminishes, or adds to God's commandments; is to be rejected as if he did not exist for you, as if he is dead. We are not to make idols of any person or thing to put them before God, not even a member of our own family.

Deuteronomy 13:6 If thy brother, the son of thy mother, or thy son, or thy daughter, or the wife of thy bosom, or thy friend, which is as thine own soul [body], entice thee secretly, saying, Let us go and serve other gods, which thou hast not known, thou, nor thy fathers;

13:7 Namely, of the gods of the people which are round about you, nigh unto thee, or far off from thee, **from the one end of the earth even unto the other end of the earth;**

13:8 Thou shalt not consent unto him, nor hearken unto him; neither shall thine eye pity him, neither shalt thou spare, **neither shalt thou conceal him**: **13:9** But thou shalt surely kill him; thine hand shall be first upon him to put him to death, and afterwards the hand of all the people.

13:10 And thou shalt stone him with stones, that he die; because he hath sought to thrust [or to deceive] thee away from the LORD thy God, which brought thee out of the land of Egypt, from the house of bondage.

It is the Eternal God who is sovereign not man. It is the Eternal's will that we are to perform, not men's will. It is the Eternal's laws that we are to obey and his Word, not men's words.

No man has the right to change God's Word, or to bind or loose God's commandments in the sense of changing them.

No man can exalt himself above the great Majesty on High who has created the universe, who can hold the world in the hollow of His hands. And before whom a man, any man; is merely a speck of dust in comparison.

God the Son is to be obeyed because he gave up his God-hood to become flesh and die for us, redeeming and freeing us from bondage to sin, because he also created us being the implementing Creator and because he is the Husband of our baptismal covenant.

God the Father is to be obeyed because he is a Great King, the King of the entire universe, because he is our spiritual Father being the executive creating authority, and because he is the figurative Father of our espoused Husband Jesus Christ. Our Husband obeys His Father and has commanded us to do likewise; and we obey our Husband, therefore we obey His Father also!

We can discern between good and evil and between the doers of good and evil; by comparing all things against the standard of the Word of God Almighty! Whatever is consistent with every Word of God is righteous and good, and any departure from any part of the Word of God is evil!

The Way to Peace and Eternal Life

God created man with an awesome purpose. God intends to grant humanity the gift of eternal life in peace and prosperity. Therefore God first made mankind flesh so that man can learn through experience that he does not have the experience and wisdom to decide everything for himself.

As every person or groups decides right and wrong for themselves they clash because other individuals or groups decide differently.

We need an ultimate moral authority which:

- All people will respect and obey,
- Who has the experience and wisdom to decide correctly.
- Who loves all people deeply and equally so as to be uncompromisingly just and fair, and
- He should have the power to enforce his decisions if that is required.

The ONLY way to lasting peace and prosperity is for every person and group of people to accept such an ultimate moral authority.

Yet every person or group wants to decide for themselves, and to decide and to have their own ways for themselves; and that leads to strife and much sorrow.

God made man flesh so that man could experience every person living according to their own ways and the strife and sorrow that such behavior brings. It is through this experience that mankind will learn that the true way to life, peace and prosperity comes through all people believing, respecting, obeying and following one ultimate moral authority.

Mankind belongs to God by virtue of being created by God, yet God has such passionate love for all people, that the Father gave up the life of his only begotten son and the son gave his own life to reconcile all repentant people to God.

God the Father and the Son have proved their love for mankind and together they are the only ultimate moral authority with the experience and wisdom of the ages. The two Beings of God the Father and the Son are in full complete and perfect unity of character, nature and purpose with one another.

At this time their mission and purpose to bring humanity into the same full, complete, perfect unity of character and nature with themselves which they have with one another.

To accomplish that purpose people must be allowed to experience bot their own ways and God's ways so that they can make an informed decision to follow and live by every Word of God which brings life eternal in peace and prosperity, or to do whatever seems right to us with our limited experience.

The choice is:

- Do as we please and reap the results of doing so, or
- Do as God says and reap the rewards for doing so.

To properly prepare people to make that choice, God allowed Adam and Eve to decide for themselves instead of forcing them to obey him, and since that time mankind has been allowed to decide his own ways for himself.

For the past six thousand years people in the flesh have largely lived and died by their own decisions. Where is there any hope for these people? God's arm is not shortened nor his power limited that mankind should perish with the flesh! The hope of all humanity is that God will resurrect us from the dead!

Physical fleshly people who have died in godliness will be resurrected not back to flesh but will be raised up as eternal spirit! While those who have died in their own ways will be resurrected to flesh and given a chance to sincerely repent and be reconciled to God and godliness!

To illustrate this marvelous thing we have been given the caterpillar which lives its life and then enters its cocoon figurative of death to break forth into new life as a wonderfully beautiful butterfly.

This is the ultimate future of mankind for those who are reconciled to God: The death of the old sinful person to be reborn as something so much more beautiful that we could not imagine it by looking at the present flesh; and more than a person could think that a worm could become a butterfly if he did not already know! And even better than the butterfly the spirit body which is God's gift to a repentance humanity is permanent!

For the past six thousand years since Able was called to God the Father through the Son, God has been calling selected persons to himself through the son.

Those who have sincerely repented and persevered to internalize the character and nature of God through learning and living by every Word of God will be resurrected an d given a new body composed of eternal spirit at the end of the six thousandth year.

Later all those who have lived and died and were not yet called to reconcile with God will be raised back to physical life and then given their opportunity to decide to live by every Word of God and receive eternal life in peace with God and man, or to continue to go their own ways which leads to sorrows, decay and death.

Why are only a few called to God ahead of time? So that they can help to bring the vast numbers to God when their time comes!

This early and latter harvest of mankind is explained in the Spring and Fall Festivals books. The purpose of this book to explain the way to salvation and eternal life on a personal level for all people regardless of when they are called to God.

The question being answered in this volume is: "What must we do to inherit eternal life?"

The way to, and peace with and reconciliation to God and eternal life:
1. God calls people to himself through the Son
2. Some believe the Word and begin to act on what they learn

3. As they begin to put aside past misconduct and turn to live by God's Word faith grows, until
4. They are ready to make a formal commitment to live by every Word of God
5. They then make a baptismal commitment to live by every Word of God
6. The sacrifice of the Lamb of God, Jesus Christ is then applied paying the debt of all past sins sincerely repented of and they are justified before God and reconciled to God the Father
7. The gift of God's Holy Spirit is provided, enabling one to retain and understand God's Word and empowering us to live by God's Word through the Spirit dwelling in us
8. We do not know all things instantly and from this point we must diligently study and ask God for growth in understanding of his Word and Will, which will be increased as we APPLY what we learn
9. We must then persevere in internalizing the nature of God through continually learning, growing and living by every Word of God as long as we live.

God's Calling

Humanity has been cut off from God the Father by our sins.

Isaiah 59:1 Behold, the Lord's hand is not shortened, that it cannot save; neither his ear heavy, that it cannot hear: **59:2** But your iniquities have separated between you and your God, and your sins have hid his face from you, that he will not hear.

Sin Separates Humanity From God, Requiring an Intercessor (Is 59:1)

Mankind being separated from God the Father by their sin; humanity needed a High Priest [A Mediator between humanity and God the Father] to reconcile humanity back to God the Father!

God, knowing that man could sin and would therefore need reconciliation, from the very beginning the two Beings who became the Father and the Son, together established the means that such a reconciliation could be effected.

That plan of reconciliation between man and God required the sincere repentance of the sinner, an effective sacrifice for sin, and a commitment by the repentant to stop sinning and sin no more. The plan also called for a Mediator or High Priest to reconcile the repentant sinner to God the Father. This spiritual High Priest Intercessor between God the Father and humanity appeared to Adam and Eve in the form of a man and spoke with Cain, Noah, Abraham and doubtless others.

The last time we hear of him in the scriptures before he became flesh, was by the name of Melchizedek when he spoke to Abraham, and later a few times he was seen by Ezekiel and certain prophets. Later this spirit High Priest of God was made flesh and known as Jesus Christ the Lamb of God allowed himself to be sacrificed for the sincerely repented sins of humanity, thus opening the way for reconciliation with God the Father.

The plan for the harvest of created humanity involves the two harvests in Judea with a smaller spring harvest and a much larger main harvest. The Feast of Unleavened Bread pictures God calling out a small number of people for seven thousand years from righteous Abel. This is studied in the "Spring Festivals" book.

The purpose of calling a few people to God and allowing them to live in a wicked world is so they can learn to love godliness and to hate and loathe evil, and to train and prepare them to be resurrected to become laborers to help bring in the main harvest. For this reason many are called but most of them will fail and only a few will be chosen to have a part in the resurrection to spirit of this early harvest of humanity.

Matthew 22:14 For many are called, but few are chosen.

Once changed to spirit they will become kings and priests of God.

The godly priesthood of the resurrected chosen is the priesthood of Jesus Christ, and works to reconcile the sinner to God the Father by teaching people to live by every Word of God. The priests are the teachers of godliness reconciling the people to God by calling all people to God and to the reconciling atoning sacrifice of Christ.

Godly kings are righteous judges and administers over the physical needs of the people.

From righteous Able to the end of the seventh thousandth year God calls people to Christ and to himself. At the end of six thousand years a resurrection of the chosen takes place and ten over the remaining one thousand years God's calling will expand to include all flesh then living, and those who were chosen at the end of the first six thousand years will work to bring in the millennial harvest, during which millennium every person will be changed to spirit at the age of 100 or destroyed if they will not sincerely repent.

The word "call" or "calling" refers to opening the mind of a person to godliness. During the first six thousand years only a very tiny number will have their minds opened to godliness while the vast majority of mankind will live out their lives with no understanding of the things of God. Then during the millennium God will call all humanity then living by pouring out his Spirit on all flesh (Joel 2:28).

After that time the main harvest of humanity who have not yet been called to God as pictured by the High Days and Festivals of the fall main harvest, will be resurrected back to flesh and will also be called to sincere repentance and godliness in their billions.

Calling and Reconciliation to God the Father

Jesus Christ is the Door (John 10) which controls access to God the Father. This is because access to God the Father can come ONLY through sincere repentance and the atoning sacrifice of the Lamb of God, Jesus Christ. Only by the application of the sacrifice of the Lamb of God, Jesus Christ can we be reconciled to and access God the Father.

John 14:6 Jesus saith unto him, I am the way, the truth, and the life: no man cometh unto the Father, but by me.

No person can understand godliness and sincerely repent, coming to accept the application of the sacrifice of the Lamb of God, Jesus Christ, unless God the Father draws or calls him to himself through Christ and sincere repentance.

John 6:44 No man can come to me, except **the Father which hath sent me draw him**: and I will raise him up at the last day.

Only God the Father chooses those individuals whom he wants to call to sincere repentance and reconciliation to himself, through the sacrifice of the Lamb of God Jesus Christ.

How does this work?

The first step in the reconciliation of any individual to God the Father, is that we must be called out of bondage to sin, just like physical Israel was called out of physical bondage in Egypt. They could not deliver themselves just as we cannot deliver ourselves from sin.

Sin has separated mankind from God and being cut off from God, human beings cannot understand spiritual things

The mind of man, cut off from God; simply cannot understand spiritual things:

1 Corinthians 2:14 But the natural man receiveth not the things of the Spirit of God: for they are foolishness unto him: neither can he know them, because they are spiritually discerned.

Romans 8:6 For to be carnally minded [cut off from God] is death; but to be spiritually minded is life and peace. **8:7** Because the carnal mind is enmity [hostile against] against God: for it is **not subject to the law of God, neither indeed can be**.

How then can mankind be called to follow Jesus Christ out of bondage to sin?

John 6:44 **No man can come to me, except the Father which hath sent me draw him**: and I will raise him up at the last day.

John 6:65 And he said, Therefore said I unto you, that **no man can come unto me, except it were given unto him of my Father.**

God the Father himself calls us to sincere repentance and to follow Christ's example in living by every Word of God, by sending his Spirit to work with people opening up an initial understanding of the way of life eternal. At this point God's Spirit does not dwell in us, but works with us revealing to us the transitory nature of physical life and the need for something more.

Sowing the Seed of the Word of God

We are called to reconciliation to God the Father through Jesus Christ the Lamb of God, yet God tells his faithful to spread the seed of the Word of God and God sends the Holy Spirit to call and work with individuals. At this point God's Holy Spirit is not IN a person but is outside the person; working with the person by opening minds to a very slight initial understanding of the Word of God. It is God that calls people and opens minds, men can only spread the Word, no human person has ever called anyone to salvation.

Very many have studied the scriptures all of their lives and have not found the way, although they longed for it, and many have even had these things explained to them by God's servants and have not understood.

Sometimes people say "I was called by such a person and I will remain loyal to him." Is it wise to follow the messenger and not the God who sent the message?

It is God the Father who calls us to sincerely repent and to live by every Word of God, so that the redeeming blood sacrifice of Jesus Christ the Lamb of God may be applied to us; thereby reconciling us to himself! We are not called to follow messengers who are mere mortal men subject to error!

We are called to live by every Word of God (Mat 4:4), and to follow men ONLY as they are faithful to follow Jesus Christ and to live by every Word of God (1 Cor 11:1). We are to prove all things and to be faithful to live by every Word of God (1 Thess 5:21) and to be as the Berean's (Acts 17:11).

The Parable of the Sower and the Seed

Luke 8:4 And when much people were gathered together, and were come to him out of every city, he spake by a parable:

8:5 A sower went out to sow his seed: and as he sowed, some fell by the way side; and it was trodden down, and the fowls of the air devoured it. **8:6** And some fell upon a rock; and as soon as it was sprung up, it withered away, because it lacked moisture [spiritually the water of God's Word]. **8:7** And some fell among thorns; and the thorns sprang up with it, and choked it. **8:8** And other fell on good ground, and sprang up, and bare fruit an hundredfold. And when he had said these things, he cried, He that hath ears to hear, let him hear.

8:9 And his disciples asked him, saying, What might this parable be? **8:10** And he said, Unto you it is given to know the mysteries of the kingdom of God: but to others in parables; that seeing they might not see, and hearing they might not understand.

The explanation begins with explaining that the seed is the whole WORD OF GOD; ALL SCRIPTURE; not just some talk of a coming kingdom.

8:11 Now the parable is this: **The seed is the word of God.**

Some hearers immediately forget or dismiss what they have heard. These are those who turn away from the message, which is most of humanity; and refuse to sincerely repent because they have NOT been called by God the Father and do not understand.

8:12 Those by the way side are they that hear; then cometh the devil, and taketh away the word out of their hearts, lest they should believe and be saved.

Some who hear initially respond with repentance and a baptismal commitment, but later fall under trials and stress. These are people, many of whom have been called to repentance by God, but Satan brings trials and persecutions on them and they fall away.

Baptism and membership in some corporation is NO GUARANTEE of salvation; for many are called but few remain faithful to the end and are chosen.

Matthew 22:11 And when the king came in to see the guests, he saw there a man which had not on a wedding garment: **22:12** And he saith unto him, Friend, how camest thou in hither not having a wedding garment [is not clothed with the righteousness of godliness] ? And he was speechless. **22:13** Then said the king to the servants, Bind him hand and foot, and take him away, and cast him into outer darkness, there shall be weeping and gnashing of teeth. **22:14 For many are called, but few are chosen.**

Revelation 19:7 Let us be glad and rejoice, and give honour to him: for **the marriage of the Lamb is come, and his wife hath made herself ready. 19:8 And to her was granted that she should be arrayed in fine linen, clean and white: for the fine linen is the righteousness of saints.**

It is zeal for all the things of God, and a diligent study of God's Word, together with faithfully living by every Word of God, through every temptation and even through serious trials and persecutions if necessary: which brings eternal salvation.

The sacrifice of Christ will only be applied to and will only justify: Those who live by every Word of God!

Romans 2:13 (For not the hearers of the law are just before God, but **the doers of the law shall be justified.**

Luke 8:13 They on the rock [the seed falling on the stony ground are those] are they, which, when they hear, receive the word with joy; and these have no root, which for a while believe, and in time of temptation fall away.

Many, who are called by God and respond positively with repentance and baptism, are later tempted back into sin by the pleasures of this society. They hedge on God's Sabbath to save a job or make money or they pollute the Sabbath for their own pleasures. They are unable to cope with trials or lust after physical pleasures etc; or they follow men and their traditions rather than living by every Word of God.

8:14 And that which fell among thorns are they, which, when they have heard, go forth, and are choked with cares and riches and pleasures of this life, and bring no fruit to perfection.

It is those who live by every Word of God persevering and overcoming through the strength of God's Holy Spirit dwelling in them who shall be resurrected to eternal life!

8:15 But that [which falls] on the good ground are they, which **in an honest and good heart, having heard the word, keep it, and bring forth fruit with patience.**

What are we called to do?

The vast majority of people in corporate assemblies attend services and are involved with a church congregation because of the social benefits and because they want to avoid God's correction or to gain a reward.

Most people just go along for the social benefits and because they want eternal life and a reward of leadership over others for eternity. The brethren are constantly reminded of these rewards for holding fast and continuing with their organization.

Of course this is a deceit, for all spiritual reward comes from God and is given by God, because of our loyalty to God; and not because of any loyalty to any idol of men or corporate entities.

The statement that "We are God's chosen leaders and you must obey us" becomes nonsense as soon as such men depart from the Word of God: Were not king Saul and Judas Iscariot chosen leaders of God?

Those episodes were recorded for us so that we would learn to prove all things by the Word of God and NOT to follow any man into sin.

Back to the purpose of our calling

What is the godly purpose to which all of the called out have been called to focus on? Was it really this selfish "GET" motive of acquiring eternal life and a kingdom and dominating others? NO!

Yes, God's kingdom will come and it will be glorious and it would be great to have a part in it; but we are putting the reward before the job!

Eternal life and an office of responsibility is the reward; and that is great to remember; but we cannot allow this reward to be a distraction from the purpose of our calling!

The destination is wondrous, but the key issue for us is The Getting There, which is achieved only by learning to live by Every Word of God and by fully internalizing the very nature and Spirit of godliness!

We have been deceived into a certain idea that if we just obey the elder we have a ticket to enter eternal life and the kingdom of God.

No, we must each work out our own salvation personally through sincere repentance and living by every Word of God; and we will each be held accountable for what we personally do, and the excuse that "I was only following the elder" is not going to get us anywhere at the judgment.

Jesus warned that just going through the motions and doing what we feel we must; **is NOT ENOUGH!** (Luke 19).

We must consistently and diligently seek spiritual treasure in heaven [eternity]. We must focus on overcoming all sin and on becoming LIKE God our Father in heaven and becoming LIKE the Son!

Brethren, our calling is to the hard work of internalizing the very nature of God the Father!

Which comes through a continual night and day zealous study of, and meditation on, God's Word; and through passionately living by every Word of God, and through teaching the Word of God to others beginning with our children.

We must be practicing for the job of setting an example for the rest of mankind, for leading the nations to righteousness as kings and priests, and practicing to be teachers of the Word of God to humanity forever!

Yes, keep the goal in mind, but do not neglect the job at hand; which is to:

Our Calling

We are called to: **1 Peter 1:15** But as he which hath called you is holy, so be ye holy in all manner of conversation [conduct]; **1:16** Because it is written, **Be ye holy; for I am holy**.

Leviticus 19:2 Speak unto all the congregation of the children of Israel, and say unto them, **Ye shall be holy: for I the Lord your God am holy**.

Holiness means "of or pertaining to the God who cannot sin", therefore holiness is purity and freedom from sin: To be holy is to become like God, to internalize the very nature of God, so that we think and act as God would!

Brethren put out all sin from among you and be pure from all sin, just as God is pure from all sin.

Leviticus 11:44 For I am the Lord your God: ye shall therefore sanctify yourselves, and ye shall be holy; for I am holy:

1 Peter 1:15 But as he which hath called you is holy, so be ye holy in all manner of conversation [conduct]; **1:16** Because it is written, Be ye holy; for I am holy.

Belief
The good ground are those who wholeheartedly BELIEVE the Word, and begin to work to learn and to diligently live by every Word of God, enduring all trials and patiently persevering to the end of their lives.

We are to let the light that God has lighted in us shine forth; and we are to live as an example of true godliness which will light up the world!

God sends messengers to spread the Word of God and those who respond positively and receive the Word with joy; BELIEVING God's Word and hungering and thirsting after every Word of God to learn it and to live by it; will learn and grow, being led by God's Spirit to a point of conversion where a decision is made to STOP sinning and to go forward living by every Word of God.

What is God calling us to do?
First God calls on us to BELIEVE the Gospel, to BELIEVE every Word of God! God's calling is foundational to belief, and belief is foundational to faith and the works of faith, which are sincere repentance from all sin and a dedicated commitment to live by every Word of God forever more!

How can we follow Christ to live by every Word of God if we do not believe in him? and how can we obey God if we do not believe the Word of God?

Mark 1:14 Now after that John was put in prison, Jesus came into Galilee, preaching the gospel of the kingdom of God, **1:5** And saying, The time is fulfilled, and the kingdom of God is at hand: **repent ye, and believe the gospel**.

Summary

1. People are cut off from God by sin, therefore they cannot understand spiritual things,
2. God must call people out of sin and does so by granting an initial small understanding,
3. If we respond to God's calling by hungering and thirsting for more understanding and by acting on what we learn, more understanding will be given, until
4. We reach a point where we believe God's Word and we are ready to make a solid sincere commitment [sincerely repent] to stop sinning and to begin to live by every Word of God,
5. We then make a baptismal commitment to continually work to internalize the very nature of God, to become holy as God is holy, rooting out all sin, and
6. Then Jesus Christ will apply his atoning sacrifice to us, reconciling us to God the Father,
7. Who will then give us the gift of the indwelling of his Spirit enabling us to live as Christ lived, by every Word of God, and
8. If we remain faithful throughout our lives, continually overcoming and growing more and more in godliness, God will give us the gift of eternal life!
9. God is calling out only a very few over the fist six thousand years of human history, then
10. After Christ comes God will call all humanity then living, and
11. Finally God will resurrect back to flesh and will call all of humanity who have not yet had their chance, during the Feast of Tabernacles main harvest.

Belief and Faith

A person is called out of bondage to sin, and to reconciliation with God the Father, by being given an initial limited understanding of spiritual things. God the Father calls us to himself through the Door [the atoning sacrifice] of Jesus Christ (John 10).

The called of God, are called to reconciliation with God the Father, they are called to become like God, by internalizing the very nature of God through learning and living by every Word of God.

When a person is called to God his mind is opened to understand certain basic spiritual things. He learns that as a transitory physical being living according to his own will, he has no lasting hope and is subject to decay and death

See the "Ecclesiastes Job" book.

When people hear the Word of God, they must choose to believe it, or to reject it.

If they recognize the value of God's Word and the hope of deliverance from Satan, sin and the grave into eternal life and they actually BELIEVE the Word of God, they will quickly begin seeking greater and greater spiritual understanding. They will want to devour the words of HOPE contained in the Word of God like a starving person desires food, hungering and thirsting after every Word of God (Mat 5); and they will be blessed with more and more understanding.

At some point belief will become FAITH. The King James folks translated the meaning somewhat awkwardly as:

Hebrews 11:1 Now faith is the substance of things hoped for, the evidence of things not seen.

True godly faith is to believe every Word of God and to completely TRUST in the Word and promises of God; trusting enough to actually follow and obey every Word of God! After all, why would we obey God if we did not trust that his Word is true and his promises unshakable? On the other hand, if we do trust that God's Word is true and that God's promises are unshakably sure, we are full of faith that God will perform what he has set out to do!

Then if we believe God and the Word of God we must act on that faith and perform the works of faith, which are sincere repentance and a commitment to stop living contrary to the Word of God and to start living by every Word of God.

The word "Repent" means to deeply regret having done something, to regret it so much that we STOP doing it and start living differently!

Faith is a gift of God, and faith comes by obedience, which is the works of faith.

Then after we begin to stop sinning and start to live a godly life, God's gift of faith increases and grows through a process of believing and living by every Word of God and learning through practical experience, that God knows best!

When we believe and then we obey, we LEARN and we GROW in godly faith! Without the study of God's Word and without belief in that Word, there can be no obedience; and with no obedience there will be no faith.

Faith is a sure and certain knowledge that God's Word is TRUE and that God keeps all of his promises; which faith is learned and grows through much experience in obedience to God.

God's chosen will have an unfeigned dedicated faith in God, coupled with the works of faith.

Hebrews 11:1 Now faith is the substance of things hoped for, the evidence of things not seen. For by it the elders obtained a good report.

The entire chapter of Hebrews 11 is about a great company of men and women who lived believing and obeying every Word of God; and grew in faith while proving their faith by the works of faith.

Faith in Action; the Works of Faith are Obedience to Live by Every Word of God

James 2:14 What doth it profit, my brethren, though a man say he hath faith, and have not works? can faith save him?

2:15 If a brother or sister be naked, and destitute of daily food, **2:16** And one of you say unto them, Depart in peace, be ye warmed and filled; notwithstanding ye give them not those things which are needful to the body; what doth it profit? **2:17 Even so faith, if it hath not works, is dead, being alone.**

2:18 Yea, a man may say, Thou hast faith, and I have works: shew me thy faith without thy works, and **I will shew thee my faith by my works**.

2:19 Thou believest that there is one God; thou doest well: the devils also believe, and tremble [but they will not repent and STOP rebelling against God]. **2:20** But wilt thou know, O vain man, that **faith without works is dead**?

2:21 Was not Abraham our father justified by works [the works of faith], when he had offered Isaac his son upon the altar? **2:22 Seest thou how faith wrought with his works, and by works was faith made perfect? 2:23** And the scripture was fulfilled which saith, Abraham believed God [and Abraham acted on that belief and obeyed God], and it was imputed unto him for righteousness: and he was called the Friend of God.

2:24 Ye see then how that by works a man is justified, and not by faith only.

2:25 Likewise also was not Rahab the harlot justified by works, when she had received the messengers, and had sent them out another way?

2:26 For as the body without the spirit is dead, so faith without works is dead also.

The natural man is cut off from God, so that he may through experience learn the sorrows of sin and never again be tempted to sin once he is delivered.

God instructs his faithful to teach all men to live by every Word of God, and in this way the seed of God's Word is spread and God calls people to reconciliation with God.

God calls us by opening up our understanding and giving the gift of belief and faith in God and in every Word of God. The gift of faith does not initially come through keeping the law; it is the gift of God to those that God is calling. Nevertheless the gift of faith brings with it a desire to live by the law of God and by every Word of God, because if we believe God we will want to please him.

God's gift of faith then, is the foundation of law keeping, and the more we internalize the very nature of God the Father through living by every Word of God, the more our initial faith grows. How? Because in the process of learning and of LIVING in a godly manner, we experience godliness more and more; and as we do so we learn to trust and believe God more and more, which is an increase of faith.

Now if we believe God we will have faith that God loves us and that his Word if for our good, therefore we will want to do what God says. We will also believe in the promises of God, and believing in the resurrection of Jesus Christ to eternal spirit, we can also believe God's promise that if we persevere in godliness we will also be raised up to eternal life.

Romans 8:11 But if the Spirit of him that raised up Jesus from the dead dwell in you, he that raised up Christ from the dead shall also quicken your mortal bodies by his Spirit that dwelleth in you.

Which is Greater; the Message and the God who sent it, or the men who helped to spread that message?

I must ask: When a messenger spreads the Word of God; who is the greater; the messenger or the author of the Word being spread, God Almighty?

I must ask this because many have fallen astray by idolizing the messenger and not exalting the author of the message. What do I mean? Many have said that "I was called by such a person and I will always be loyal to him."

This is just NOT true: we were not called by any person! We are called to God, by God the Father to come to him through Jesus Christ! We may have heard the word from some person, but we never would have understood and turned to godliness unless God the Father had called us and opened up our understanding.

Brethren this exalting messengers above the author or the message is the sin of idolatry, exalting the messenger above the message and the author of the message. Teachers of the Word of God are only human and at times make mistakes, and how can one discern false teachers from true teachers except by holding them up to the standard of every Word of God?

Repentance

To repent means to be sincerely sorry, to deeply regret offending another, to regret the act so intensely that we will never do it again.

Sin is the transgression of the law and the law commands us to honor our father and our mother. Spiritually God is our Father in heaven and our mother is the New Jerusalem which is the seat of God's throne and the fountainhead of God's will. To do anything contrary to God the Father's Word or Will dishonors our Father and therefore transgresses the commandment.

Exodus 20:12 Honour thy father and thy mother: that thy days may be long upon the land which the Lord thy God giveth thee.

This physical commandment has its spiritual corollary, since spi9ritually God the Father in heaven is our ultimate Father.

Whenever Israel followed God, they were victorious; and whenever they tried to fight the enemy their own way, while not being faithful to God, they were defeated.

This is also true in the spiritual sense concerning our fight against sin. Satan is far smarter and stronger than we are; and whenever we try to fight sin on our own; we are guaranteed to fail!

No matter how we struggle on our own with temptation and sin, we fail and continually slip, to do the thing that we are struggling to stop doing. Paul presents the answer in Romans 8 where he says that we must walk [live] in the spirit, and the flesh must be brought into submission to the spirit of God to overcome sin. 1 John 2:6 also says that we are to walk [live as Christ walks [lives].

Acts 2:38 Then Peter said unto them, **Repent, and be baptized** every one of you in the name of Jesus Christ for the remission of sins, and **ye shall receive the gift of the Holy Ghost** [Spirit].

Once God calls us and opens our minds to a small initial understanding of spiritual things, and we begin to respond positively, believing and accepting what we are learning; our belief begins to develop into a trusting faith. We must then make a commitment to STOP living contrary to the Word of God.

The word "repent" means to deeply regret what we have done, to regret it so much that we are filled with sorrow and shame over our past conduct ad wish that we had never done the ting. Godly sorrow brings true regret that we have performed the deed, while the carnal sorrow regrets not doing the deed itself but having been caught.

2 Corinthians 7:9 Now I rejoice, not that ye were made sorry, but that ye sorrowed to repentance: for ye were made sorry after a godly manner. . .

Paul commended the Corinthians for sorrowing to genuine repentance for their toleration of sin in their assembly. They had been rebuked and had deeply regretted their sin and were moved to STOP doing the evil deed of tolerating open sin in their assemblies.

Godly repentance means to regret our evil actions so deeply that we loathe what we have done to the point that we make a wholehearted decision to never do the thing again.

Godly repentance comes from realizing that any actions contrary to the Word of God brings suffering, sorrows, decay and death, and that the only way to peace between God and man and between human beings is to live by every Word of God.

When God calls us we are called to sincere repentance of our refusal to honor God our Father by living contrary to his Word of Life Eternal. Our minds are opened at our calling to understand that our previous doings were detestable and gendered to suffering and death.

Once our minds and eyes are opened, if we respond positively to God's calling to learn and internalize the very nature of God; we will deeply regret our past wickedness and we will turn to embrace godliness with a whole heart.

Repentance means to stop doing the thing that we regret doing and turn around to do something else. Spiritually true repentance means to stop doing whatever we want and think is right, and change direction to learn and to live by every Word of God.

Once we make an unshakable commitment to STOP living contrary to the Word of God, we must also make a positive commitment to live by every Word of God henceforth and forever.

When we are forgiven God the Father erased the indictment against us, He erased the list of our past sins; by our sincere repentance and the application of the sacrifice of Christ.

In no way does Christ's sacrifice do away with the law of sacrifice, rather it fulfils that law; by offering a PERFECT sacrifice for sincerely repented PAST sins; obligating us to go forward and sin no more. For if we seek the application of Christ's sacrifice and then continue in sin, we make a mockery of that sacrifice and have not truly repented at all.

Hebrews 10:26 For if we sin wilfully after that we have received the knowledge of the truth, there remaineth no more sacrifice for sins, **10:27** But a certain fearful looking for of judgment and fiery indignation, which shall devour the adversaries.

10:28 He that despised Moses' law died without mercy under two or three witnesses: **10:29** Of how much sorer [greater] punishment, suppose ye, shall he be thought worthy, who hath trodden under foot the Son of God [by continuing in sin], and hath counted the blood of the [the sacrifice of the New Covenant Jesus Christ the Lamb of God] covenant, wherewith he was sanctified, an unholy thing [asking for its application without real repentance], and hath done despite [has been contemptuous of Christ's sacrifice and God's mercy, by continuing in sin] unto the Spirit of grace?

Colossians 2:14 Blotting out the handwriting of ordinances that was against us, which was contrary to us, and took it out of the way, nailing it to his cross;

The ordinances which were against us is the indictment - the list of our sins for which we faced eternal death - which list is paid in full with our sincere repentance and the application the sacrifice of the Lamb of God to us.

The list of our sins, the indictment against us; was paid in full by the death of Christ for the sincerely repentant.

Jesus Christ through his perfect sinless life and his willingness to obey the Father to the death, was worthy to be given all power in the universe [under God the Father]

2:15 And having spoiled principalities and powers, he made a shew of them openly, triumphing over them in it.

The primary teaching of both John Baptist and Jesus Christ [the true Gospel] was to repent of living according to our own natural inclinations, and to change direction to live by every Word of God.

Matthew 3:1 In those days came John the Baptist, preaching in the wilderness of Judaea, **3:2** And saying, Repent ye: for the kingdom of heaven is at hand.

After John had taught this and many people were baptized many leaders decided it would be a good idea to be baptized also, but they thought to do this in order to impress the people and had not really changed their evil behavior. Therefore john said that they must first prove the sincerity of their repentance by a change in their behavior.

Matthew 3:8 Bring forth therefore fruits meet for repentance [demonstrate a change in behavior towards godliness]:

Six months after John Baptist began preaching Jesus also began preaching the same thing. Repent, and change direction from living according to your own ideas and start living by every Word of God (Mat 4:4)

Matthew 4:17 From that time Jesus began to preach, and to say, Repent: for the kingdom of heaven is at hand.

Acts 3:19 Repent ye therefore, and be converted [change our attitude and behavior], that your sins may be blotted out [regret and stop sinning so that we might be forgiven], when the times of refreshing shall come from the presence of the Lord.

This is the same thing that God inspired Ezekiel to write for his day and for us in our day as well

Ezekiel 14:6 Therefore say unto the house of Israel, Thus saith the Lord God; Repent, and turn yourselves from your idols [everyone including today's Ekklesia needs to turn from following idols of men to embrace and live by every Word of God]; and turn away your faces from all your abominations.

God tells us through Ezekiel that God will judge us for exalting anything, including false traditions and idols of men, above a passionate zeal to learn and to live by every Word of God.

Ezekiel 18:30 Therefore I will judge you, O house of Israel, every one according to his ways, saith the Lord God. Repent, and turn yourselves from all your transgressions; so iniquity shall not be your ruin.

To repent means to STOP doing what we have been doing, and begin to live a different way. In spiritual terms repentance means to STOP doing what we decide and START living by every Word of God the Father.

Ezekiel 18:30 Therefore I will judge you, O house of Israel, every one according to his ways, saith the Lord God. Repent, and turn yourselves from all your transgressions; so iniquity shall not be your ruin.

Joel 2:12 Therefore also now, saith the Lord, turn ye even to me with all your heart, and with fasting, and with weeping, and with mourning:

What are we to repent of and turn away from? We are to repent of deciding right and wrong for ourselves and we are to repent of not living by ever Word of God.

1 John 2:3 And hereby we do know that we know him, if we keep his commandments. **2:4** He that saith, I know him, and keepeth not his commandments, is a liar, and the truth is not in him.

What did Jesus command? He taught us to live by every Word of God (Mat 4:4).

Deuteronomy 4:39 Know therefore this day, and consider it in thine heart, that the Lord he is God in heaven above, and upon the earth beneath: there is none else.

4:40 Thou shalt keep therefore his statutes, and his commandments, which I command thee this day, that it may go well with thee, and with thy children after thee, and that thou mayest prolong thy days upon the earth, which the Lord thy God giveth thee, for ever.

1 John 5:2 By this we know that we love the children of God, when we love God, and keep his commandments. **5:3** For this is the love of God, that we keep his commandments: and his commandments are not grievous.

Does this refer exclusively to the Ten Commandments? If you believe this they why do people reject God's commanded seventh day Sabbath for Sunday? That subject will be covered in our book on "Ecclesiastical Authority."

I ask again, does this refer exclusively to the Ten Commandments? The answer is a resounding NO; this refers to Every Word of God, because the Ten command us to honor our father, and our ultimate spiritual Father is God the Father in heaven! If we do not live by Every Word of God the Father then we dishonour him and we sin.

Baptism and Commitment

Once we have been called to God and we have had our minds opened to a small initial understanding of spiritual things; if we respond positively and begin to loathe our past sins and sincerely repent of them: it is time to make a solid commitment to live by every Word of God.

If we commit to STOP sinning and to follow God the Father and the Lamb of God; God will send his Holy Spirit to dwell within us and empower us to learn and to apply what we learn to overcome sin in our lives.

More about the Spirit later, but first the required baptismal commitment

The New Covenant ordinance of baptism has its origins in the law which Gad gave to Moses.

In the law anyone who became polluted by some uncleanness was required to wash and then remain unclean until the sun set and a new day began.

Here are just two examples in the law.

Deuteronomy 23:11 But it shall be, **when evening cometh** on, he shall wash himself with water: and **when the sun is down**, he shall come into the camp again.

Leviticus 15:6 And he that sitteth on any thing whereon he sat that hath the issue shall wash his clothes, and bathe himself in water, and be unclean until the even. **15:7** And he that toucheth the flesh of him that hath the issue shall wash his clothes, and bathe himself in water, and be unclean until the even.

John Baptist was faithful to God's law and taught the people to sincerely repent and wash themselves clean from all of their sincerely repented sins. In doing this he was revealing that the law of the Clean and the Unclean was really an allegory that all sin renders us spiritually unclean before God and we need to be washed clean from all sin.

This washing was called "Baptizing" in the Greek of the New Testament scriptures and means a complete immersion in water.

John called the people first to repent [to STOP sinning], and then to wash themselves [be baptized], and just six months later Jesus Christ came teaching the same thing.

Galatians 2:16 knowing that a man is not justified by the works of the law, [future law keeping; does not atone for PAST sins] but is justified by the faith of Jesus Christ, even we have believed in Jesus Christ, that we might be justified by the faith of Christ, and not by the works of the law: for by the works of the law shall no flesh be justified.

No flesh, no person; can be justified before God for their past deeds of sin by any future law keeping. That is because ALL have sinned at some point and even if we keep the law perfectly after that, we must still pay for that PAST sin and NO amount of future law abiding can atone for past sin.

For example if you murder someone and then live perfectly for many years; you are still a murderer.

We can keep all kinds of traditions and fast three days week and avoid associating with physically uncircumcised yet converted New Covenant Gentiles, which is the subject here. And that is not going to justify anyone.

People can only be justified by sincere repentance, a genuine baptismal commitment to go and sin no more, and faith in the application of the atoning sacrifice of Jesus Christ, which is circumcision of the heart!

No matter how perfectly the law is kept, it still does not atone for PAST sin.

We can wake up today, and say we are going to be perfect from here on out forever. But that doesn't pay for previous sins!

To have those PAST sins paid for, to have an atonement and reconciliation made between us and God, comes only through sincere repentance and faith in the sacrifice of Jesus Christ.

Paul says, you can't be justified, you can't be made right with God, by your own deeds. You can only be made right with God by having the sacrifice of Jesus Christ applied to you; and then going forward to diligently do the DEEDS of God; living by every Word of God in future!

The sacrifice of Christ is only APPLIED to the REPENTANT; to those who STOP sinning! and it is sincere repentance to stop sinning and the application of the atonement of Christ for our past sins; which justifies and purifies us.

After that, we are to go forward; avoiding sin and living by every Word of God. But keeping the commandments does not justify anyone from PAST sins. It is sacrifice of Christ which justifies us and makes us right with God and atones for past sins.

2:17 But if, while we seek to be justified by Christ, we ourselves also are found sinners, [that is, if we continue in sin,] **is therefore Christ the minister of sin? God forbid.**

Once we are justified by sincere repentance, a baptismal commitment to go and sin no more and faith in the sacrifice of Christ, we are NOT to continue in sin as Paul said, God forbid that we should continue in sin!

2:18 For if I build again the things, which I destroyed, [that is, if I continue in my sinful nature] **I make myself a transgressor.**

If I have destroyed my sinful nature in sincere repentance and baptism, rising up from the grave of baptism a NEW being in Christ, and then being justified by my faith in the sacrifice of Christ; if I go out and continue in sin, I have returned to my sins and I am still a transgressor.

2:19 For I through the law am dead to the law, that I might live unto God. 2:20 I am crucified with Christ: nevertheless, I live; yet not I, but Christ liveth in me: and the life which I now live in the flesh I live by the faith of the Son of God, who loved me, and gave himself for me

Christ was crucified for our sins, if that sacrifice is applied to us, our old sinful self is also dead because Christ died and the crucifixion and sacrifice of Jesus Christ has paid the penalty for PAST sincerely repented sin. Therefore we must live by every Word of God through the indwelling power of Christ; from henceforth and forever more!

Our repentance, our baptismal commitment and faith in Christ and his sacrifice, atones for PAST sin. And the sinful man, our sinful nature is dead and gone, and we rise up new persons in Christ.

Jesus Christ can then dwell in us through the power of God's Holy Spirit, and when he [Christ] is dwelling in us, Christ will do the things he has always done, now doing them within us, that is, he will live by every Word of God and we will live by every Word of God in Christ-like zeal as we are led by the Spirit of Christ.

This is the New Covenant circumcision of the heart:

Colossians 2:11 In whom also ye are circumcised with the **circumcision** made without hands, in putting off the body of the sins of the flesh by the **circumcision** of Christ:

God's Spirit is not divided against God. God's Spirit is the Spirit and nature of God. God is not divided against himself. He keeps his own Word.

Christ says, "I have kept my Father's commandments" and the Holy Spirit of God will empower us and lead us to also keep God's commandments; to turn away from sin.

John 15:10 If ye keep my commandments, ye shall abide in my love; even as I have kept my Father's commandments, and abide in his love.

Galatians 2:21 I do not frustrate the grace of God: for if righteousness come by the law, then Christ death is in vain.

If we have sinned, and we could stop sinning today and be perfect from this point onward: What about past sins?

Keeping the law from this point forward does not atone for our PAST law breaking. Only sincere repentance and the application of the sacrifice of Jesus Christ can atone for past law breaking; and then, the Holy Spirit is given to us, and empowers us to go forward, putting away all sin and living by every Word of God in the future.

To summarize: We must sincerely repent of all PAST sin and then STOP sinning; then to really get that point across we must make a formal baptismal commitment to stop sinning and destroy our PAST sinful self; going down into the grave of water and destroying the old person of sin, and then rising up out of the water a NEW person in Christ and Christ-like zeal to Live by Every Word of GOD.

Then the atoning sacrifice of Jesus Christ the true Lamb of God, will be applied to us and we must go forward in Christ-like zeal to live by every Word of God through the strength of the ultimate overcomer dwelling in us, henceforth and forever!

Physical circumcision is only a symbolic removal of a piece of flesh and avails nothing unless God is obeyed [except that physical circumcision is a prophecy of spiritual circumcision into the New Covenant]; but it is the spiritual circumcision of the New Covenant which removes our sins which have separated us from God!

The true doctrine of Salvation through Jesus Christ, is that we must become spiritually circumcised, removing all of the sin which separates us from God the Father through sincere repentance, a baptismal commitment to sin no more and the application of the sacrifice of Jesus Christ the Lamb of God.

Anyone who teaches the false doctrine that we need not be passionately faithful and obedient to the whole Word of God, just as Jesus Christ was and is; teaching that we can tolerate compromise with the Word of God; is teaching that we need not be spiritually circumcised and is an anti-Christ and is under a curse from God!

Galatians 3:1 O foolish Galatians, who hath bewitched you, that you should not obey the truth, before whose eyes Jesus Christ hath been evidently set forth, crucified among you? **3:2** This only would I learn of you, Received you the Spirit, [did the Holy Spirit come] by the works of the law, [Does keeping the commandments in future, atone for PAST sin?] or by the hearing of faith?

God's Spirit works with us when God calls us, but God does not give his Holy Spirit to dwell within us until we sincerely repent and make a baptismal commitment to STOP sinning. It is only then that the sacrifice of Christ is applied to us justifying us by paying for our sincerely repented past sins.

Did you receive the indwelling of the Holy Spirit, by now starting to keep the commandments; or did the penalty for sin have to be paid first by the application of the sacrifice of Christ before we could be reconciled to God?

Yes, we had to sincerely repent first and then the sacrifice of Jesus Christ the Lamb of God must be applied to all our repented sins, BEFORE we can receive the gift of God's Spirit to dwell in us?

Therefore we do not receive the gift of the Holy Spirit by any future law keeping; we receive the gift of God's Spirit through sincere repentance and the application of Christ's sacrifice for all our sincerely repented PAST sins.

It is our repentance and faith in Christ's atoning sacrifice, which reconciles us to God the Father, which then brings us into a relationship with God the Father, so that he may then give us his Spirit. Our future law keeping then maintains our proper relationship with God, which was established by Gods calling, our sincere repentance and baptism and the application of Christ's sacrifice.

3:3 Are you so foolish? Having begun in the Spirit, are you now made perfect by the acts of the flesh? **3:4** Have you suffered so many things in vain? If it be yet in vain. **3:5** He, theretofore, [or he, therefore,] that ministers to you the Spirit, and works miracles among you, doeth he it by the works of the law, or by the hearing of faith? **3:6** Even as Abraham believed God, and [obeyed God] it was accounted to him for righteousness. **3:7** Know you therefore that they which are of faith, the same are the children of Abraham.

Paul teaches us about being saved by faith and the act of faith which is sincere repentance, and being forgiven through the atoning sacrifice of Christ and living by faith in Christ, and then keeping the commandments through the indwelling of Christ, to show the difference between physical circumcision and the circumcision of the heart.

In fact Paul is explaining the difference between keeping God's Word in future and the need for an atonement for PAST sin.

People who do what Abraham did, being full of faith and marrying that faith to the actions of obedience to the whole Word of God; are Abraham's children. **Galatians 3:7** Know you not therefore that they which are of faith, the same are the children of Abraham."

Paul is teaching us that it is not just physical Israel who are the children of Abraham, but it is everyone who has sincerely repented and had the atoning sacrifice of Christ applied to them.

Everyone who commits to obey God the Father in all things and who is then filled with God's Spirit, everyone who is filled with faith in God, all of them, both Jew and Gentile including ALL races, are people of faith and are therefore the children of Abraham.

It is not those who are the physical descendants of Abraham; but those who do what Christ teaches and what Abraham did as our example; those who are like Abraham in faith, words and deeds; are truly Abraham's children. Physical descent means nothing in the New Covenant: Believing and living by every Word of God is all in all!

In Hebrews 12:8 Paul explains that those who will not endure correction are not truly son's at all but bastards. Why does any father correct his children? Why, to mould their behavior into what HE wants it to be; to cause the child to act as the father would have him act.

Therefore if we will not do what Abraham did for our example, he is not truly our father in a spiritual sense; and if we do not obey our Father in heaven; then he is NOT our Father in the spiritual sense; and if we will not keep the whole Word of God our Father in heaven; then we are rebellious children in need of severe correction.

Hebrews 12:8 But if ye be without chastisement, whereof all are partakers, then are ye bastards, and not sons.

If we become the children of God our Father in heaven and are reconciled to him in faith; and turn away from all sin to live by every Word of God; we also become reconciled to Abraham and become heirs of the promises made to him.

Paul is trying to heal the rift between certain Jews and certain Gentiles in saying that; if we have faith in God and in Christ and keep all of God's Word as Abraham did; then we are circumcised in heart: Regardless of our race we are grafted into a spiritual Israel of the New Covenant and we ARE the children of Abraham.

Circumcision of the flesh has a fault, which is that those circumcised in the flesh still could not obey their father Abraham nor their Father in heaven; therefore circumcision of the flesh was replaced by a much better circumcision: A circumcision of the heart through the sacrifice of Christ which atoned for sin, removing the barrier of sin [foreskin of our heart] which comes between us and God the Father.

The foreskin of our hearts [which is our sins] must be removed!

Isaiah 59:1 Behold, the LORD's hand is not shortened, that it cannot save; neither his ear heavy, that it cannot hear: **59:2 But your iniquities have separated between you and your God, and your sins have hid his face from you, that he will not hear.**

As it is written:

Deuteronomy 10:16 Circumcise therefore the **foreskin of your heart**, and be no more stiffnecked [stubborn and self-willed].

Those sins are removed by our sincere repentance and our baptismal commitment to go and sin no more; through faith in the sacrifice of Jesus

Christ the Lamb of God; which then reconciles us to God the Father and makes us the seed of Abraham in a spiritual sense.

It is the circumcision of the heart [the removal of sin by the application of the sacrifice of Christ] which makes us Abraham's seed,: not the circumcision of the flesh; which does not remove sin, nor does it make us truly spiritual sons of Abraham, or sons of God our Father in heaven.

Galatians 3:8 And the scripture, foreseeing that God would justify the heathen through faith, preached before the gospel unto Abraham, saying, In thee shall **all nations** be blessed. **3:9** So, then they which be of faith are blessed with faithful Abraham.

ALL those who repent [whether of physical Israel or Gentiles] and turn away from rebellion against God the Father; who STOP sinning: Will then have the sacrifice of the Lamb of God applied to them!

Psalm 22:27 All the ends of the world shall remember and turn unto the LORD: and all the kindreds of the nations shall worship before thee.

Our faith in Christ; which must be a living faith of sincere repentance from evil works, to become obedient to the whole Word of God the Father, as Christ was obedient to God the Father: will result in the application of Christ's atoning sacrifice to us. And being justified by that sacrifice we will be reconciled to God the Father in heaven.

Romans 2:13 (For not the hearers of the law are just before God, but the doers of the law shall be justified.

We are only justified by sincere repentance and the application of Christ's sacrifice! The unrepentant sinner will NOT have the sacrifice of Christ applied to him or her and will NOT be justified before God!

The true circumcision of the New Covenant is spiritual, of the heart and spirit, and not of the flesh.

Circumcision of the flesh profits nothing spiritually, even baptism and ordination, or attending some corporate church organization profits nothing at all; UNLESS we are circumcised of the heart; through sincere repentance from all sin and compromising with any part of the whole Word of God followed by a commitment to diligently believe and live by every Word of God; and the application of the sacrifice of Jesus Christ.

If we are baptized, ordained, or attend corporate church services, or are physically circumcised: It means absolutely NOTHING unless we do the deeds of Abraham and have his faith to trust and obey Almighty God!

Circumcision of the flesh was a sign of the Mosaic Covenant and when that Covenant passed away because of its weakness: It was replaced with a New and better Covenant, a spiritual Covenant.

The sign of the New Covenant is the circumcision of the heart: Which is repentance from rebellion and sin, a commitment to obey God the Father and the application of the atoning sacrifice of Christ! This circumcises our hearts by removing all PAST sins and reconciles us to God the Father by removing that barrier of sin hat existed between us and God the Father; which barrier is our rebellion and sin!

This message about circumcision is an explanation of the process of salvation!

Yes, the truly converted Gentiles are grafted into a New Covenant spiritual Israel, being filled with faith in God. They are obedient in faith and are the seed of Abraham, for Abraham believed God and coupled that belief with obedience!

Abraham believed God. Abraham acted on that belief and obeyed God showing forth the works of his faith. That is faith.

Faith is not just belief, it is action based on belief. We can believe all we want to and if we do nothing about it, it has done us absolutely no good. We must believe God, and we must act on that belief by doing what God says.

If we believe in the sacrifice of Christ, then we must act to stop sinning so that his sacrifice may then be applied to us! This is called "SINCERE REPENTANCE"!

3:10 For as many as are of the works of the law are under a curse: for it is written, Cursed is every one that continues not in all things which are written in the book of the law to do them.

If we do not have faith in the atoning sacrifice of Christ, his perfect sinless life and resurrection, and if we justify breaking the law in even the smallest point, we are cursed [facing death] and we must pay the penalty for having broken the Word of God.

There is no remission of PAST sin without sincere repentance from all past sin, a commitment to sin no more in future and the application of the sacrifice of Christ!

The penalty for transgressing the law or any part of the Word of God is death; Adam died for his rebellion against God! And the only way to be saved from being forced to pay the penalty we have earned; is to sincerely repent of all PAST sins, resolve to STOP sinning in future, be baptized, and have faith in the promises and the sacrifice of Jesus Christ.

Galatians 3:11 But that no man is justified by the law in the sight of God, it is evident: for, the just shall live by faith. **3:12** And the law is not of faith: but, the man that does them shall live in them. **3:13** Christ hath redeemed us from the curse of the law, [If we sincerely repent and STOP sinning, Christ will redeem us from the penalty for having broken the law,] being made a curse for us, having died for us: for it is written, Cursed is every one that hangeth on a tree.

The law itself is not a curse: It is a great blessing. But there is a curse of the law, and the curse of the law is the penalty that must be paid when the law is broken. And when the law is broken, the penalty to be exacted is death.

We can only be saved from that penalty through sincere repentance for not obeying God and then to dedicate ourselves to live by every Word of God from henceforth and forever more.

Then the atoning sacrifice of Jesus Christ will be applied to us; at which point we will be given God's Spirit; and the Spirit of Christ and of God the Father will dwell in us, empowering us to live by every Word of God the Father and of Jesus Christ.

And if we should slip now and then, or here and there unintentionally sin; we have faith that Christ's sacrifice will atone for us if we sincerely repent. That does not justify continuing in sin. It does not justify habitual sin. But it is there to save us, when and if we do unintentionally slip.

3:14 That the blessing of Abraham might come also on the Gentiles through Jesus Christ; that we might receive the promise of the Spirit through faith.

The Spirit of God empowers us to keep God's Word imparts us with the very nature of God. The Holy Spirit is given through our sincere repentance and faith in the sacrifice of Christ and our willingness to obey Christ and God the Father, to turn from our sins and to diligently live by every Word of God the Father in future (Mat 4:4).

3:15 Brethren, I speak after the manner of men; Though it be but a man's agreement or covenant, yet if it be confirmed, no man disannuls, or adds to it.

When you have a firm covenant or a contract with somebody, nobody can break it, or disannul it, or change it; without a penalty. It is a commitment made between two people.

3:16 Now, to Abraham and his seed were the promises made. He said not, and to seeds, as of many; but as of one, And to **thy seed, which is Christ.**

The promise of God to Abraham was that through your seed God shall bless all people; which includes ALL races. This is fulfilled physically by the nations of Israel through Isaac.

Jesus was implanted in Mary and was not her biological son, yet this promise to Abraham was fulfilled spiritually by Jesus Christ since Abraham is the father of the faithful, and there is none more faithful than Jesus Christ.

Therefore Paul when speaking of spiritual things said:

Galatians 3:16 Now to Abraham and his seed were the promises made. He saith not, And to seeds, as of many; but as of one, And to thy seed, which is Christ.

Galatians 3:17 And this I say, that the covenant, that was confirmed before of God in Christ, the law, which was four hundred and thirty years later, cannot disannul that covenant or that promise that God made to Abraham, that it should make the promise of no effect.

That is, Jesus Christ was God before he was made flesh, and he promised Abraham in Ur: "in your seed shall all flesh be blessed." And the law coming 430 years [after the promise was made in Ur] later at Sinai cannot dissannul the promise that God made to Abraham.

The New Covenant of spiritual Israel is for all those who would respond to God the Father's call, all who would believe and sincerely repent and turn from sin, dedicating themselves to diligently keep and live by the whole Word of God.

This promise made to Abraham, that all flesh shall be blessed through his seed; one of his descendant's; is firm and cannot be altered or changed by subsequent covenants or laws.

Therefore, the Mosaic Covenant cannot alter the promise of the spiritual New Covenant which God made to Abraham, concerning the blessing of atonement through his seed; Jesus Christ.

3:18 For if the inheritance be of the law, it is no more of a promise: but God gave it to Abraham by promise.

God's promise to Abraham was a promise; and was not part of the Mosaic Covenant and the various laws. It was a personal promise of God to Abraham.

3:19 Wherefore, then, serveth the law? The law was added because of transgressions [or wickedness,] till the seed, [that is, the one seed] should come to whom the promise was made; and it was ordained by angels in the hand of a mediator. **3:20** Now, a mediator is not a mediator of one, but God is one.

That is, a mediator mediates between two parties. A mediator does not deal with just one party. And there is one mediator between God and man, and that is Jesus Christ. He came as our mediator, and our deliverer, and our sacrifice. And he mediates between us and God the Father.

No, Mary is not a mediatrix and the saints do not mediate for people, here is no other mediator between God and man, than Jesus Christ.

1 Timothy 2:5 For there is one God, and **one mediator between God and men, the man Christ Jesus;**

Galatians 3:21 Is the law then against the promises of God? . . .

Are God's commandments and the Covenants, somehow contrary to or against the promises of God? Of course not.

As Paul says, . . . God forbid: for if there had been a law given which could have given life, truly righteousness should have been by the law.

No keeping the law in future does not provide payment for past sin: What provides atonement and forgiveness is our repentance coupled with the application of the actual sacrifice of the Creator.

3:22 But the scripture hath concluded that all are under sin, that the promise of faith of Jesus Christ might be given to them who believe. **3:23** But before faith came, we were kept under [the penalty of having broken the law] law and shut up [faith in Christ was hidden] unto the faith which should afterwards be revealed.

Paul says, until faith came in, and until the sacrifice of Jesus Christ came into the picture, until Christ actually fulfilled his mission; we were all under the curse [because the penalty of breaking the law must be paid] of the law. We all face the penalty for having broken the law. We were all facing death for having broken the commandments until Christ's sacrifice and faith entered.

Christ's sacrifice was made and he was resurrected to spirit, and we can have faith in that sacrifice and resurrection; faith that Christ lived a sinless life and his sacrifice atoned for our sincerely repented sin and that we, if Christ lives in us keeping the whole Word of God in us, can also be resurrected to spirit as he was. Faith then enters into the picture and the concept of having to die for our PAST sin fades away, as we are justified by our sincere repentance and faith in the atoning sacrifice of Christ, that he paid the penalty in our place.

3:24 Wherefore the law was our schoolmaster to bring us to Christ, that we might be justified by faith. **3:25** For after faith is come, we are no longer under a schoolmaster.

We needed to learn not to sin and therefore we faced a penalty for our sin, to teach us not to sin.

When we learn not to sin any more and to REPENT of our PAST sin; then FAITH in the atoning sacrifice of Christ enters the picture and delivers the REPENTANT from the need to pay the penalty for PAST sin. This DOES NOT JUSTIFY continuing in sin!

3:26 For you are all the children of God through faith in Christ Jesus. **3:27** For as many of you as have been baptized into Christ have put on Christ.

If we have been called by God and have sincerely repented of all past sins, then the sacrifice of Jesus Christ will pay for our repented PAST sins and God the Father and Jesus Christ will dwell in us through the power of God's Spirit; empowering us to live as Christ lived, living by every Word of God (Mat 4:4).

3:28 There is neither Jew nor Greek, there is neither bond nor free, there is neither male nor female: for you are all one in Christ Jesus. **3:29** And if you be in Christ, then are ye all Abraham's seed, and heirs according to the promise.

The sign of the New Covenant is not circumcision in the flesh; **it is circumcision of the heart** [which is heartfelt REPENTANCE from sin and going forward to faithfully live by every Word of God like Christ did!].

The sign of the New Covenant is REPENTANCE, FAITH and the diligent keeping of every Word of God! It is FAITH in Christ, married to the works of REPENTANT OBEDIENCE that saves: Faith in Jesus Christ, faith in

God the Father, faith in the sacrifice that was applied to blot out our REPENTED sins.

Faith that the Spirit of God is given to us and dwells in us and empowers us to live by every Word of God, and empowers us to please God; and fills us with the love of God, which is to live by every Word of God.

We must now live by faith; because before, we were dead in sin having broken the law and under the penalty of death; and sin is the transgression of the law (1 John 3:4).

Sin is the transgression of the law. We have all broken the law at some point in our lives. Therefore, we are all under the penalty of having broken the law which is death.

It is a stopping of sinning [REPENTANCE] and faith in Jesus Christ and the application of his sacrifice to atone for our past sins; that brings into a proper relationship with God and circumcises our hearts; removing the BARRIER of sin which separates us from Almighty God.

And it is through sincere repentance, faith and the application of the sacrifice of Christ reconciling us to God; that the Holy Spirit can be given to us; and that Spirit then empowers us to live by every Word of God in the future.

Once a penalty for breaking a law has been paid, that does not in any way justify continuing to break the law.

If you have a habit of going through red lights, and you go and pay a fine, and the next time you are caught, you tell the judge, "Well, I paid the fine last time; I have a right to do this from now on." He is going to laugh at you, and probably take away your license, and maybe give you a few days to cool off in a cell.

The fact is, when we pay a fine, it only pays for PAST law breaking. It does not pay for any future law breaking. And that is true with God as well. The sacrifice of Christ applied to us, only atones for sincerely repented PAST law breaking. It does not permit us to indulge ourselves in future law breaking.

If we inadvertently break the law in future, we must repent, and have the sacrifice applied again, or we will face the penalty for that particular act of law breaking.

And there will come a time, if we willfully break the law and justify ourselves in doing so; that Christ is going to run out of patience with us.

If we are not sincere; we are not honest; we don't really want to live by God's Word; we are not really trying to please God then God's patience will end with serious correction. His sacrifice is not going to be applied to us anymore; until we straighten up, and wake up, and start really genuinely repenting, and start really genuinely trying to please God.

Sincere repentance, faith and the works of faith save us from the penalty of sin, which is death. It is faith and the sacrifice of Christ which saves us.

That faith does not entitle us to then go out and incur the penalty a second time, and a third, and a fourth, and on and on, and on.

No, Faith in the sacrifice, must be married to the works of faith, married to sincere repentance and a dedicated commitment to STOP sinning brings atonement for PAST sin, PAST law breaking; and allows us to be reconciled with God the Father.

Which atonement for sin places us into a proper relationship with God; and through faith, we are given God's Holy Spirit which will then empower us to live by every Word of God from then on.

Paul continues with his guidance and instruction to the people, trying to reconcile the Jews and the Gentile converts with each other, and to make them realize that they are all part of the same body, and through faith, they are all the children of Abraham.

1 Corinthians 7:19 Circumcision is nothing, and uncircumcision is nothing, but the keeping of the commandments of God. [is everything]

Physical circumcision, baptism and even ordination are absolutely NOTHING if we are not zealous to live by every Word of God!

Spiritual circumcision is the removal of the sin that separates us from God and the writing of the whole Word of God on our hearts and in our minds through the Holy Spirit enabling us to live by every Word of God.

Jeremiah 31:33 But this shall be the covenant that I will make with the house of Israel; After those days, saith the Lord, I will put my law in their inward parts, and write it in their hearts; and will be their God, and they shall be my people.

Those who compromise or reject any part of the Word of God, as is commonly done in today's spiritual Ekklesia, will have no part in the New Covenant resurrection to spirit.

The Lessons of Baptism

This washing of baptism is first a washing away of the uncleanness of all sincerely repented past sins.

Baptism is a symbolic death of the sinful man, who then rises out of the watery grave of baptism a new person dedicated to continually learn and to live by every Word of God.

Romans 6:3 Know ye not, that so many of us as were baptized into Jesus Christ were baptized into his death?

That is, sincere repentance and a baptismal commitment to live by every Word of God; brings the application of the sacrificial death of the Lamb of God to atone for all of our past repented sins.

Romans 2:13 (For not the hearers of the law are just before God, but the doers of the law [who have repented and turned from breaking the law and Word of God] shall be justified [by the application of the sacrifice of Jesus Christ, the Lamb of God].

Baptism is the symbol of a firm commitment to live by every Word of God which then espouses the person to Jesus Christ [the full marriage comes at the resurrection to spirit]. Effectual baptism must be the voluntary act of a mature sincerely repentant person who fully understands what they are committing themselves to.

Baptism is not for children or for persons who are not fully aware that they are committing themselves to live by every Word of God forever.

Baptized persons are not members of any corporate church, they are individual persons in a spiritual covenant with God.

John's baptism restored a person into the Mosaic Covenant, but the baptism of Christ washed away sins on a spiritual level because it represented a sincerely repentant commitment to the spiritual New Covenant of Jeremiah 36:34 and Ezekiel 36:26.

New Covenant Baptism is the making of a Covenant with God the Father to espouse oneself to Christ, and to live by every Word of and to internalize the very nature of God the Father.

How to Baptize: To be properly baptized a person must be well informed, sincerely repentant and fully committed to live by every Word of God forever. Baptism is to be completely immersed in water for a few seconds by a converted male, while the words "I baptize you into the New

Covenant and into God the Father, the Son and the Holy Spirit, in the name of Jesus Christ (Acts 19:5)" are spoken.

Matthew 28:19 Go ye therefore, and teach all nations, **baptizing them in the name of the Father, and of the Son, and of the Holy Ghost**

Once a person is raised up out of the water at least one and preferable two converted males are to place their hands on the person's head, anointing them with oil [symbolic of the Holy Spirit] and consecrating them into the New Covenant and asking for the gift of the Holy Spirit.

Acts 8:14 Now when the apostles which were at Jerusalem heard that Samaria had received the word of God, they sent unto them Peter and John: **8:15** Who, when they were come down, prayed for them, that they might receive the Holy Ghost: **8:16** (For as yet he was fallen upon none of them: only they were baptized in the name of the Lord Jesus.) **8:17** Then laid they their hands on them, and they received the Holy Ghost.

This is the proscribed formula, however God can call anyone in any circumstance, and God can give his Spirit without baptism in extraordinary circumstances (Acts 10:44-48). Remember that no person was baptized in this way until Christ began teaching and yet a great many - from Abel to Christ - had received the Holy Spirit.

Circumstances making baptism impossible may occur in isolated areas even today. Nevertheless this procedure must be followed unless one is converted on his deathbed or in similar extreme circumstances. I am trying to say that even in extreme conditions like the tribulation, one should still sincerely repent and trust God.

After baptism, if we remain faithful, continually learning and growing spiritually and overcoming sin; we will be resurrected to spirit and then married to Jesus Christ restored to his Spirit form before God the Father in heaven (Rev 15, 19), before returning to the earth with Christ.

Galatians 3:27 For as many of you as have been baptized into Christ have put on [have committed to be united an done in unity with Christ] Christ.

There are many, many places throughout both the Old and New Testaments where we are told to stop sinning (1 Corinthians 15:34, 1 John 2:1, Ephesians 4:26, Ezekiel 18:4, Deuteronomy 30:19).

Once we commit ourselves to STOP sinning and to go forward to live by every Word of God, we will then be justified and redeemed through the application of the atoning sacrifice of Jesus Christ the Lamb of God.

We then are fully reconciled to God the Father and he gives us the gift of his Holy Spirit which enables us to comprehend and retain a good understanding of the Word of God, empowering us to live just as Christ lived, overcoming all sin and living by every Word of God (Mat 4:4).

Deuteronomy 5:32 Ye shall observe to do therefore as the Lord your God hath commanded you: ye shall not turn aside to the right hand or to the left.

1 John 2:6 He that saith he abideth in him ought himself also so to walk [live], even as he walked [lives].

Romans 6:1 What shall we say then? **Shall we continue in sin, that grace may abound? 6:2 God forbid. How shall we, that are dead to sin, live any longer therein?**

If we have been delivered from the slavery of sin [spiritual Egypt] why would we seek to remain in bondage? To love God is to seek to please him and to become like him, as he has defined himself by his Word. If we reject any part of, or compromise with any of God's Word, we love the slavery of Egypt and sin; MORE than we love God the Father of Jesus Christ, for they are in complete UNITY with one another!

Baptism represents the death and burial of the old sinful man; and a truly converted person will rise up from baptism a new being, burning with Christ-like zeal to live by every Word of God just as Jesus Christ did.

Baptism is a commitment of sincere repentance from sin and represents the death of the existing sinful man and his allegorical resurrection to godliness; and is a total commitment to God the Father and Jesus Christ; to please God, to keep the whole Word of God with passionate zeal and to become like God in every way.

Baptism is a complete and unshakable commitment of espousal in marriage to Jesus Christ for all eternity! A commitment to internalize the very nature of God by keeping his Word with a zeal to become like our LORD.

6:3 Know ye not, that so many of us as were baptized into Jesus Christ were baptized into his death?

The old man of sin is dead and buried in baptism; so that we may rise up from the water a new person in Christ; keeping the whole Word of God just like Christ did and does.

Matthew 4:4 But he answered and said, It is written, **Man shall not live by bread alone, but by every word that proceedeth out of the mouth of God**.

Romans 6:4 Therefore we are buried with him **by baptism into death**: that like as Christ was raised up from the dead by the glory of the Father, even so **we also should walk in newness of life**.

We commit ourselves at baptism to destroy the old man of sin and to arise a NEW person in Christ-like godliness! It is our calling to becoming Christ-like; loving and obeying God the Father as Christ did, walking and living by every Word of God as Jesus Christ walked and lived!

6:5 For if we have been planted [if we have been buried in baptism] together in the likeness of his death, we shall be also [rise from the grave of baptism as he rose from the dead] in the likeness of his resurrection: **6:6 Knowing this, that our old [sinful] man is crucified with him, that the body of sin might be destroyed, that henceforth we should not serve sin.**

After our baptismal commitment we are: TO NO LONGER SERVE SIN!

After baptism we should serve [obey] God; so that we may then be raised up in a resurrection to spirit just as Jesus Christ was raised up to spirit.

The dead sin not [they can do nothing]; therefore those who bury the old sinful self in baptism cannot continue in wilful sin.

We are to live as Christ lived, by following the Holy Spirit of Christ dwelling in us; and that Spirit will NEVER lead us to compromise with any part of the Word of God, or to tolerate sin and false doctrine. Any spirit that leads into tolerating sin or false teachings contrary to the Word of God is NOT of Christ: It is the spirit of Anti-Christ and is of Satan!

6:7 For he that is dead is freed from sin.

Being buried in baptism is a symbolic death of the old sinful person and frees us from PAST sin!

Why should we, being liberated from PAST sin; desire to compromise with God's Word and to lose our Christ-like zeal for the whole Word of God, and associate with worldliness; thereby going back into bondage?

There is only one reason: Because we love serving sin unto decay and death, more than we love serving God unto eternal life!

It is because we are willing to sell the birthright of our calling, which is eternal life in peace and harmony with God and all his children; for the temporary pleasures of sin; that we are subject to eternal death.

Like Esau, many do not value their freedom from slavery to sin; and many sell their birthright for a temporary and transitory relief from trials, or fall to temptations to take pleasure in evil doing.

6:8 Now if we be dead with Christ [in baptism], we believe that we shall also live with him [free from sin as he lives]: **6:9** Knowing that Christ being raised from the dead dieth no more; death hath no more dominion over him.

Christ died for our sin once; and was then raised up to eternal life to serve God the Father; therefore we are to destroy the old man of sin and enter a baptismal commitment to serve God the Father and to: "go and sin no more."

Once raised up from baptism, we are raised up to a new life, free from sinning; to serve God the Father and to live by every Word of God with Christ-like passion.

Jesus Christ died once and now lives again; serving God the Father; and we who symbolically destroyed our past sinful selves in the watery grave of baptism; are to rise up new persons to serve God the Father

6:10 For in that he died, he died unto sin once: but in that he liveth, **he liveth unto God**.

The birthright of our calling is the same eternal life that was given to Jesus Christ when he was raised up from physical death and changed back to spirit.

UNDERSTAND the appalling price that Christ Jesus paid for us: Jesus Christ GAVE UP his Godhood and eternal life to be made flesh for us! He then GAVE UP his physical life for us!

He did this with COMPLETE FAITH, that God the Father would strengthen him against all temptation to live by every Word of God the Father; making him a worthy sacrifice for his creation: In COMPLETE FAITH that his Father could and would raise him up and restore him back to eternal life!

6:11 Likewise reckon ye also yourselves to be **dead indeed unto sin**, but **alive unto God** [We are to be sincerely repent and we are to become spiritually sensitive and passionate to keep the Word of God.] **through Jesus Christ our Lord.**

We are to become like the dead in regards to all temptation to sin and compromise with the commandments and Word of God. We are to destroy the old sinful man and become a new Christ-like person!

If we love God the Father and the Son and internalize the very nature of BOTH God the Father and the Son through Christ-like love and obedience to God the Father and his Word; our beloved Father will also raise us up to eternal life just as he raised Jesus up!

6:12 Let not sin [any transgression of the Word of God] **therefore reign in your mortal body,** that ye should obey it in the lusts thereof. **6:13 Neither yield ye your members as instruments of unrighteousness unto sin: but yield yourselves unto God,** as those that are alive from the dead [freed from the bondage of sin and death], and your members [keep the whole Word of God with all our mind and deeds] as instruments [subject our whole being to serve God the Father] of righteousness [The righteousness of God is the keeping of the Word of God] unto God.

Shun all sin and compromise with the Word of Almighty God; who alone is able to save and deliver us out of all sin. Allow his very mind, spirit and nature to dwell within us; overcoming all sin through the power of God!

As baptized persons we are to consider ourselves symbolically resurrected back to a new physical life after the death of the old sinful person, and delivered out of the spiritual Egypt of bondage to sin!

We are not to turn back into that spiritual Egypt of bondage to sin, or we shall be destroyed as those Israelites who wanted to turn back were destroyed!

If we truly loved Christ; we would do those things pleasing to Christ; we would be as zealous for God the Father's Word as Jesus Christ was and is!

We are the servants of those that we follow and obey. We are NOT to follow any man into wilful sin against any part of the Word of God, we are not to allow sin to have dominion over us and we are not to turn back into bondage to sin and death.

6:14 For sin shall not have dominion over you: for ye are not under the law [facing a penalty for breaking the law], but under grace [having stopped sinning and having been forgiven for our sincerely repented PAST sins]. **6:15 What then? shall we [continue in sin] sin, because we are not under the law, but under grace? God forbid.**

Anyone who has made a baptismal commitment to espouse themselves to Jesus Christ, and then compromises with any part of the Word of God even to the slightest degree, is in danger of being rejected as a suitable part of his resurrected spiritual bride.

Just as a bride is to become one flesh with her husband and is to faithfully follow him; so we are to become of one spirit, mind and actions with our Husband, Jesus Christ.

We are to internalize his very nature, which is the lesson of eating Unleavened Bread every day of the Feast of Unleavened Bread; representing the internalizing of Jesus Christ: The Bread of LIFE.

What was the nature of Jesus Christ? He loved God the Father with all his heart, and he kept all of his Fathers commandments, Word and instructions, without compromise or deviation to the slightest degree.

If we go willingly back into sin through deliberate compromise with God's Word, we are in danger of being rejected as a part of the bride; and if we do not repent, we are in danger of damnation.

If we reject portions of God's Word to justify our sins [like rejecting the commandments regarding the New Moons, rejecting God's Biblical Calendar, rejecting Nehemiah and the sanctity of the Sabbath and rejecting Luke on the Passover]; Jesus Christ will reject us!

If we return to the spiritual Egypt of bondage to sin from which we had been delivered by the application of the awesome sacrifice of Christ; we are returning back to the filthy burden of bondage to sin which we have been delivered out of; and we make a mockery of the sacrifice of Christ who died to deliver us.

If we prefer such filth to the Holy Law of Liberty from sin; we are NOT worthy of Jesus Christ and we will not be a part of his bride.

James 1:22 But be ye doers of the word, and not hearers only, deceiving your own selves. 1:23 For if any be a hearer of the word, and not a doer, he is like unto a man beholding his natural face in a glass: **1:24** For he beholdeth himself, and goeth his way, and straightway forgetteth what manner of man he was.

1:25 But whoso looketh into the perfect law of liberty [God's law liberates us from bondage to sin], **and continueth therein, he being not a forgetful hearer, but a doer of the work** [Word and law of God], **this man shall be blessed in his deed.**

My beloved brethren, it is time to wake up and to see how far we have fallen when we compromise and commit spiritual adultery against our LORD, by idolizing men and false traditions above the Word of God and the Glorious Law of Liberty!

Galatians 6:7 Be not deceived; God is not mocked: for whatsoever a man soweth, that shall he also reap.

Hebrews 10:26 For if we sin wilfully after that we have received the knowledge of the truth, there remaineth no more sacrifice for sins,

2 Peter 2:20 For if after they have escaped the pollutions of the world through the knowledge of the Lord and Saviour Jesus Christ, they are again entangled therein, and overcome, the latter end is worse with them than the beginning.

2:21 For it had been better for them not to have known the way of righteousness, than, after they have known it, to turn from the holy commandment delivered unto them. **2:22** But it is happened unto them according to the true proverb, **The dog is turned to his own vomit again; and the sow that was washed to her wallowing in the mire.**

Romans 6:16 Know ye not, that to whom ye yield yourselves servants to obey, his servants ye are to whom ye obey; whether **of sin unto death, or of obedience unto righteousness** [righteousness is passionately living by every Word of God]?

A minister once said to me: "I am a minister of Jesus Christ, I can do anything I want and God has to back me up."

I tell you that a minister of Jesus Christ would be doing what Jesus Christ wants, and NOT anything that HE himself wants.

If he is doing anything HE wants, Almighty God will NOT back him up, because he is NOT a minister of Jesus Christ; he is the servant of another.

We are to prove all things by the Word of God which is also the Word of Jesus Christ; and we are to follow and obey God our Father and our espoused Husband totally; and to follow men ONLY as they follow God the Father and Jesus Christ.

6:17 But God be thanked, that ye were the servants of sin, but ye have **obeyed from the heart that form of doctrine which was delivered you** [which is the sound doctrine of the Holy Scriptures to keep the whole Word of God]. **6:18** Being then made free from sin, **ye became the servants of righteousness.**

Godly righteousness is to live by every Word of God.

Let us rejoice that some have chosen to become like Jesus Christ, instead of continuing in sin; and have become the servants of righteousness through a passionate love of God, to enthusiastically wholeheartedly live by every Word of God.

Those who would compromise with any part of God's Word; and those who would love or fear this world more than they love their spiritual Father and their espoused Husband: Will be corrected by God.

6:19 I speak after the manner of men because of the infirmity of your flesh: for as ye have [in the PAST we committed many sins and were in bondage to sin] yielded your members servants to uncleanness and to iniquity unto iniquity; even so **now yield your members servants to righteousness unto holiness.**

Turn away from our PAST zeal for sin and the pleasures of this world and die the symbolic baptismal death of the old sinful person, and rise up a new person in Christ; seeking the righteousness of God by keeping all of God's Word with an even greater zeal then we had for the pleasures of this world!

If we serve sin by not keeping a certain part of the Word of God, we are empty of the righteousness of God.

James 2:10 For whosoever shall keep the whole law, and yet offend in one point, he is guilty of all.

Romans 6:20 For when ye were the servants of sin, ye were free from righteousness. **6:21** What fruit had ye then in those things whereof ye are now ashamed? for **the end of those things is death**.

6:22 But now being made free from sin, and [once freed from sin we are to] become servants to God, ye have your fruit unto holiness, and the end everlasting life. **6:23** For **the wages of sin is death**; but **the gift of God** [given to those who follow the whole word of God] **is eternal life through Jesus Christ our Lord.**

Sin and compromise with God's Word leads to all manner of decay and death: God's commandments bring harmony, peace and eternal life!

If we have been called to come to God the Father through Jesus Christ, and we sincerely repent and make a genuine baptismal commitment to live by every Word of God; God the Father WILL apply the atoning sacrifice of Jesus Christ the Lamb of God to us, and God the Father will give us his empowering Spirit.

If we have responded to God's call with sincere repentance and a commitment to go and sin no more, living by every Word of God and to follow the example that Christ set for us: We will receive God's Holy Spirit and we must no longer live according to our own desires, but we must live spiritual lives; loathing all sin and passionately loving the spiritual things of God.

Romans 8:9 But ye are not [to live in carnality] in the flesh, but [to live godly in God's Spirit] in the Spirit, if so be that the Spirit of God dwell in you. Now if any man [if we do not live as Christ lived, by every Word of God] have not the Spirit of Christ, he is none of [we have no part on Christ, because we live contrary to the way that Christ lived] his.

Romans 8:14 For as many as are led by [and faithfully follow] the Spirit of God, they are the sons of God.

When we initially receive God's Spirit to dwell within us after baptism we do not yet know or understand all godly things. From the time that we receive the gift of God's Spirit we must diligently study the Holy Scriptures, passionately embracing godliness and all truth, and removing every taint of error from our minds and behavior.

Learning godliness and internalizing the nature of God, while removing all sin and falsehood is a lifetime endeavour.

Yet if we diligently labor to learn and to practice what we learn over our lifetime, we will receive the gift of eternal life in a resurrection to spirit: Eternal life with God, at peace with God and with all others who have also overcome and turned to the Eternal with a whole heart.

The Lamb of God Sacrificed for Humanity

The Passover in Egypt was a graphic allegorical instruction that the very Creator God wold give up his Godhood to be made flesh as Jesus Christ the Lamb of God and would die as a sacrifice to cover the sincerely repented sins of humanity. In the beginning God knew that man would sin and so provision was made from the very creation for an effectual sacrifice to cover the repented sins of all humanity. The Passover is covered in detail in "The Biblical Spring Festivals" book.

Revelation 13:8 And all that dwell upon the earth shall worship him, whose names are not written in the book of life of **the Lamb slain from the foundation of the world**.

John 1:29 The next day John seeth Jesus coming unto him, and saith, **Behold the Lamb of God, which taketh away the sin of the world**.

The Implementing Creator; The Spirit High Priest

Genesis 1:26 And God (Elohim, plural: Mighty Ones) said, Let us make man in **our** image, after **our** likeness:.. [From the very beginning, creation is represented as a collaborative effort of two Mighty Beings.]

Genesis 3:22 reflects the same plurality of Beings in the same Family of Beings, And the LORD God said, Behold, the man is become as **one of us**, to know good and evil: and now, lest he put forth his hand, and take also of the tree of life, and eat, and live for ever:..

Genesis 1:1 In the beginning God [Elohim; Mighty Ones] created . . . The term translated as "God" here means "Mighty Ones": The singular of Elohim being El meaning a Lord or Mighty One, a judge or ruler.

Later, because men had made many gods [mighty ones] it was no longer adequate to simply call the true God Elohim [Mighty Ones] since one Elohim would only be one of multitudes of gods; and the Creator Mighty One therefore identified himself to Moses as YHVH to separate YHVH from all the other mighty ones or gods of the nations, and to separate himself from the mighty ones of Egypt.

This introduced a specific name for the True God Family to differentiate the Creator from other mighty ones [Elohim].

The term Elohim originally meant - until men perverted it - a family of at least two Creator beings; one the Executive Creating Authority who later became God the Father and one the Implementing Creating Authority who later gave up his God-hood to become the Son.

The term Elohim meant at least two creating Beings and the word YHVH also refers to the same two Creator Beings as eternally existing and as separate from all other mighty ones.

The name YHVH means simply "I AM" or "I Am self existent and eternal;" and this description fits and is applicable to BOTH God the Father and the one who became the Son.

In the beginning there were two eternal God Beings called Elohim who characterized themselves as being the YHVH FAMILY of self existing eternal ones.

The Being who was later called God the Father was and is the Executive Authority over the entire universe, and the One who was the actual Implementing Creator and gave up his Godhood to be made flesh and after dying for the sins of mankind was resurrected and ascended back to the Father.

Once the man was created God, the Father left the One who later gave up his Godhood to become flesh as the Son, to care for the man and his wife.

God the Father left because mankind sinned separating humanity from God the Father by their sin and rebellion against the Word of God to do as they would decide for themselves instead of living by every Word of God.

The moment that the woman and the man sinned by acting contrary to the Word of God [the tree in the garden was a test of obedience for them which they failed], that sin separated them from God the Father.

Sin Separates Humanity From God, Requiring an Intercessor (Is 59:1)

Mankind being separated from God the Father by their sin; humanity needed a High Priest [A Mediator between humanity and God the Father] to reconcile humanity back to God the Father!

God, knowing that man could sin and would therefore need reconciliation, from the every beginning the two Beings who became the Father and the Son, together established the means that such a reconciliation could be effected.

That plan of reconciliation between man and God required the sincere repentance of the sinner, an effective sacrifice for sin, and a commitment by the repentant to stop sinning and sin no more. The plan also called for a Mediator or High Priest to reconcile the repentant sinner to God the Father.

When man sinned humanity was cut off and separated from God the Father by that sin (Is 59:1-2); yet the Being who became the Son remained with humanity working to reconcile mankind to God the Father fulfilling the role of a spiritual High Priest [at that time a High Priest made of spirit].

In that role the Implementing Creator was still spirit, yet he appeared in human form from time to time and spoke with many people over many centuries.

The One who became Jesus Christ was the Implementing Creator and after man sinned, this Implementing Creator became the High Priest of God the Father, a Mediator [which mediation between God and man is the job of a High Priest] between God the Father and humanity.

This spiritual High Priest or Intercessor between God the Father and humanity appeared to Adam and Eve in the form of a man and spoke with Cain, Noah, Abraham and doubtless others.

The Lamb of God

This Spirit High Priest who interceded for man with God the Father was the true spiritual High Priest of which the physical high priesthood of Aaron was only an instructional allegory.

We can learn about the duties and functions of our Spirit High Priest by looking at the duties of the physical high priest. The function of a high priest is to intercede for mankind with God the Father.

This intercession requires that:

1. The people be taught the righteousness of God, that
2. The people be brought to sincere repentance for all past sins and commit themselves to STOP sinning and to go and sin no more, and that
3. A sacrifice be made to pay for all sincerely repented past sins and so redeem the sinner from the blood debt which he owes for his sin; thereby reconciling the repent with God the Father

These three things are the duty and the function of a high priest, whether the physical Aaronic high priest or the spirit High Priest of God in heaven.

The Spirit High Priest of God the Father in heaven was the very Implementing Creator who created all things under the Executive Authority of God the Father in heaven.

Then to fully fulfil the office of Spirit High Priest by experiencing life as a human being so that he could fully understand the pulls of the flesh, and so that he could offer himself as a perfect sinless sacrifice for his creation; This Being resigned his God hood to become flesh as the man we call Jesus Christ.

John 1:14 And the Word was made flesh, and dwelt among us, (and we beheld his glory, the glory as of the only begotten of the Father,) full of grace and truth.

The Son of God

Matthew 1-2 concerns the genealogy and the events around the birth of Christ as proofs of his Messiah-ship. The genealogy shows that Christ fulfilled the prophets by having a son of David through Joseph his physical surrogate family parent.

Luke restates this genealogy right back to Adam in Luk 3:23; Luke also confirms in verses 31-32 that the Christ Family was of the line of David.

The biblical term used here "conceived" does not mean what it does in modern English, as a meeting of egg and sperm; it simply means "being with child".

Isaiah 7:14 Therefore the Lord himself shall give you a sign; Behold, a virgin ["young woman"] shall conceive [Strong's 02030 meaning being with child, not necessarily meaning conceive], and bear a son, and shall call his name Immanuel.

This is actually a prophecy of the birth of Immanuel the son of Isaiah as a fore-type of the birth of Christ. The Hebrew actually means a young woman [the wife of Isaiah] will be with child and the translators substituted the misleading words "virgin" for "young woman" and "conceive" for "be with child," not understanding the concept of surrogate motherhood [pas Mary was] at that date.

The correct translation is: "Therefore the Lord himself shall give you a sign; Behold, a young woman shall be with child, and bear a son, and shall call his name Immanuel."

Immanuel [meaning God is with us] was the prophesied son of Isaiah as a fore-type of Jesus [Hebrew: Yeshua; Salvation, Saviour]. See chapter 7 in the Isaiah study for more.

The virgin birth of Jesus comes from the New Testament: **Luke 1:34** Then said Mary unto the angel, How shall this be, seeing I know not a man?

The concept of surrogate pregnancy that we understand today was unknown by the translators in the days of the King James translators; and John himself records that Mary was a virgin, not "known" by ANYONE.

It was the God personality who became God the Father, who by a miracle, reduced the actual Creator to the size of an embryo and placed him in the womb of Mary. There was NO sexual activity between God and Mary, such as placing his sperm inside Mary: which would have been adultery on the part of God.

While Jesus was born of a virgin of David and supposedly into the line of David; he himself said that he was not a son of David at all but only appeared to be so through being born into the family of David.

Jesus denied being a literal son of David. He was only a son of David by being born into the family of David and not by conception with God's sperm and Mary's egg which would be rape and adultery by God the Father!

Jesus was a son of David, because he was born into the family of David. Yes, Jesus was born to Mary; but he was not conceived as a sperm uniting with an egg of Mary. She was his surrogate mother! Therefore we may say that Christ was born to a woman of the line of David, but was not conceived by Mary, David's descendant!

Jesus told the Pharisees that he was not the son of David.

While in the flesh he was NOT a God, because he had given up his Godhood to be made flesh! Yet he was still the Creator of humanity! This God being, the very Implementing Creator of humanity and all things, voluntarily gave up his Godhood to be made flesh like his human creation!

Matthew 22:41 While the Pharisees were gathered together, Jesus asked them, **22:42** Saying, What think ye of Christ? whose son is he? They say unto him, The son of David.

The Pharisees did not accept Jesus [Hebrew: Yeshua] as Christ and he asked them what they thought of Christ to teach them that Christ was the son of God and not the literal son of David.

22:43 He saith unto them, How then doth David in spirit call him Lord, saying, **22:44** The LORD said unto my Lord, Sit thou on my right hand, till I make thine enemies thy footstool? **22:45** If David then call him Lord, how is he his son?

22:46 And no man was able to answer him a word, neither durst any man from that day forth ask him any more questions.

Christ was the God of David, and was called Lord by David. This proves that Christ was the God of Israel who spoke to Moses and the very Creator; as well as the sacrificial Passover Lamb of God who gave himself FOR HIS creation!

He then grew up to manhood experiencing all of the temptations and trials that Satan offered, while calling out and teaching a people to live by both the letter and the intent of every Word of God the Father. Finally voluntarily giving up his life for his creation.

Then after three full days and three full nights in the grave he was resurrected back to life by God the Father, but not back to physical life as a man!

At his resurrection this God who have given up his Godhood was restored to his original place as fully spirit and fully God!

Was Jesus God?

- Before being made flesh and being placed in the womb of Mary; he was the very Implementing Creator God!
- After he was made flesh, he had voluntarily given up his Godhood and he became a 100% physical human being!
- At his resurrection, this man of flesh was restored back to his original state as a spirit God!

All of the imaginations of men that Jesus was half man and half God or the fantastic idea that Jesus was both 100% man and 100% God are simply nonsense.

He was ALL God until he gave up has Godhood to be made flesh, and once made flesh he was a 100% physical human being, then after he died he was resurrected back to spirit and became a God again!

How was this done?

Think; vapor, liquid, solid; being different states of the same thing.

God is spirit and spirit is pure energy, matter is made out of energy. God the Father simply transformed the Messiah from pure energy to matter and then placed him inside the womb of Mary as the tiniest possible form of human being. He then grew from that to birth and then to the age of 33 when he allowed himself to be sacrificed to atone for sin and redeem humanity from the wages of sin which is death.

As the spirit High Priest of God the Father, the Implementing Creator gave up his Godhood to be made flesh so that he could experience life in the flesh and then give himself in sacrifice for his creation as the Lamb of God.

Then after three literal days and three literal nights he was resurrected back to spirit and back to the glory which he had before being made flesh!

Jesus prayed that the Father would resurrect him back to the glory that he had given up to offer himself in sacrifice for humanity.

John 17:5 And now, O Father, glorify thou me with thine own self with **the glory which I had with thee before the world was.**

Hebrews 5:1 For every high priest taken from among men is **ordained for men in things pertaining to God, that he may offer both gifts and sacrifices for sins:**

The job of a high priest is to offer sacrifices for sins, to intercede with God for the people, to bring us into harmony with God by offering atonement for our sins and to be a mediator between mankind and God the Father.

5:2 Who can have compassion, [that is a high priest should have compassion] on the ignorant, and on them that are out of the way; for that he himself also is compassed with infirmity.

Because a human high priest is subject to the same things as all people, he understands the human condition. It was therefore necessary for our spirit High Priest to experience the trials and temptations of the flesh, in order to best understand the human condition; and it was necessary that he have an effectual sacrifice to offer God the Father to redeem humanity from sin.

Jesus Christ being without sin, need not offer an atonement for his own sins, but offered HIMSELF as a perfect sinless offering for the people!

When Christ gave up his God-hood to be made flesh and then gave his life for the people in obedience to God the Father; it was because his life had been perfect and without sin that he was raised up by God the Father back to the glory which he had had before as a spirit with eternal life; and was called by God the Father to be a High Priest forever, of the order of Melchizedek [the name of the spirit High Priest by which this being was called before being made flesh].

5:6 As he saith also in another place, Thou art a priest for ever after the order of Melchisedec. **5:7** Who in the days of his [Christ's] flesh, when he had offered up prayers and supplications with strong crying and tears unto him that was able to save him from death, and was heard in that he feared.

The Son respected and obeyed God the Father right up to and including dying for the people according to God the Father's will.

Jesus Christ the eternal High Priest gave up his divinity to become mortal flesh and offered up himself as the Creator of Humanity, who being worth more that all humanity and being without any sin; was a perfect sacrifice and needed be offered only once to atone for all the sincerely repented sins of all humanity. While the physical sacrifices of animals only served to keep people in the physical Mosaic Covenant and had NO spiritual promises, and animals needed to be killed on a continual basis

Hebrews 7:27 Who needeth not daily, as those high priests, to offer up sacrifice, first for his own sins, and then for the people's: for this he did once [being a perfect sinless sacrifice of the Creator himself], when he offered up himself.

7:28 For the law maketh men high priests which have infirmity; but the word of the oath, which was since the law, maketh the Son, who is consecrated [an eternal spirit High Priest] for evermore.

Our High Priest, Jesus Christ will now live forever and will be able to make continual intercession for us, for all eternity. His sacrifice being perfect, no longer has to be made again and again. He doesn't have to be killed day after day, year after year. No!

However, every time someone repents, that perfect sacrifice needs to be REAPPLIED to the repentant sinner.

The difference is in the actual dying as opposed to the actual applying of the sacrifice. They are two different things.

Christ died, regardless of whether any man ever repents or not. He was dead and He was resurrected. That has nothing to do with whether men repent, or turn from sin or not. However, when men do sincerely repent, the sacrifice is now there and available to be applied to them.

The Passover Sacrifice

The need for a Passover Sacrifice began in the Garden of Eden when sin first entered humanity, and the need for both an atoning sacrifice and a reconciling High Priest entered the picture .

Genesis 1:1 In the beginning God created the heaven and the earth. **1:2** And the earth was without form, and void; and darkness was upon the face of the deep. And the Spirit of God moved upon the face of the waters.

In the beginning God made the universe and then God made the earth into a suitable environment for humanity. After that God created physical man in God's own likeness.

Genesis 1:26 And God said, Let us make man in our image, after our likeness: and let them have dominion over the fish of the sea, and over the fowl of the air, and over the cattle, and over all the earth, and over every creeping thing that creepeth upon the earth. **1:27 So God created man in his own image, in the image of God created he him; male and female created he them.**

God saw that all the things that He had created were very good including the man and the woman. Humanity and all creatures were vegetarian and there was no sin and no death in the world, and there being no sin there was no need of any sacrifice.

Sin entered the world cutting humanity off from God the Father and death also entered the world, bringing the need for sincere repentance and a High Priest to offer a Reconciling Sacrifice

Romans 3:10 As it is written, There is none righteous, no, not one: **3:11** There is none that understandeth, there is none that seeketh after God. **3:12** They are all gone out of the way, they are together become unprofitable; there is none that doeth good, no, not one.

Romans 3:23 For all have sinned, and come short of the glory of God;

The Scriptures tell us that the penalty for sin is death:

Ezekiel 18:20 The soul that sinneth, it shall die....

Jeremiah 17:9 The heart is deceitful above all things, and desperately wicked: who can know it? **17:10** I the LORD search the heart, I try the reins, **even to give every man according to his ways, and according to the fruit of his doings.**

But Elohim, which consists of God the Father and the One who would become Jesus Christ, had devised a plan from the very foundation of the world. Knowing that sin would enter the world, planned from the very beginning that Jesus Christ would mediate between humanity and God the Father as the spirit High Priest called Melchizedek, and would also be the perfect sacrificial Lamb of God, slain from the foundation of the world (Isaiah 46:10, 1 Peter 1:20, Revelation 13:8).

It had been decided long before creation that one of them would take on the sins of the whole world and would die as a perfect sacrifice so that humans could be redeemed from the awful penalty of eternal death.

The God being who later gave up his Godhood to become flesh as Jesus Christ was the one that chose to come down as a man and provide a way for mankind to be forgiven and reconciled to God the Father by offering himself as a perfect atoning sacrifice for all sincerely repented sin.

The Annual Festivals

The plan of God for the harvest of physical humanity into the spirit family of God is typified by the Annual High Days and Festivals. When God created Lucifer that angel later rebelled leading many other angels into rebellion and causing massive damage.

In the beginning God existed, God created the angels and then God created the present physical universe. God is a family consisting of two Beings, one who was the Executive authority and the other who was the Implementing Creator with one submitting to the other but both working together in full unity as if they were one Being.

They worked to a detailed plan, first creating many millions of angels and then organizing those angels to help them in creating the physical universe. Then one of the three leading angels called Lucifer [Light Bringer] became filled and lifted up with pride rebelling against his Maker.

After a war in the heavens Lucifer was cast down to the earth and declared to be the Adversary [Satan] of God. At some point God decided that he would make mankind as physical beings and give humanity an opportunity to rebel and decide his own ways for himself so as to make his own mistakes while in the flesh. In that way, with the very limited power of physical beings having no power commensurate with mighty angels, mankind could make his mistakes without endangering the universe or other beings.

It was an intrinsic part of the plan of God to make man flesh so that man could rebel against God and experience first hand the decay and death which such rebellion against the way of God which brings life brings. Since God knew that mankind would rebel and sin which would bring death, that would be the end of man; therefore God designed a way to save humanity.

First it was imperative that all humanity learn the lesson that God's way brings life, and that going contrary to the way of God brings decay, ultimate destruction and death. Man must learn that God being truth, light and life cannot coexist with the darkness of falsehood and evil which brings death.

Therefore the beginning of man's lesson was for humanity to be exposed to sin and being tempted to be allowed to sin.

Isaiah 59:1 Behold, the Lord's hand is not shortened, that it cannot save; neither his ear heavy, that it cannot hear: **59:2** But your iniquities have separated between you and your God, and your sins have hid his face from you, that he will not hear.

God does not want another such situation on his hands, therefore God created mankind physical and allowed humans to sin and to experience life outside of godliness while limiting human ability to do harm.

Mankind would be allowed to do whatever he wanted short of destroying all life on the planet, so that humans could learn through experience that humanity needs an ultimate and benevolent universal authority.

Sin Separates Humanity From God (Is 59:1), Requiring an Intercessor [a High Priest] and a Sacrifice to Redeem People From Repented Sin

Mankind being separated from God the Father by their sin; humanity needed a High Priest [A Mediator between humanity and God the Father] to reconcile humanity back to God the Father!

God, knowing that man could sin and would therefore need reconciliation, from the every beginning the two Beings who became the Father and the Son, together established the means that such a reconciliation could be effected.

That plan of reconciliation between man and God required the sincere repentance of the sinner, an effective sacrifice for sin, and a commitment by the repentant to stop sinning and sin no more. The plan also called for a Mediator or High Priest to reconcile the repentant sinner to God the Father.

When man sinned, humanity was cut off and separated from God the Father by that sin (Is 59:1-2); yet the Being who became the Son remained with humanity working to reconcile mankind to God the Father, fulfilling the role of a spiritual High Priest [at that time a High Priest made of spirit].

In that role the Implementing Creator was still spirit, yet he appeared in human form from time to time and spoke with many people over many centuries.

The One who became Jesus Christ was the Implementing Creator and after man sinned, this Implementing Creator became the High Priest of God the

Father, a Mediator [which mediation between God and man is the job of a High Priest] between God the Father and humanity.

This spiritual High Priest Intercessor between God the Father and humanity appeared to Adam and Eve in the form of a man and spoke with Cain, Noah, Abraham and doubtless others.

The last time we hear of him in the scriptures before he became flesh, was by he name of Melchizedek when he spoke to Abraham, and later a few times he was seen by Ezekiel and certain prophets. Later this spirit High Priest of God was made flesh and known as Jesus Christ the Lamb of God allowed himself to be sacrificed for the sincerely repented sins of humanity, thus opening the way for reconciliation with God the Father.

The plan for the harvest of created humanity involves the two harvests in Judea with a smaller spring harvest and a much larger main harvest. The Feast of Unleavened Bread pictures God calling out a small number of people for seven thousand years from righteous Abel. This is studied in our articles on the Feast of Unleavened Bread which are found at the Spring Festivals category on the sidebar.

The purpose of calling a few people to God and allowing them to live in a wicked world is so they can learn to love godliness and to hate and loathe evil, and to train and prepare them to be resurrected to become laborers to help bring in the main harvest. For this reason many are called but most of them will fail and only few will be chosen to have a part in the resurrection to spirit of this early harvest of humanity.

Once changed to spirit they will become kings and priests of God.

The godly priesthood of the resurrected chosen is the priesthood of Jesus Christ, and works to reconcile the sinner to God the Father by teaching people to live by every Word of God. The priests are the teachers of godliness reconciling the people to God by calling all people to God and to the reconciling atoning sacrifice of Christ.

Godly kings are righteous judges and administers over the needs of the people.

From righteous Able to the end of six thousand years God has been calling a people to himself and a resurrection of the chosen takes place and then over the remaining one thousand years God's calling will expand to include all flesh then living, and those who were chosen at the end of the first six thousand years will work to bring in the millennial harvest, during which millennium every person will be changed to spirit at the age of 100 or destroyed if they will not sincerely repent.

The word "call" or "calling" refers to opening the mind of a person to godliness. During the first six thousand years only a very tiny number will have their minds opened to godliness while the vast majority of mankind will live out their lives with no understanding of the things of God. Then during the millennium God will call all humanity then living by pouring out his spirit on all flesh (Joel 2:28).

After that time the main harvest of humanity who have not yet been called to God as pictured by the High Days and Festivals of the fall main harvest, will be resurrected back to flesh and will also be called to sincere repentance and godliness in their billions.

That sin which was rebellion against God the Father the Executive Authority of the universe, also immediately resulted in mankind being cut off from God the Father and thrust out of the paradise of God, and necessitated the means for reconciliation with God, if humanity was to be saved.

To bring about a reconciliation with God the Father, an Intercessor or Mediator between the Father and mankind was needed and was established in the person of the Implementing Creator. This mediatorial office is the office of a High Priest, and this office was called the office of Melchisedec by Abraham.

No person can come to [be reconciled to] God the Father, except through the mediatorial High Priest Jesus Christ.

John 14:6 Jesus saith unto him, I am the way, the truth, and the life: **no man cometh unto the Father, but by me**.

This Implementing Creator set up various lessons to teach us about how reconciliation with God was to be achieved. First sacrifices were instituted during the life of Adam as revealed in the story of Cain and Abel, Noah's and Abraham's sacrifices, etc; to teach us that the penalty for sin is death and that penalty must be paid.

Ezekiel 18:4 Behold, all souls are mine; as the soul of the father, so also the soul of the son is mine: **the soul that sinneth, it shall die**.

Romans 6:23 For **the wages of sin is death; but the gift of God is eternal life** through Jesus Christ our Lord.

The penalty that all humanity has earned by their sin must be paid, and God in his infinite mercy has prepared a way for the penalty of sin to be paid by another on our behalf. The system which allows another to die in our place, so redeeming us from death is the Law of sacrifice.

God had planned from the very beginning that a people would be enslaved in Egypt and would be called out of bondage in Egypt as an allegorical lesson that God is calling a people out of bondage to sin. Once called out of Egypt Israel was married to the very Implementing Creator who was the spirit High Priest Melchisedec at Mount Sinai. This Mosaic Marriage Covenant was to teach us about another New Covenant (Jer 31:31, Ezek 36:26).

The priesthood of Aaron was then instituted to teach us about a higher spirit priesthood of mediation between God the Father and humanity.

Physical sacrifices were instituted with Adam, and the law of sacrifice was further detailed for the Levitical priesthood, to teach us more about the sacrifice of Jesus Christ the Lamb of God.

Israel was also given the Biblical festivals to teaching us about God's overall plan for salvation. The Feast of Unleavened Bread pictures God calling out a kind of early harvest of human first fruits for seven thousand years, while the rest of humanity would remain cut off from God. In the way the few early called out to God would see the sin all around them and would learn the lesson that doing things our own way brings much sorrow and death; and that God's Word brings life.

The fall Feast of Tabernacles teaches us that a time will come when over another seven thousand years God will resurrect the main body of humanity in their courses and will also call them to God. Then with the help of the previously converted early harvest of human first fruits the main harvest of humanity will be taught to live a godly life.

The Allegory of Abraham and His Son Isaac

Prophetic pictures and references to the coming Lamb of God are scattered throughout the Old Testament. One reference is a dramatic portrayal that was played out by Abraham who was willing to sacrifice his son when God told him to take his beloved son Isaac up to the mountain and offer him as a sacrifice.

Abraham was to be an allegory of the fact that the heavenly Father was going to send His only begotten Son to be offered up as a sacrifice to atone for the sins of mankind. The account of Abraham being willing to obediently offer up his "son of promise" is symbolic that God would provide His own lamb (symbolic of Christ) for the burnt offering in place of Abraham's son.

In Genesis 22 we read that God tested Abraham by commanding him to offer his beloved son Isaac as a sacrifice to Him. This was an inference depicting that the Father was going to provide an offering by sending His own beloved Son to pay the penalty for the sins of mankind. In this test Abraham showed that he was obedient to God to the point of giving up Isaac, the son that God had promised to him and for whom Abraham and Sarah had waited for many years. This was a test of faith for Abraham and he proved his obedience to his Lord but this incident also looked forward to what the Father was willing to do to save the world almost 2000 years later.

Genesis 22:1 And it came to pass after these things, that God did tempt Abraham, and said unto him, Abraham: and he said, Behold, here I am.

22:2 And he said, Take now thy son, thine only son Isaac, whom thou lovest, and get thee into the land of Moriah; and offer him there for a burnt offering upon one of the mountains which I will tell thee of.

22:3 And Abraham rose up early in the morning, and saddled his ass, and took two of his young men with him, and Isaac his son, and clave the wood for the burnt offering, and rose up, and went unto the place of which God had told him.

As they were walking on the way to the mountain, Isaac asked his father "Look, the fire and the wood, but where is the lamb for a burnt offering?" In response, Abraham prophetically spoke these words: "My son, God will provide himself a lamb for a burnt offering: so they went both of them together" (Genesis 22:7-8).

When they arrived at the mount Abraham prepared an altar and bound Isaac and laid him on the altar to offer him as a sacrifice to the Lord. But just as Abraham raised his knife to slay his beloved child, God told him not to do him any harm. At the last minute God spared Abraham's dear son. We read:

Genesis 22:9 And they came to the place which God had told him of; and Abraham built an altar there, and laid the wood in order, and bound Isaac his son, and laid him on the altar upon the wood.

22:10 And Abraham stretched forth his hand, and took the knife to slay his son. **22:11** And the angel of the Lord called unto him out of heaven, and said, Abraham, Abraham: and he said, Here am I. **22:12** And he said, Lay not thine hand upon the lad, neither do thou any thing unto him: for now I know that thou fearest God, seeing thou hast not withheld thy son, thine only son from me.

22:13 And Abraham lifted up his eyes, and looked, and behold behind him a ram caught in a thicket by his horns: and Abraham went and took the ram, and offered him up for a burnt offering in the stead of his son. **22:14** And Abraham called the name of that place Jehovahjireh: as it is said to this day, In the mount of the Lord it shall be seen.

After offering up the ram in place of his son Issac, Abraham prophesied of a future event (when the Lamb of God would be sacrificed for the sincerely repentant) by calling the place Jehovahjire meaning "In the mount of the Lord it shall be seen, i.e., Jehovah will see; will provide. The name literally means 'The Lord who sees, or The Lord who will see to it'." (*Bible.org*)

The Hebrew for **Jehovah-jireh is** "Yhvh Yireh" (Strong's #3070) From Yhovah and ra'ah; Jehovah will see (to it); Jehovah-Jireh, a symbolical name for Mount Moriah. (*Strong's Concordance*)

The Passover Lamb

The physical sacrifices were instituted at creation and later refined into various details when physical Israel was called out of Egypt. Every one of these sacrifices reflected and typified a facet of the work and sacrifice of Jesus Christ the Lamb of God.

These physical sacrifices were only instructional allegories of the perfect sacrifice of the Lamb of God, they could keep one in good standing in the Mosaic Covenant but they could not atone for sin on the spiritual plain. Only the perfect sacrifice of the Creator God made flesh as the man Jesus Christ could atone for the sincerely repented sins of his creation.

The account of Abraham and Isaac was an allegory of God the Father giving up His beloved Son, the Christ, whom He would provide as the Lamb of God for humanity.

John 3:16 For God so loved the world, that he gave his only begotten Son, that whosoever believeth in him should not perish, but have everlasting life. **3:17** For God sent not his Son into the world to condemn the world; but that the world through him might be saved.

In the book of Exodus and we read that physical Israel was called out from hard bondage in Egypt. On the night that God would send the last plague and kill the firstborn in the homes of the Egyptians, He instituted the Passover ordinance for His people.

The Passover looked forward to and is allegorical of the sacrifice of Christ the Lamb of God, and if we sincerely repent ad commit to sin no more we will; be forgiven and reconciled to God the Father being covered by Christ's atoning blood on the door posts of our hearts, just like the blood on the doorposts of Israel in Egypt.

The sacrifice of the Passover lamb on the Feast of Passover is a dramatic account of what happened on the night that the death angel passed through the land of Egypt in Exodus 12.

The Passover Feast occurs each year on the 14th day of the month of Abib, also called Nisan. As long as the tabernacle/temple stood the Passover lamb was slain and eaten in remembrance of the Lord "passing over" the houses of those who had sacrificed the Passover lamb and sprinkled its blood on their wooden doorposts and mantles.

At the same time, the angel of death visited those who had not sprinkled the blood of the lamb, symbolic of the fact that it is only those who have been called out of bondage to Satan and sin, and sincerely repented of all past sin and committed to sin no more, who will have the atoning sacrifice of Christ applied to them that will be given eternal life. All those who refuse to repent after they have been given a chance to know God's truth will ultimately die in the Lake of Fire. (Revelation 21:8.)

Approximately 1,500 years after the angel of death destroyed the first born in Egypt on the 14th day of Abib; the Passover Lamb of God, Jesus Christ, was sacrificed upon a wooden stake for the sins of all mankind.

The killing of the lambs on that first Passover and the pouring of their blood upon the door posts, pointed to the perfect sacrifice of Christ who shed His blood in sacrifice for the spiritually called out of bondage to sin. Even the timing of Christ's death was on the same Passover day.

Exodus 12:29 And it came to pass, that at midnight the Lord smote all the firstborn in the land of Egypt, from the firstborn of Pharaoh that sat on his throne unto the firstborn of the captive that was in the dungeon; and all the firstborn of cattle.

God had instructed Moses to tell every household of the Israelite people to select a male lamb in its first year and without any defect on the tenth day of the first month.

Exodus 12:3 Speak ye unto all the congregation of Israel, saying, In the tenth day of this month they shall take to them every man a lamb, according to the house of their fathers, a lamb for an house:

12:4 And if the household be too little for the lamb, let him and his neighbour next unto his house take it according to the number of the souls; every man according to his eating shall make your count for the lamb.

12:5 Your lamb shall be without blemish, a male of the first year: ye shall take it out from the sheep, or from the goats:

12:6 And ye shall keep it up until the fourteenth day of the same month: and the whole assembly of the congregation of Israel shall kill it in the evening.

The head of the household was to slaughter the lamb at the very beginning of the Passover at sunset on the evening part beginning the Passover day, taking care that none of its bones were broken, and to apply some of its blood to the tops and sides of the door posts of his family's house. The lamb was to be roasted with fire and eaten with unleavened bread and bitter herbs and if any of it remained it was to burned up before the morning.

Exodus 12:6 And ye shall keep it up until the fourteenth day of the same month: and the whole assembly of the congregation of Israel shall kill it in the evening. **12:7** And they shall take of the blood, and strike it on the two side posts and on the upper door post of the houses, wherein they shall eat it.

12:8 And they shall eat the flesh in that night, roast with fire, and unleavened bread; and with bitter herbs they shall eat it. **12:9** Eat not of it raw, nor sodden at all with water, but roast with fire; his head with his legs, and with the purtenance thereof.

12:10 And ye shall let nothing of it remain until the morning; and that which remaineth of it until the morning ye shall burn with fire.

God also gave specific instructions as to how the Israelites were to eat the lamb, fully dressed with their shoes on, in other words, they had to be ready to travel when it was time to leave Egypt, as we are to be ready to journey out of our bondage to sin.

Exodus 12:11 And thus shall ye eat it; with your loins girded, your shoes on your feet, and your staff in your hand; and ye shall eat it in haste: it is the Lord's passover.

God said that when He saw the lamb's blood on the door posts of a house, He would "pass over" that home and not permit "the destroyer" to enter and kill the firstborn children. Any home without the blood of the lamb would have their firstborn struck down that night.

Exodus 12:12 For I will pass through the land of Egypt this night, and will smite all the firstborn in the land of Egypt, both man and beast; and against all the gods of Egypt I will execute judgment: I am the Lord.

12:13 And the blood shall be to you for a token upon the houses where ye are: and when I see the blood, I will pass over you, and the plague shall not be upon you to destroy you, when I smite the land of Egypt.

After that first Passover night, God commanded the observance of the Passover Feast as a lasting memorial throughout all generations.

Exodus 12:14 And this day shall be unto you for a memorial; and ye shall keep it a feast to the Lord throughout your generations; ye shall keep it a feast by an ordinance for ever.

Our annual keeping of the Passover is a depiction of God's great plan of redemption and is the first of the appointed festivals that reminds us that a sacrifice must be made to atone for our sincerely repented sins to reconcile us to God the Father and to redeem us from the death penalty that we have earned by rebelling against God.

Just as the firstborn of Israel were spared from the death angel that night, so, too, the spiritually called out who are sincerely repentant and faithful to the end and will be saved from the sentence of eternal death by the reconciling atoning blood sacrifice of Jesus Christ the Lamb of God.

Behold the Lamb of God

When John Baptist saw Jesus walking toward him, John called Him "the Lamb of God" referring to Jesus as the One that God the Father had sent to be the Saviour Redeemer, the atoning reconciling sacrifice for all of the sincerely repentant called out from bondage to Satan and sin.

John recognized that this was He who was to come (the Messiah) that would give His life as the perfect and ultimate sacrifice for the sins of humanity (Genesis 3:15, Isaiah 53).

John 1:29 The next day John seeth Jesus coming unto him, and saith, **Behold the Lamb of God, which taketh away the sin of the world. 1:30 This is he of whom I said, After me cometh a man which is preferred before me: for he was before me.**

John 1:35 Again the next day after John stood, and two of his disciples; **1:36 And looking upon Jesus as he walked, he saith, Behold the Lamb of God!**

By calling Jesus "the Lamb of God who takes away the sin of the world" John's disciples could immediately associate "the Lamb of God" with the slaying of the Passover lamb and the applying of its blood to the doorposts of the Israelites' houses which protected the firstborn from being slain.

John the Baptist and his disciples could make the connection for they would have also been familiar with the prophets Jeremiah and Isaiah who foretold of the Coming One who would be brought "like a lamb led to the slaughter" and whose sufferings and sacrifice would provide redemption for all called out and sincerely repentant people.

Jeremiah 11:19 But I was like a lamb or an ox that is brought to the slaughter; and I knew not that they had devised devices against me, saying, Let us destroy the tree with the fruit thereof, and let us cut him off from the land of the living, that his name may be no more remembered.

Isaiah 53:7 He was oppressed, and he was afflicted, yet he opened not his mouth: he is brought as a lamb to the slaughter, and as a sheep before her shearers is dumb, so he openeth not his mouth.

Isaiah 53:10 Yet it pleased the Lord to bruise him; he hath put him to grief: when thou shalt make his soul an offering for sin, he shall see his seed, he shall prolong his days, and the pleasure of the Lord shall prosper in his hand. **53:11** He shall see of the travail of his soul, and shall be satisfied: by his knowledge shall my righteous servant justify many; for he shall bear their iniquities.

The writers of Scripture were referring to the Messiah that was to come, and that person was the very Creator God who divested Himself of His glory and majesty and came down to live a perfect life in the flesh as a man and then die an agonizing death so that you and I could have the opportunity to be forgiven of our sins.

Even though we all must die a physical death, if we are one of God's children and we remain faithful to God all of our lives, we will go on to have eternal life at the resurrection to spirit.

Many scriptures establish a relationship between the Passover lamb that was slain and sacrificed at the Feast of Passover as commanded in Egypt, and the consummate Passover Lamb, Jesus Christ; who died and shed His blood to reconcile the sincerely repentant to God the Father.

1 Peter 2:24 Who his own self bare our sins in his own body on the tree, that we, being dead to sins, should live unto righteousness: by whose stripes ye were healed. **2:25** For ye were as sheep going astray; but are now returned unto the Shepherd and Bishop of your souls.

1 Corinthians 5:7 Purge out therefore the old leaven, that ye may be a new lump, as ye are unleavened. **For even Christ our passover is sacrificed for us:**

5:8 Therefore let us keep the feast, not with old leaven, neither with the leaven of malice and wickedness; but with the unleavened bread of sincerity and truth.

The apostle Peter compares the lamb that was chosen for sacrifice, which was to have no defect (Exodus 12:5), with Christ, whom he calls "a lamb without blemish and without spot".

1 Peter 2:19 But with the precious blood of Christ, as of a lamb without blemish and without spot:

In Revelation, John the apostle saw a vision of Christ as "a Lamb.... appearing as if it had been slain".

Revelation 5:6 And I beheld, and, lo, in the midst of the throne and of the four beasts, and in the midst of the elders, stood a Lamb as it had been slain, having seven horns and seven eyes, which are the seven Spirits of God sent forth into all the earth.

Jesus Christ was "without blemish and without spot" because His life was completely free from all taint of sin. This qualified Him to be a perfect sacrifice for all repented sin; and to be resurrected as our spirit High Priest who would reconcile us to God the Father by approaching unto God and offering himself as a perfect atonement and redemption for all sincerely repented sin.

Hebrews 4:14 Seeing then that we have a great high priest, that is passed into the heavens, Jesus the Son of God, let us hold fast our profession. **4:15** For we have not an high priest which cannot be touched with the feeling of our infirmities; **but was in all points tempted like as we are, yet without sin. 4:16** Let us therefore come boldly unto the throne of grace, that we may obtain mercy, and find grace to help in time of need.

Just as the Passover was to be held in remembrance as an annual Feast in Mosaic Israel, in the New Covenant of Jeremiah 31:31 the spiritually called out are to memorialize the Lord's death on the yearly Passover Festival. Today we have no tabernacle/temple and therefore we cannot offer a physical sacrifice so we are to follow Christ's example as closely as possible with an unleavened bread and wine service in memory of all these things on every Passover.

1 Corinthians 11:20 When ye come together therefore into one place, this is not to eat the Lord's supper. **11:21** For in eating every one taketh before other his own supper: and one is hungry, and another is drunken. **11:22** What? have ye not houses to eat and to drink in? or despise ye the church of God, and shame them that have not? what shall I say to you? shall I praise you in this? I praise you not.

11:23 For I have received of the Lord that which also I delivered unto you, that the Lord Jesus the same night in which he was betrayed took bread: **11:24** And when he had given thanks, he brake it, and said, Take, eat: this is my body, which is broken for you: this do in remembrance of me.

11:25 After the same manner also he took the cup, when he had supped, saying, this cup is the new testament in my blood: this do ye, as oft as ye drink it, in remembrance of me. **11:26 For as often as ye eat this bread, and drink this cup, ye do shew the Lord's death till he come.**

Scripture says that the spiritually called out who have sincerely repented and committed themselves to follow Christ to live by every Word of God the Father and to sin no more, will be justified by the application of the sacrifice of the Lamb of God made flesh.

Romans 2:13 (For not the hearers of the law are just before God, but the doers of the law shall be justified.

Hebrews 9:11 But Christ being come an high priest of good things to come, by a greater and more perfect tabernacle, not made with hands, that is to say, not of this building;

9:12 Neither by the blood of goats and calves, but by his own blood he entered in once into the holy place, having obtained eternal redemption for us. **9:13** For if the blood of bulls and of goats, and the ashes of an heifer sprinkling the unclean, sanctifieth to the purifying of the flesh:

9:14 How much more shall the blood of Christ, who through the eternal Spirit offered himself without spot to God, purge your conscience from dead works to serve the living God?

9:15 And for this cause he is the mediator of the new testament, that by means of death, for the redemption of the transgressions that were under the first testament, **they which are called might receive the promise of eternal inheritance.**

Just as the Egyptian Passover lamb's applied blood applied to the doorposts caused the death angel to pass over each Israelite households, Christ's applied blood causes God's judgment to pass over sinners and gives life to the sincerely rep0entant.

Romans 6:23 For the wages of sin is death; **but the gift of God is eternal life through Jesus Christ our Lord.**

Because of what Christ has done for us we must no longer let sin reign over us, but we are to walk in a new lifestyle, zealously living by every Word of God.

Romans 6:1 What shall we say then? Shall we continue in sin, that grace may abound? **6:2** God forbid. How shall we, that are dead to sin, live any longer therein?

6:3 Know ye not, that so many of us as were baptized into Jesus Christ were baptized into his death? **6:4** Therefore we [the old sinful person] are buried with him by baptism into death: that like as Christ was raised up from the dead by the glory of the Father, even so we also should walk in newness of life [having sincerely repented, we are now committed to live by every Word of God just as Christ lived and lives].

6:5 For if we have been planted together in the likeness of his death, we shall be also [if we are faithful we will rise in a resurrection to spirit like

Christ did] in the likeness of his resurrection: **6:6** Knowing this, that our old [sinful] man is crucified with him, **that the body of sin might be destroyed, that henceforth we should not serve sin. 6:7** For he that is dead is freed from sin. **6:8** Now if we be dead with Christ, we believe that we shall also live [we are to live as Christ lived, 1 John 2:6] with him :

6:9 Knowing that Christ being raised from the dead dieth no more; death hath no more dominion over him. **6:10** For in that he died, he died unto [for our sins] sin once: but in that he liveth, he liveth unto God.

6:11 Likewise reckon ye also yourselves to be dead indeed unto sin [after repentance and baptism we must reject all sin to live by every Word of God] , but alive unto God through Jesus Christ our Lord. **6:12** Let not sin [sin is not living by every Word of God, Mat 4:4] therefore reign in your mortal body, that ye should obey it in the lusts thereof. **6:13** Neither yield ye your members as instruments of unrighteousness unto sin: but yield yourselves unto God, as those that are alive from the dead, and your members as instruments of righteousness unto God.

6:14 For sin shall not have dominion over you: for ye are not under the [no longer facing the penalty for past sins, now being repentant and justified by Christ] law, but under grace.

As the first Passover marked the Hebrews' release from Egyptian slavery, so the sacrifice of Christ applied to the sincerely repentant releases us from bondage to Satan and sin.

Romans 8:1 There is therefore now no condemnation to them which are in Christ Jesus, who walk not after the flesh, but after the Spirit. **8:2** For the law of the Spirit of life in Christ Jesus hath made me free from the law of sin and death. **8:3** For what the law could not do, in that it was weak through the flesh, **God sending his own Son in the likeness of sinful flesh, and for sin, condemned sin in the flesh:**

In our modern world many of us do not live on farms and are not familiar with the slaying of animals, but the concept of payment or restitution for wrong doing is one we can readily identify with. We know that the wages of sin is death (Romans 6:23) and that our sin separates us from God.

Isaiah 59:2 But your iniquities have separated between you and your God, and your sins have hid his face from you, that he will not hear.

Because of our sins, all of us have been separated from God, and we stand guilty before Him. Therefore, the only hope we have is for God to provide a way for us to be reconciled to Himself, and that is what the Father did in sending His Son Jesus Christ to die on a stake for us. Jesus Christ the Lamb of God died to make atonement for sin and to pay the penalty for our sins of all who sincerely repent of all past sin and follow Him to sin now more.

In stopping the sin that separates us from God and being redeemed by the atoning sacrifice of the Lamb of God, committing to follow the example of Jesus Christ and sin no more; we will find everlasting life as the children of God!

The Mosaic Passover lamb, although a reality in the lives of the people of that time, were a mere foreshadowing of the actual Passover Lamb which is Jesus Christ who died once and for all.

Hebrews 9:26 For then must he often have suffered since the foundation of the world: but now once in the end of the world hath he appeared to put away sin by the sacrifice of himself.

Through His sinless life and sacrificial death, Jesus became the only person qualified to give mankind a way to escape death and a sure hope of eternal life.

1 Peter 1:20 Who verily was foreordained before the foundation of the world, but was manifest in these last times for you,

1:21 Who by him do believe in God, that raised him up from the dead, and gave him glory; that your faith and hope might be in God.

1:22 Seeing ye have purified your souls in obeying the truth through the Spirit unto unfeigned love of the brethren, see that ye love one another with a pure heart fervently:

1:23 Being born again, not of corruptible seed, but of incorruptible, by the word of God, which liveth and abideth for ever.

The fact that our heavenly Father gave His only begotten Son to be the perfect sacrifice which atones for our sin is part of the glorious Good News of the Gospel that is so eloquently stated by Peter in his epistle to the brethren:

1 Peter 1:17 And if ye call on the Father, who without respect of persons judgeth according to every man's work, pass the time of your sojourning here in fear:

1:18 Forasmuch as ye know that ye were not redeemed with corruptible things, as silver and gold, from your vain conversation received by tradition from your fathers; **1:19** But with the precious blood of Christ, as of a lamb without blemish and without spot:

1:20 Who verily was foreordained before the foundation of the world, but was manifest in these last times for you, **1:21** Who by him do believe in God, that raised him up from the dead, and gave him glory; that your faith and hope might be in God.

After Christ's crucifixion and death, God the Father raised him up from the grave and accepted Him and placed Him at His (the Father's) right hand. It is because of their incredible love for us that Elohim ordained that Jesus Christ would be the Messiah who would go through the excruciating pain of a terrible death and the agonizing separation from His Father because of the sins that He bore for us.

Every one of us has sinned and deserve God's judgment of the death penalty for our sins, but God the Father sent His only begotten Son to satisfy that judgment for those who sincerely repent and follow Jesus Christ to live by every Word of God just as Jesus Christ did, setting an example for us to follow.

Throughout history the world around us has been filled with sin and evil of every kind, and it has been that way since Adam and Eve rebelled against God and disobeyed His command to not to eat of the Tree of the Knowledge of Good and Evil.

For God to fulfil His plan of bringing humanity to godliness and eternal life as his children, God had to implement a means by which men and women could be forgiven for their sins. Out of God's great mercy and incredible love, He wanted to make a way to redeem humanity from the misery of sin and death, providing a way for them to go on to eternal life if they choose to sincerely repent [stop living contrary to the Word of God] and commit to go and sin no more.

Romans 5:7 For scarcely for a righteous man will one die: yet peradventure for a good man some would even dare to die. **5:8 But God commendeth his love toward us, in that, while we were yet sinners, Christ died for us.**

5:9 Much more then, **being now justified by his blood, we shall be saved from wrath through him.**

1 John 4:9 In this was manifested the love of God toward us, because that God sent his only begotten Son into the world, that we might live through him. **4:10** Herein is love, not that we loved God, but that he loved us, and sent his Son to be the propitiation for our sins.

For those who truly believe and sincerely repent of all their past sins and commit to go and sin no more, remaining faithful unto death; it is they who will be saved at the resurrection to spirit and they will spend eternity with God.

What a glorious future we have ahead of us; all because Jesus Christ was willing to be our Passover Lamb, the One who truly is the Lamb of God who takes away the sins of the world.

What an honor it is to be given this precious knowledge of what Passover and the Passover lamb depicts. Let us keep this solemn Feast day with gladness in our hearts and with a grateful heart for what our Lord and Saviour has done for each one of us who sincerely repent and who follow Him whither-so-ever He goes.

In Conclusion

God began (way back in the Book of Genesis, the very day that Adam and Eve sinned) to implement a Wonderful Plan, a plan that included the coming and redeeming sacrifice of the Messiah which would make it possible to undo what Satan did in enticing mankind to sin against God.

All have sinned like our first parents, but for those who want to truly be like God, holy and righteous forever, a Sacrifice has been provided that atones for all of our past sins: we that we can be forgiven and fallow Christ's lead back to the Tree of Life.

The whole chapter of Isaiah 53 explains the role of the Lamb of God and what He would do for us and how He came to set the captives free from their sins.

Isaiah 53:1 Who hath believed our report? and to whom is the arm of the Lord revealed? **53:2** For he shall grow up before him as a tender plant, and as a root out of a dry ground: he hath no form nor comeliness; and when we shall see him, there is no beauty that we should desire him.

53:3 He is despised and rejected of men; a man of sorrows, and acquainted with grief: and we hid as it were our faces from him; he was despised, and we esteemed him not.

53:4 Surely he hath borne our griefs, and carried our sorrows: yet we did esteem him stricken, smitten of God, and afflicted. **53:5** But he was wounded for our transgressions, he was bruised for our iniquities: the chastisement of our peace was upon him; and with his stripes we are healed.

53:6 All we like sheep have gone astray; we have turned every one to his own way; and the Lord hath laid on him the iniquity of us all. **53:7** He was oppressed, and he was afflicted, yet he opened not his mouth: he is brought as a lamb to the slaughter, and as a sheep before her shearers is dumb, so he openeth not his mouth.

53:8 He was taken from prison and from judgment: and who shall declare his generation? for he was cut off out of the land of the living: for the transgression of my people was he stricken. **53:9** And he made his grave with the wicked, and with the rich in his death; because he had done no violence, neither was any deceit in his mouth.

53:10 Yet it pleased the Lord to bruise him; he hath put him to grief: when thou shalt make his soul an offering for sin, he shall see his seed, he shall prolong his days [be resurrected to eternal life], and the pleasure of the Lord shall prosper in his hand. **53:11** He shall see of the travail of his soul, and shall be satisfied: by his knowledge shall my righteous servant justify many; for he shall bear their iniquities.

53:12 Therefore will I divide him a portion with the great, and he shall divide the spoil with the strong; because he hath poured out his soul unto death: and he was numbered with the transgressors; and he bare the sin of many, and made intercession for the transgressors.

The story of sinful man and the need for a Messiah began in Genesis and ends in Revelation, but that is not the end for those were passed over by the angel of eternal death, because they have chosen eternal life by choosing to live by every Word of God in this present evil world.

Revelation 21:1 And I saw a new heaven and a new earth: for the first heaven and the first earth were passed away; and there was no more sea.

21:2 And I John saw the holy city, new Jerusalem, coming down from God out of heaven, prepared as a bride adorned for her husband. **21:3** And I heard a great voice out of heaven saying, Behold, the tabernacle of God is with men, and he will dwell with them, and they shall be his people, and God himself shall be with them, and be their God.

21:4 And God shall wipe away all tears from their eyes; and there shall be no more death, neither sorrow, nor crying, neither shall there be any more pain: for the former things are passed away.

21:5 And he that sat upon the throne said, Behold, I make all things new. And he said unto me, Write: for these words are true and faithful.

21:6 And he said unto me, It is done. I am Alpha and Omega, the beginning and the end. I will give unto him that is athirst of the fountain of the water of life freely. **21:7** He that overcometh shall inherit all things; and I will be his God, and he shall be my son.

21:8 But the fearful, and unbelieving, and the abominable, and murderers, and whoremongers, and sorcerers, and idolaters, and all liars, shall have their part in the lake which burneth with fire and brimstone: which is the second death.

Revelation 22:1 And he shewed me a pure river of water of life, clear as crystal, proceeding out of the throne of God and of the Lamb.

22:2 In the midst of the street of it, and on either side of the river, **was there the tree of life**, which bare twelve manner of fruits, and yielded her fruit every month: and the leaves of the tree were for the healing of the nations.

22:3 And there shall be no more curse: but the throne of God and of the Lamb shall be in it; and his servants shall serve him:

Perseverance and Overcoming

The sacrifice of Christ is only APPLIED to the REPENTANT; to those who STOP sinning! and it is sincere repentance to stop sinning and the application of the atonement of Christ for our PAST sins; which justifies and purifies us.

After that, we are to go forward; avoiding sin and living by every Word of God. But keeping the commandments does not justify anyone from PAST sins. It is sacrifice of Christ which justifies us and makes us right with God and atones for past sins.

2:17 But if, while we seek to be justified by Christ, we ourselves also are found sinners, [that is, if we continue in sin,] is therefore Christ the minister of sin? God forbid.

Once we are justified by sincere repentance, a baptismal commitment to go and sin no more and faith in the sacrifice of Christ, we are NOT to continue in sin as Paul said, God forbid that we should continue in sin!

2:18 For if I build again the things, which I destroyed, [that is, if I continue in my sinful nature] I make myself a transgressor.

If I have destroyed my sinful nature in sincere repentance and baptism, rising up from the grave of baptism a NEW being in Christ, and then being justified by my faith in the sacrifice of Christ; if I go out and continue in sin, I have returned to my sins and I am still a transgressor.

2:19 For I through the law am dead to the law, that I might live unto God. 2:20 I am crucified with Christ: nevertheless, I live; yet not I, but Christ liveth in me: and the life which I now live in the flesh I live by the faith of the Son of God, who loved me, and gave himself for me

Christ was crucified for our sins and if that sacrifice is applied to us, our old sinful self is also dead because Christ died and the crucifixion and sacrifice of Jesus Christ has paid the penalty for PAST sincerely repented sin. Therefore we must live by every Word of God through the indwelling power of Christ; from henceforth and forever more!

Our repentance, our baptismal commitment and faith in Christ and his sacrifice, atones for PAST sin. And the sinful man, our sinful nature is dead and gone, and we rise up new persons in Christ.

Jesus Christ can then dwell in us through the power of God's Holy Spirit, and when he [Christ] is dwelling in us, Christ will do the things he has always done, now doing them within us, that is, he will live by every Word of God and we will live by every Word of God in Christ-like zeal as we are led by the Spirit of Christ.

This is the New Covenant circumcision of the heart:

Colossians 2:11 In whom also ye are circumcised with the **circumcision** made without hands, in putting off the body of the sins of the flesh by the **circumcision** of Christ:

God's Spirit is not divided against God. God's Spirit is the Spirit and nature of God. God is not divided against himself. He keeps his own Word.

Christ says, "I have kept my Father's commandments" and the Holy Spirit of God will empower us and lead us to also keep God's commandments; to turn away from sin.

John 15:10 If ye keep my commandments, ye shall abide in my love; even as I have kept my Father's commandments, and abide in his love.

Galatians 2:21 I do not frustrate the grace of God: for if righteousness come by the law, then Christ death is in vain.

If we have sinned, and we could stop sinning today and be perfect from this point onward: What about past sins?

Keeping the law from this point forward does not atone for our PAST law breaking. Only sincere repentance and the application of the sacrifice of Jesus Christ can atone for past law breaking; and then, the Holy Spirit is given to us, and empowers us to go forward, putting away all sin and living by every Word of God in the future.

We must sincerely repent of all PAST sin and then commit to STOP sinning; and then to really get that point across we must make a formal baptismal commitment to stop sinning and destroy our PAST sinful self; going down into the grave of water and destroying the old person of sin, and then rising up out of the water a NEW person in Christ and Christ-like zeal to Live by Every Word of GOD.

Then the atoning sacrifice of Jesus Christ the true Lamb of God, will be applied to us and we must go forward in Christ-like zeal to live by every Word of God through the strength of the ultimate overcomer dwelling in us, henceforth and forever!

Physical circumcision is only a symbolic removal of a piece of flesh and avails nothing unless God is obeyed [except that physical circumcision is a prophecy of spiritual circumcision into the New Covenant]; but it is the spiritual circumcision of the New Covenant which removes our sins which have separated us from God!

The true doctrine of Salvation through Jesus Christ, is that we must become spiritually circumcised, removing all of the sin which separates us from God the Father through sincere repentance, a baptismal commitment to sin no more and the application of the sacrifice of Jesus Christ the Lamb of God.

It is our repentance and faith in Christ's atoning sacrifice, which reconciles us to God the Father, which then brings us into a relationship with God the Father, so that he may then give us his Spirit.

Romans 2:13 (For not the hearers of the law are just before God, **but the doers of the law shall be justified.**

We are only justified by the application of Christ's sacrifice if we STOP sinning and begin to live by every Word of God! The unrepentant sinner will NOT have the sacrifice of Christ applied to him or her and will NOT be justified before God!

The true circumcision of the New Covenant is spiritual, of the heart and spirit, and not of the flesh.

Circumcision of the flesh profits nothing spiritually, even baptism and ordination, or attending some corporate church organization profits nothing at all; UNLESS we are circumcised of the heart; through sincere repentance from all sin and compromising with any part of the whole Word of God followed by a commitment to diligently believe and live by every Word of God; and the application of the sacrifice of Jesus Christ.

If we are baptized, ordained, or attend corporate church services, or are physically circumcised: It means absolutely NOTHING unless we do the deeds of Abraham and have his faith to trust and obey Almighty God!

Circumcision of the flesh was a sign of the Mosaic Covenant and when that Covenant passed away because of its weakness: It was replaced with a New and better Covenant, a spiritual Covenant.

The sign of the New Covenant is the circumcision of the heart: Which is repentance from rebellion and sin, a commitment to obey God the Father and the application of the atoning sacrifice of Christ! This circumcises our hearts by removing all PAST sins and reconciles us to God the Father by removing that barrier of sin hat existed between us and God the Father; which barrier is our rebellion and sin!

Galatians 3:27 For as many of you as have been baptized into Christ have put on [have committed to be united and one in unity with Christ] Christ.

There are many, many places throughout both the Old and New Testaments where we are told to stop sinning. Just to mention a few: 1 Corinthians 15:34, 1 John 2:1, Ephesians 4:26, Ezekiel 18:4, Deuteronomy 30:19.

Once we commit ourselves to STOP sinning and to go forward to live by every Word of God, we will then be justified and redeemed through the application of the atoning sacrifice of Jesus Christ the Lamb of God.

We then are fully reconciled to God the Father and he gives us the gift of his Holy Spirit which enables us to comprehend and retain a good understanding of the Word of God, empowering us to live just as Christ lived, overcoming all sin and living by every Word of God (Mat 4:4).

Deuteronomy 5:32 Ye shall observe to do therefore as the Lord your God hath commanded you: ye shall not turn aside to the right hand or to the left.

1 John 2:6 He that saith he abideth in him ought himself also so to walk [live], even as he walked [lives].

Romans 6:1 What shall we say then? **Shall we continue in sin, that grace may abound? 6:2 God forbid. How shall we, that are dead to sin, live any longer therein?**

If we have been delivered from the slavery of sin [spiritual Egypt] why would we seek to remain in bondage? To love God is to seek to please him and to become like him, as he has defined himself by his Word. If we reject any part of, or compromise with any of God's Word, we love the slavery of Egypt and sin; MORE than we love God the Father of Jesus Christ, for they are in complete UNITY with one another!

Baptism represents the death and burial of the old sinful man; and a truly converted person will rise up from baptism a new being, burning with Christ-like zeal to live by every Word of God as Jesus Christ did.

Baptism is a commitment of sincere repentance from sin and represents the death of the existing sinful man and his allegorical resurrection to godliness; and is a total commitment to God the Father and Jesus Christ; to please God, to keep the whole Word of God with passionate zeal and to become like God in every way.

Baptism is a complete and unshakable commitment of espousal in marriage to Jesus Christ for all eternity! A commitment to internalize the very nature of God by keeping his Word with a zeal to become like our LORD.

The old man of sin is dead and buried in baptism; so that we may rise up from the water a new person in Christ; keeping the whole Word of God just like Christ did and does.

Matthew 4:4 But he answered and said, It is written, **Man shall not live by bread alone, but by every word that proceedeth out of the mouth of God**.

Romans 6:4 Therefore we are buried with him **by baptism into death**: that like as Christ was raised up from the dead by the glory of the Father, even so **we also should walk in newness of life**.

We commit ourselves at baptism to destroy the old man of sin and to arise a NEW person in Christ-like godliness! It is our calling to becoming Christ-like; loving and obeying God the Father as Christ did, walking and living by every Word of God as Jesus Christ walked and lived!

6:5 For if we have been planted [if we have been buried in baptism] together in the likeness of his death, we shall be also [rise from the grave of baptism as he rose from the dead] in the likeness of his resurrection: **6:6 Knowing this, that our old [sinful] man is crucified with him, that the body of sin might be destroyed, that henceforth we should not serve sin.**

After our baptismal commitment we are: TO NO LONGER SERVE SIN!

After baptism we should serve [obey] God; so that we may then be raised up in a resurrection to spirit just as Jesus Christ was raised up to spirit.

The dead sin not [they can do nothing]; therefore those who destroy and bury the old sinful self in baptism must not continue in willful sin.

We are to live as Christ lived, by following the Holy Spirit of Christ dwelling in us; and that Spirit will NEVER lead us to compromise with any part of the Word of God, or to tolerate sin and false doctrine. Any spirit that leads into tolerating sin or false teachings contrary to the Word of God, is NOT of Christ; It is the spirit of Anti-Christ and is of Satan!

Why should we, being liberated from PAST sin; desire to compromise with God's Word and to lose our Christ-like zeal for the whole Word of God, and associate with worldliness; thereby going back into bondage?

There is only one reason: Because we love serving sin unto decay and death, more than we love serving God unto eternal life!

It is because we are willing to sell the birthright of our calling, which is eternal life in peace and harmony with God and all his children; for the temporary pleasures of sin; that we are subject to eternal death.

Like Esau, many do not value their freedom from slavery to sin; and many sell their birthright for a temporary and transitory relief from trials, or fall to temptations to take pleasure in evil doing.

6:8 Now if we be dead with Christ [in baptism], we believe that we shall also live with him [free from sin as he lives]: **6:9** Knowing that Christ being raised from the dead dieth no more; death hath no more dominion over him.

Christ died for our sin once; and was then raised up to eternal life to serve God the Father; therefore we are to destroy the old man of sin and enter a baptismal commitment to serve God the Father and to: "go and sin no more."

Once raised up from baptism, we are raised up to a new life, free from sinning; to serve God the Father and to live by every Word of God with Christ-like passion.

Jesus Christ died once and now lives again; serving God the Father; and we who symbolically destroyed our past sinful selves in the watery grave of baptism; are to rise up new persons to serve God the Father

6:10 For in that he died, he died unto sin once: but in that he liveth, **he liveth unto God**.

The birthright of our calling is the same eternal life that was given to Jesus Christ when he was raised up from physical death and changed back to spirit.

UNDERSTAND the appalling price that Christ Jesus paid for us: Jesus Christ GAVE UP his Godhood and eternal life to be made flesh for us! He then GAVE UP his physical life for us!

He did this with COMPLETE FAITH that God the Father would strengthen him against all temptation to live by every Word of God the Father; making him a worthy sacrifice for his creation: In COMPLETE FAITH that his Father could and would raise him up and restore him back to eternal life!

6:11 Likewise reckon ye also yourselves to be **dead indeed unto sin**, but **alive unto God** [We are to be sincerely repent and become spiritually sensitive and passionate to keep the Word of God.] **through Jesus Christ our Lord.**

We are to become like the dead in regards to all temptation to sin and compromise with the commandments and Word of God. We are to destroy the old sinful man and become a new Christ-like person!

If we love God the Father and the Son and internalize the very nature of BOTH God the Father and the Son through Christ-like love and obedience to God the Father and his Word; our beloved Father will also raise us up to eternal life just as he raised Jesus up!

6:12 Let not sin [any transgression of the Word of God] **therefore reign in your mortal body,** that ye should obey it in the lusts thereof. **6:13 Neither yield ye your members as instruments of unrighteousness unto sin: but yield yourselves unto God,** as those that are alive from the dead [freed from the bondage of sin and death], and your members [keep the whole Word of God with all our mind and deeds] as instruments [subject our whole being to serve God the Father] of righteousness [The righteousness of God is the keeping of the Word of God.] unto God.

Shun all sin and compromise with the Word of Almighty God; who alone is able to save and deliver us out of all sin. Allow his very mind, spirit and nature to dwell within us; overcoming all sin through the power of God!

As baptized persons we are to consider ourselves symbolically resurrected back to a new physical life after the death of the old sinful person, and delivered out of the spiritual Egypt of bondage to sin!

We are not to turn back into that spiritual Egypt of bondage to sin, or we shall be destroyed as those Israelites who wanted to turn back were destroyed!

If we truly loved Christ; we would do those things pleasing to Christ; we would be as zealous for God the Father's Word as Jesus Christ was and is!

We are the servants of those that we follow and obey. We are NOT to follow any man into willful sin against any part of the Word of God, we are not to allow sin to have dominion over us and we are not to turn back into bondage to sin and death.

6:14 For sin shall not have dominion over you: for ye are not under the law [no longer facing a penalty for breaking the law], but under grace [having stopped sinning and having been forgiven for our sincerely repented PAST sins]. **6:15** What then? **shall we** [continue in sin] **sin, because we are not under the law, but under grace? God forbid.**

Anyone who has made a baptismal commitment to espouse themselves to Jesus Christ, and then compromises with any part of the Word of God even to the slightest degree, is in danger of being rejected as a suitable part of his resurrected spiritual bride.

Just as a bride is to become one flesh with her husband and is to faithfully follow him; so we are to become of one spirit, mind and actions with our Husband, Jesus Christ.

We are to internalize the very nature of God, which is the lesson of eating Unleavened Bread every day of the Feast of Unleavened Bread; representing the internalizing of God the Father, and Jesus Christ: The Bread of LIFE.

What was the nature of Jesus Christ? He loved God the Father with all his heart, and he kept all of his Fathers commandments, Word, Will and instructions without compromise or deviation to the slightest degree.

If we go willingly back into sin through deliberate compromise with God's Word, we are in danger of being rejected as a part of the bride; and if we do not repent, we are in danger of damnation.

If we reject portions of God's Word to justify our sins [like rejecting the commandments regarding the New Moons, rejecting God's Biblical Calendar, rejecting Nehemiah and the sanctity of the Sabbath and rejecting Luke on the Passover]; Jesus Christ will reject us!

If we return to the spiritual Egypt of bondage to sin from which we had been delivered by the application of the awesome sacrifice of Christ; we are returning back to the filthy burden of bondage to sin which we have been delivered out of; and we make a mockery of the sacrifice of Christ who died to deliver us.

If we prefer such filth to the Holy Law of Liberty from sin; we are NOT worthy of Jesus Christ and we will not be a part of his bride.

James 1:22 But be ye doers of the word, and not hearers only, deceiving your own selves. 1:23 For if any be a hearer of the word, and not a doer, he is like unto a man beholding his natural face in a glass: **1:24** For he beholdeth himself, and goeth his way, and straightway forgetteth what manner of man he was.

1:25 But whoso looketh into the perfect law of liberty [God's law liberates us from bondage to sin], **and continueth therein, he being not a forgetful hearer, but a doer of the work** [Word and law of God]**, this man shall be blessed in his deed.**

My beloved brethren, it is time to wake up and to see how far we have fallen when we compromise and commit spiritual adultery against our LORD, by idolizing men and false traditions above the Word of God and the Glorious Law of Liberty!

Galatians 6:7 Be not deceived; God is not mocked: for whatsoever a man soweth, that shall he also reap.

Hebrews 10:26 For if we sin wilfully after that we have received the knowledge of the truth, there remaineth no more sacrifice for sins,

2 Peter 2:20 For if after they have escaped the pollutions of the world through the knowledge of the Lord and Saviour Jesus Christ, they are again entangled therein, and overcome, the latter end is worse with them than the beginning.

2:21 For it had been better for them not to have known the way of righteousness, than, after they have known it, to turn from the holy commandment delivered unto them. **2:22** But it is happened unto them according to the true proverb, **The dog is turned to his own vomit again; and the sow that was washed to her wallowing in the mire.**

Romans 6:16 Know ye not, that to whom ye yield yourselves servants to obey, his servants ye are to whom ye obey; whether **of sin unto death, or of obedience unto righteousness** [righteousness is passionately living by every Word of God]?

We are to prove all things by the Word of God which is also the Word of Jesus Christ; and we are to follow and obey God our Father and our espoused Husband totally; and to follow men ONLY as they follow God the Father and Jesus Christ.

6:17 But God be thanked, that ye were the servants of sin, but ye have **obeyed from the heart that form of doctrine which was delivered you** [which is the sound doctrine of the Holy Scriptures to keep the whole word of God]. **6:18** Being then made free from sin, **ye became the servants of righteousness** [Righteousness is to keep the whole word of God].

Let us rejoice that some have chosen to become like Jesus Christ, instead of continuing in sin; and are now the servants of righteousness through a passionate love of God, to enthusiastically wholeheartedly live by every Word of God.

Those who would compromise with any part of God's Word; and those who would love or fear this world more than they love their spiritual Father and their espoused Husband: Will be corrected by God.

6:19 I speak after the manner of men because of the infirmity of your flesh: for as ye have [in the PAST we committed many sins and were in bondage to sin] yielded your members servants to uncleanness and to iniquity unto iniquity; even so **now yield your members servants to righteousness unto holiness.**

Turn away from our PAST zeal for sin and the pleasures of this world and die the symbolic baptismal death of the old sinful person, and rise up a new person in Christ; seeking the righteousness of God by keeping all of God's Word with an even greater zeal then we had for the pleasures of this world!

If we serve sin by not keeping a certain part of the Word of God, we are empty of the righteousness of God.

James 2:10 For whosoever shall keep the whole law, and yet offend in one point, he is guilty of all.

Romans 6:20 For when ye were the servants of sin, ye were free from righteousness. **6:21** What fruit had ye then in those things whereof ye are now ashamed? for **the end of those things is death**.

6:22 But now being made free from sin, and [once freed from sin we are to] become servants to God, ye have your fruit unto holiness, and the end everlasting life. **6:23** For **the wages of sin is death**; but **the gift of God** [given to those who follow the whole word of God] **is eternal life through Jesus Christ our Lord**.

Sin and compromise with God's Word leads to all manner of decay and death: God's commandments bring harmony, peace and eternal life!

If we have been called to come to God the Father through Jesus Christ, and we sincerely repent and make a genuine baptismal commitment to live by every Word of God; God the Father WILL apply the atoning sacrifice of Jesus Christ the Lamb of God to us, and God the Father will give us his empowering Spirit.

If we have responded to God's call with sincere repentance and a commitment to go and sin no more, living by every Word of God and to follow the example that Christ set for us: We will receive God's Holy Spirit and we must no longer live according to our own desires, but we must live spiritual lives; loathing all sin and passionately loving the spiritual things of God.

Romans 8:9 But ye are not [to live in carnality] in the flesh, but [to live godly in God's Spirit] in the Spirit, if so be that the Spirit of God dwell in you. Now if any man [if we do not live as Christ lived, by every Word of God] have not the Spirit of Christ, he is none of [we have no part on Christ, because we live contrary to the way that Christ lived] his.

Romans 8:14 For as many as are led by [and faithfully follow] the Spirit of God, they are the sons of God.

When we initially receive God's Spirit to dwell within us after baptism we do not yet know or understand all godly things. From the time that we receive the gift of God's Spirit we must diligently study the Holy

Scriptures, passionately embracing godliness and all truth, and removing every taint of error from our minds and behavior.

Learning godliness and internalizing the nature of God, while removing all sin and falsehood is a lifetime endeavour. Yet if we labor to learn and to practice what we learn over our lifetime, we will receive the gift of eternal life in a resurrection to spirit.

Victorious Overcoming

In Mosaic Israel the whole nation was the Ekklesia [nation, family] of God and people of God of that day. The army of Israel was supposed to be the host [army] of the Eternal; and YHVH was the commander of the host [army] of God [the army of Israel].

Joshua 5:14 And he said, Nay; but as captain of the host of the LORD [YHVH] am I now come. And Joshua fell on his face to the earth, and did worship, and said unto him, What saith my Lord unto his servant? **5:15** And the captain of the LORD's host said unto Joshua, Loose thy shoe from off thy foot; for the place whereon thou standest is holy. And Joshua did so.

The Eternal was the captain of the host of Israel, and is often described as the "LORD of Hosts": meaning the LORD or captain of God's armies.

In the fight against the Canaanites; Israel as the people of God called out of Egypt, was a type of a spiritual Israel called out of the spiritual Egypt of bondage to sin: while the Canaanites were a type of sin, which is to be totally destroyed.

God used these people as an allegorical example for our instruction, yet he will raise up both physical Israel and the Canaanites in their time and they shall all have a chance to sincerely repent and enter into the spiritual Israel of the New Covenant.

The Eternal was captain over the armies of Mosaic Israel, fighting to destroy the wicked Canaanites as a type of extirpating and destroying sin from off the earth.

This an allegory that the Eternal as the Captain of our Salvation is going before his faithful to fight against sin for us; just as he went before Israel to fight the Canaanites whenever Israel was faithful and followed their Captain.

You will notice that when Israel faithfully followed the Eternal as they did all the days of Joshua, they never lost a battle, except when sin was among them. When they strayed from a zeal to keep the whole Word of God, they began to lose battles.

So it is with us; when we stray from zealously, enthusiastically, following our LORD; and turn to our own ways, or try to fight the battle on our own; we begin to lose the fight against sin and are overcome by it.

It is ONLY when we are faithful to obey and diligently follow the whole word of God; that the Captain of our Salvation will go before us to fight all sin and give us his gift of victory over our greatest enemy, Satan, sin and the wages of unrepented sin which is death.

In line with this allegory, the Captain of the LORD's host gave Joshua some instructions at the beginning of his service, that are equally fitting for our spiritual battle against sin.

As Joshua was to keep the whole Word of God in the physical Mosaic sense; WE are to keep the whole Word of GOD in BOTH the physical Mosaic sense AND in all of its spirit and intent!

If we do that, then the Captain of our Salvation, will dwell in us and fight the battle against sin with us; and the Mighty Overcomer will give us the victory over sin; IF we will only follow His example and His lead!

This is the first of the principles of victory over sin; Absolute commitment and loyalty to the Captain of our Salvation; to follow the Lamb of God whithersoever he goeth (Rev 14:4)! Without any hint of compromise or of any hint of turning aside to the right or to the left!

Joshua 1:5 There shall not any man be able to stand before thee all the days of thy life: as I was with Moses, so I will be with thee: I will not fail thee, nor forsake thee. **1:6 Be strong and of a good courage**: for unto this people shalt thou divide for an inheritance the land, which I sware unto their fathers to give them.

1:7 Only be thou strong and very courageous, that thou mayest observe to do according to all the law, which Moses my servant commanded thee: turn not from it to the right hand or to the left, that thou mayest prosper withersoever thou goest.

1:8 This book of the law shall not depart out of thy mouth; but thou shalt meditate therein day and night, that thou mayest observe to do according to all that is written therein: for then thou shalt make thy way prosperous, and then thou shalt have good success.

This principle of warring against all sin; is to "Rely on God and Be Prepared!" To properly train for the fight, through learning and living by every Word of God!

This means that we are to study day and night! Study does not mean just reading the scriptures; It also means meditating and thinking about their meaning, while praying for understanding from God. It means to have our minds focused on the Word of God, its physical and spiritual meaning and how it applies to the situations that we encounter day by day.

Like a good soldier; we are to learn, learn, learn and then practice, practice, practice; until the lessons become our very nature!

A good soldier first learns Absolute Loyalty and Obedience unto death, to his Commander; and a good soldier of the LORD of Hosts [armies] in the battle against Satan and sin, is to be Absolutely Obedient and Loyal to the whole Word of our Mighty Commander, even unto death.

The next thing a good soldier learns is complete dedication to accomplishing any mission given to him. Regardless of the price or hazards, a good soldier will continue moving forward to accomplish his mission.

The same is true of the spiritual soldier; he is totally dedicated to his mission to overcome all sin; whatever the cost in trials or persecutions, in sickness or poverty; in every situation he marches on in the battle against Satan and sin; totally loyal to his LORD and to his mission to achieve complete victory over all sin and to become like his Father in heaven!

Brethren, religion is not some kind of social game! This is FOR REAL! It is a serious matter of life and death for eternity!

May we all be good soldiers of the LORD of Hosts against Satan and all sin; following our LORD to total victory! Be Strong and Persevere for the battle belongs to the Great Overcomer the LORD of Hosts!

Though we may be battered in this world, let us be strongly encouraged; for we know that our redemption is very near:

Let us prepare for the fight, fully grounding ourselves on the Sound Doctrine of every Word of God, and internalizing the very nature of God; so that the temptation to sin is so repellent and vile to us, that we can reject it without another thought!

If any are rejected by their brethren - who presently lack the light that guides us - let us go forward in godliness, being courageous to set a shining example so that in their time they will see the light of God and turn to him with a whole heart!

Another principle of being a good soldier of the LORD is having the courage to acknowledge errors and to turn to do what is right, always. A good soldier knows that his mistakes [his example] could affect the lives of many others; so he rejoices for correction, and is quick to correct his errors. The spiritual soldier is to be quick to continually correct his faults and to learn and progress in his spiritual growth.

Each sin that is corrected is another victory in the war against Satan and sin; while each refusal to accept truth and to change for the better, is a lost battle in the war.

My dear friends, let us be strong to pursue the truth of God, and be full of a good courage to acknowledge error and follow our Commander and King of kings, to total victory against the Adversary and all sin!

How to Conquer Sin

Why are we tempted to sin? Because we think that the sin is pleasurable, and we love the pleasure of sin more than we love following the Word of God.

1. Love God the Father and Jesus Christ enough to DO WHAT THEY SAY, and to live by EVERY Word of God the Father (Mat 4:4). Make pleasing God our greatest pleasure and chief delight!

2. Learn to loathe as hideous filth, anything that comes between us, and God the Father and Christ.

3. When we are tempted by certain things, AVOID those things, and so avoid [flee] temptation.

4. Do not let our thoughts dwell on the temptation; but fill your mind with good things.

5. Do Bible studies into the sin that besets us, consider how evil and filthy it really is, behind its façade of pleasure. and understand that the wages of sin is SUFFERING and DEATH.

6. When you are tempted, do not think "Oh how I would like that," but think about a field full of dead rotting bodies, or eating a pot of raw sewage; and equate that with the temptation to sin. Think how you are offending and separating yourself from your Beloved Father

and Christ when you sin: Think on the consequences of your sin to yourself and to others. Stop and THINK before you act; and immediately, instantly; reject those things that separate us from our Beloved Father and espoused Husband!

7. Replace evil with good in your mind and concentrate on all the good things and benefits of godliness.

Philippians 4:8 Finally, brethren, whatsoever things are true, whatsoever things are honest, whatsoever things are just, whatsoever things are pure, whatsoever things are lovely, whatsoever things are of good report; if there be any virtue, and if there be any praise, think on these things.

Overcoming sin is about what you love the most: God or the sin! and about putting the temptation to sin into its proper perspective of coming between us and God and of bringing eternal death, as opposed to the eternal life that our Beloved offers!

Once we have that established; we can proceed to overcome through the ultimate Overcomer dwelling in us! and we can employ the tools of overcoming:

Ephesians 6:13 Wherefore take unto you the whole armour of God, that ye may be able to withstand in the evil day, and having done all, to stand. **6:14** Stand therefore, having your loins girt about with truth [the knowledge of the whole word of God] , and having on the breastplate of righteousness [of keeping the whole word of God]

6:15 And your feet shod [walk and live the gospel of salvation and peace with God by being zealous to keep God's word as Christ kept the Father's word] with the preparation of the gospel of peace;

6:16 Above all, taking the shield of faith [believe an trust in our God, thereby quenching temptation], wherewith ye shall be able to quench all the fiery darts of the wicked. **6:17** And take the helmet of salvation [protect our minds with a knowledge of the salvation of God], and **the sword of the Spirit, which is the word of God:** [Destroy false teachings by the truth of the whole word of God.]

Pray without ceasing. Even when not praying verbally, have your minds set on the Word of God and sing godly songs and psalms carefully considering their meaning through the day. Meditate day and night on the meaning of every Word of God. And in so doing you will internalize the nature of God and cast out the temptation to sin!

6:18 Praying always with all prayer and supplication in the Spirit, and watching thereunto with all perseverance and supplication for all saints;

In our Bible Studies one thing is overwhelming clear: Whenever Israel followed God, they were victorious; and whenever they tried to fight the enemy their own way, while not being faithful to God, they were defeated.

This is also true in the spiritual sense, concerning the fight against sin. Satan is far smarter and stronger than we are; and whenever we try to fight sin on our own; we are guaranteed to fail!

No matter how we struggle on our own with temptation and sin, we fail and continually slip to do the thing that we are struggling with. Paul presents the answer in Romans 8 where he says that we must walk [live] in the spirit, and the flesh must be brought into submission to the spirit of God to overcome sin. 1 John 2:6 also says that we are to walk [live as Christ walks [lives]

How to be fully victorious over sin

The solution is to follow Christ and be zealous to live by every Word of God; then Christ the Overcomer, will dwell in us through the Spirit of God; and will go before us to give us the victory over sin; IF we will only follow him!

What I am talking about is making a fully dedicated commitment to go and sin no more, and then to seek the help of our Mighty Overcomer in our struggle with sin.

We cannot overcome Satan on our own; We need the full power of Jesus Christ in us to overcome; but with the Ultimate Overcomer dwelling in us: Full Victory over sin is assured!

Consider that in our youth we were totally committed to our spouse, in such passionate love that we had eyes for no other! If we have the same passionate love for Christ and the whole word of God; the struggle against sin would be so much easier because nothing would be a temptation to sin against and offend our LORD.

The very first point is the real depth of our commitment to Christ and every Word of God. You see, it is a mater of loving our LORD and God's Word, MORE than we love the pleasures of sin.

2 Timothy 3:1 This know also, that in the last days perilous times shall come. **3:2** For men shall be lovers of their own selves, covetous, boasters, proud, blasphemers, disobedient to parents, unthankful, unholy, **3:3** Without natural affection, trucebreakers, false accusers, incontinent, fierce, despisers of those that are good, **3:4** Traitors, heady, highminded, lovers of pleasures more than lovers of God;

3:5 Having a form [an appearance of godliness but no substance] **of godliness, but denying the power thereof** [Not accepting the authority of scripture to obey it, and therefore lacking any power to overcome.]: **from such turn away.**

When we call the Sabbath holy and proceed to habitually pollute it, when we pollute God's High Days by buying in restaurants, and by observing days as God's days, which are not sanctified by scripture but on the dates which we chose. When we idolize men, exalting their word above the Word of God and are full of many self justified sins; how is it that we expect to overcome other sins?

Brethren, we struggle with some sins and cannot overcome, lacking the power of the Holy Spirit; because we are committed to our idols of men and corporate entities, and are NOT committed to passionately love the whole word of God!

Today we are full of sin and have rejected the Word of God for our own false traditions, and then we complain that we have no power to overcome and must struggle with personal issues!

The very first means to overcome sin; is to learn and live by every Word of God and repudiate our idols and our sins; and follow on to sin no more zealously learning, keeping every Word of God !

Only then will Christ go before us to cleanse us and give us victory over sin! We struggle with sin and cannot overcome, because we love the pleasures of sin more than we love the word of God. Therefore we find ourselves tempted to sin, and seeing sin as pleasurable we fall to temptation, because we are not fully committed to the word of God.

We ask and receive not, because we are not pleasing to God!

Let me be absolutely clear; if we show your contempt for the Word of God by buying in restaurants on Sabbath or High Days; and exalt the false words and false traditions of men above the Word of God; We have quenched God's Spirit and the power to overcome sin will leave us.

The very first thing that is needed to be victorious in a personal struggle over sin; is to sincerely repent of all our many sins, and to adamantly and passionately commit ourselves to turn from ALL SIN; and to zealously learn, keep and teach the whole Word of God; and to follow our Mighty Overcomer, who will give us the victory!

Then ASK for, and use the spirit of power, that God the Father gives to all those who obey Him (Acts 5:32). Only then will Christ empower us to overcome, for the breaking of one point of the law is the breaking of the whole law.

Today's Ekklesia is full of sin and the brethren exalt their idols and teach to tolerate sin for the sake of organizational unity; and then they wonder why they have no power!

The truly converted have little struggle with sin, for they depend on their God to deliver them and simply reject all temptation as an offense against their Beloved.

Our relationship with our Mighty One is supposed to be one of intense intimate passionate love; always longing to be held in his protective loving arms and never being tempted to do anything to displease him. To overcome sin, we must start with a proper relationship with our Glorious espoused Husband!

If we would only put our trust in our Mighty One who killed the first born of Egypt and parted the sea; we could reject any temptation to sin, as unthinkable!

The Resurrection

Definition "Soul": The word "soul" has two very different meanings

1. Any physical being; for example thirty souls sailed on the ship is simply a reference to thirty persons;
2. A spirit, by definition "life or mind".

Bible study on the soul or spirit can be confusing at times due to the difficulty of clearly understanding the intended meaning; however there is no confusion in the Hebrew and Greek.

The Hebrew word "nephesh" in Genesis 2:7 means a physical being and refers to any physical life from butterflies to elephants, from chickadees to man. The Hebrew word "ruach" refers to the breath, mind, or spirit of life.

The Greek words "psuche" or pneuma" also refer to the breath, mind, or spirit of life.

The only way to really understand the intended meaning and establish biblical doctrine correctly is to go to the Hebrew or Greek words in their proper context. With this in mind let us go to the most interesting passage of Genesis 2:7

Genesis 2:7 And the Lord God formed man of the dust of the ground, and **breathed into his nostrils the breath** [breath or spirit] **of life; and man became a living soul** [nephesh, creature].

We all know that breathing air into a dead person does not bring life if the spark of that something which we call life is not present. God may well have breathed air into the man, but he also breathed the spark or spirit which we call life into the man.

The passage teaches us that man is flesh like every other animal and also has the spark or spirit of life like every other animal. Yet there is a vast difference in intellect and capacity between men and animals, which tells us that the spirit in man is superior - or there is far more of it - to the spirit of life in the animals. Animals have a certain spirit of life and capacity to do things, but mankind has a vastly superior spirit of life and capacity for accomplishment.

The things of man are so far above the animal intellect that the animals simply cannot understand the things of men.

Yes, there is a spirit in man that is superior to the spirit of animals, and there is also a Spirit of God which is so superior to the spirit in man, that man simply cannot understand the things of God.

1 Corinthians 2:11 For what man knoweth the things of a man, save the **spirit of man which is in him?** even so the things of God knoweth no man, but the **Spirit of God**.

The Holy Spirit of God is further above the spirit in man, than the spirit in man is above the amoeba.

1 Corinthians 2:14 But the natural [the spirit "the life and mind" of man] man receiveth not the things of the Spirit of God: for they are foolishness unto him: neither can he know them, because they are spiritually discerned.

God made Adam perfect in every way and Adam lay there in all his perfect splendour, absolutely useless; UNTIL God turned the power on, but giving him the spirit or spark of power that is life.

The spirit in all physical creatures is the spark or essence of life, and that spirit can be provided at several different levels.

The caterpillar lives but it does not have the capacity of a sheep dog; A sheep dog at work is a wonder to behold but it does not have the intellect of a man. A man is a true wonder in the things which he can do; but he is not even close to understanding the wisdom of the Creator God.

Therefore we can say that the spirit not only gives life but at an ascending level it imparts an improved intellect and thinking ability. It is also self-evident that an improved intellect and ability to think is based on memory capacity, if we cannot remember what we learn we cannot progress.

Spirit is the essence of life and as its power [or quantity of presence] is increased, the power to think, learn and remember is increased. That is to say; when the amount of the spirit of life is increased, the level of intelligence also increases. God has 100% full power and man has maybe 3% power and the animals even less.

God is fully spirit but man is flesh with a very tiny amount of human spirit in that flesh, and when the flesh wears out the plug is pulled, the spirit leaves and the flesh perishes.

Just as the flesh must have the spirit of man to function; the spirit must be plugged into the flesh to function. Once the spirit in man is separated from the flesh of man it becomes inanimate.

By way of illustration; we could all get together and build the most awesome computer ever made and it would sit there absolutely useless: UNTIL the power was turned on! Or an audio tape cannot function or be played unless it is plugged into a player.

Ecclesiastes 9:5 For the living know that they shall die: but **the dead know not any thing**,

What happens at death?

Ecclesiastes 12:7 Then shall the dust [flesh] return to the earth as it was: and the spirit shall return unto God who gave it

From the point of the death of our flesh, our spirits are removed by God and kept in a secure place against the appointed time when they will be judged, either immediately being given a new body of spirit and eternal life, or being placed back into a new body of flesh so as to receive an opportunity to sincerely repent and turn to godliness and then also be given a new spirit body and eternal life.

Revelation 6:9 And when he had opened the fifth seal, **I saw under the altar** [Context: In heaven] **the souls** [pneuma, spirits] **of them that were slain for the word of God, and for the testimony which they held:**

Did you catch that? The spirits of the godly are waiting, being stored in heaven, under the altar before the throne of God the Father!

They are not animate, not having bodies of either flesh or a spirit body at this time; yet they are figuratively crying out for deliverance, to be given their reward of eternal spiritual bodies, and for the bloodshed of the called out on the earth to stop. This scripture speaks of the overcoming spirits of godly people being kept under the heavenly altar, but it is not clear where the other still uncalled spirits are being kept.

If the spirits of the godly dead are stored in heaven, why will the graves be opened on the earth?

The context must be understood. God's two servants have been preaching the true Gospel for 3 1/2 years and in that time have attracted the attention of the whole world. Then they are killed and lie dead for 3 1/2 days before the whole world.

Without doubt these two have spoken to the world about the power of God to raise the dead who are faithful to God. The whole mass of humanity has heard their preaching and is now waiting to see if the resurrection will really happen! Through them and the miracles and doctrine God has provided to them; God has caught the attention of the whole of humanity.

Billions are watching: Will these two come back to life and stand on their feet to rise up into heaven, or have they lied and is the Miracle worker from the Vatican the true man of God after all.

Then Christ will come with his angels and raise these two up, and also change those in Christ who are alive; and there will be massive earthquakes worldwide and Christ will bring the spirits of the dead in Christ - the Chosen - with him to change them to spirit in the sight of all the nations.

The event will be astonishing to the whole of humanity and Israel will repent and seek Christ and his deliverance with all their hearts. Israel will remember the preaching of God's two which they had laughed at; and they will be dumbstruck at the resurrection or change of probably millions.

Then they and all humanity will see the power of God to deliver them from their existential distress and will cry out to Christ to deliver them. The account is in Revelation 11 and in Revelation 11:13 we see the end result of these things in the sincere repentance and acceptance of the Saviour.

Revelation 11:13 . . . .and the remnant were affrighted [amazed, astonished], and gave glory to the God of heaven.

Is the Spirit in Man Immortal?

Many believe that man has an immortal soul [spirit] which after physical death goes to a place of judgment where a decision is made by God to cast this immortal soul into eternal torment or into eternal bliss.

The word "soul" means the breath of life, the mind, or spirit of man and animals. [Psuche] meaning spirit See Strong's G 5590 The "soul" is really the mind or spirit of life in a living body; whether man or animal.

Ezekiel 18:4 Behold, all **soul**s are mine; as the **soul** of the father, so also the **soul** of the son is mine: **the soul that sinneth, it shall die.**

Romans 6:23 **For the wages of sin is death; but the gift of God is eternal life through Jesus Christ our Lord.**

All who have sinned have earned the wages of sin which is death, but through sincere repentance and the GIFT of the application of the sacrifice of Jesus Christ and the gift of the Holy Spirit, people can be saved from the death which they deserve.

We see from Jesus' own words that men are not able to kill the soul or spirit in man; but that God is able to kill and destroy the soul [spirit in man].

Matthew 10:28 And fear not them which kill the body, but are not able to kill the soul: but rather **fear him which is able to destroy both soul** [psuche, mind, life force] **and body** [flesh] **in hell.**

Yes, the word "soul" does mean the mind and life force or spirit in man; and animals. No, the word "soul" does not mean an immortal or eternal being.

Man is not and does not have an eternal immortal soul or spirit; God can destroy the "soul" both spirit and body.

Romans 6:23 For the wages of sin is death; but the gift of God is eternal life through Jesus Christ our Lord.

Eternal life is the gift of God and is given to all those who sincerely repent of all PAST sin and commit to go and sin no more.

Acts 5:32 And we are his witnesses of these things; and so is also the Holy Ghost, **whom God hath given to them that obey him**.

If we sincerely repent and enter a baptismal commitment to STOP sinning, and we then follow through with that commitment, God's Holy Spirit will be given to dwell within us and we will be resurrected to an eternal spirit body.

Romans 6:4 Therefore we are buried with him by baptism into death: that like as Christ was raised up from the dead by the glory of the Father, even so we also should walk in newness of life.

Romans 8:11 But if the Spirit of him that raised up Jesus from the dead dwell in you, he that raised up Christ from the dead shall also quicken your mortal bodies by his Spirit that dwelleth in you.

Jesus Christ gave his life to redeem us from all repented PAST sins, and if we STOP sinning and go forward to diligently internalize the nature of God the Father and Jesus Christ through diligently learning and living by every Word of God; then God's Spirit will dwell in us and we shall be raised to a new life just like Jesus Christ was raised from the dead to a glorious eternal spirit body!

1 Thessalonians 4:16 For the Lord himself shall descend from heaven with a shout, with the voice of the archangel, and with the trump of God: and the dead in Christ shall rise first: **4:17** Then we which are alive and remain shall be caught up together with them in the clouds, to meet the Lord in the air: and so shall we ever be with the Lord. **4:18** Wherefore comfort one another with these words.

The promise of an eternal throne made to David, was a promise of a resurrection to eternal life, to sit upon his throne FOREVER!

David was a man after God's own heart (Acts 13:22) because he NEVER worshiped other gods, and because whenever he sinned he quickly and sincerely repented just as soon as he realized that he had sinned.

The resurrection of David

Hosea 3:5 Afterward shall the children of Israel return, and **seek the Lord their God, and David their king**; and shall fear the Lord and his goodness in the latter days.

When Christ comes, he will set a resurrected David back upon his throne, to rule all Israel FOREVER, thus fulfilling God's promise to David!

Ezekiel 34:23 And I will set up one shepherd over them, and he shall feed them, **even my servant David;** he shall feed them, and he shall be their shepherd. **34:24** And I the Lord will be their God, and my servant David a prince among them; I the Lord have spoken it.

Ezekiel 37:21 And say unto them, Thus saith the Lord God; Behold, I will take the children of Israel from among the heathen, whither they be gone, and will gather them on every side, and bring them into their own land:

37:22 And I will make them one nation in the land upon the mountains of Israel; and one king shall be king to them all: and they shall be no

more two nations, neither shall they be divided into two kingdoms any more at all.

37:23 Neither shall they defile themselves any more with their idols, nor with their detestable things, nor with any of their transgressions: but I will save them out of all their dwellingplaces, wherein they have sinned, and will cleanse them: so shall they be my people, and I will be their God.

37:24 And **David my servant shall be king over them**; and they all shall have one shepherd: they shall also walk in my judgments, and observe my statutes, and do them [thus showing that the whole law and every Word of God will also be kept forever!]. **37:25** And they shall dwell in the land that I have given unto Jacob my servant, wherein your fathers have dwelt; and they shall dwell therein, even they, and their children, and their children's children for ever: and my servant David shall be their prince for ever.

Let us diligently live by every Word of God, and let us be as quick to repent as David was, so that God's Spirit will dwell in us also; and we shall be raised up to eternal life with David, just as God the Father raised up Jesus Christ!

God is molding us into beings fit to inherit eternal life and our present trials in this temporary physical life are as nothing compared to an eternal life of prosperity and peace with God!

The Holy Spirit

The first mention of the Spirit of God is found in Genesis 1:2 where the Hebrew word Ruach is used, which word means "the mind, the life, the presence". The Holy Spirit is the "mind, the life, the presence and power of God" of God.

The spirit in a particular person is the life, mind, all past experiences and the memories and the nature of that particular person

The spirit of Abraham is the mind, the intellect, and contains the nature and experiences of the person Abraham, and when Abraham is resurrected it is that spirit of Abraham which will be plugged into a new body and will become a functional living person again: The SAME person with a new body.

This is also true for all humanity, because each person has his very OWN spirit of man; the same kind of spirit as other people yet unique to himself, because it has recorded his unique personal experiences, nature and thoughts. Then when each person is resurrected, his own personal version of the spirit in man - containing all that he is - will be plugged into his own new personal body and he will become fully functional and will live again.

Therefore the Holy Spirit of God is the mind, the life, the experience and the wisdom from that intellect combined with that experience it is also the presence, the very nature and power of BOTH God the Father and Jesus Christ.

The Trinity

There are those that teach that the Holy Spirit is a unique individual being like Jesus Christ and God the Father, misunderstanding and using one main scripture to appear to support the idea of a Trinity.

The scripture used to support a trinity

1 John 5:6 This is he that came by water and blood, even Jesus Christ; not by water [baptism] only, but by water and blood [sacrifice]. And it is the Spirit that beareth witness [God's Spirit dwelling in us and empowering us to live by every Word of God is a true proof that we are of God.], because the Spirit is truth.

Meaning, that the Holy Spirit dwelling in us through our calling and repentance and the water of baptism and the blood sacrifice of Jesus Christ the Lamb of God; is proof positive of our conversion.

The fact that the presence of God's Spirit is a witness of the power of God in no way indicates that the Holy Spirit is a unique individual; quite the contrary, since it dwells within us just like the spirit of man dwells within us, we know that God's Spirit is simply the nature of God added to the nature of man in us.

5:7 For there are three that bear record in heaven, the Father, the Word [the Son Jesus Christ and every Word of God], and the Holy Ghost: and these three are one.

The three being one has nothing to do with three beings somehow being one being; it merely means that these three are united as one in their witness that the converted are the children of God.

Our calling by God the Father, our baptism [the water] and the application of the sacrifice of the Lamb of God [the blood] and the presence of the Holy Spirit in us, all bear witness to the fact that we have sincerely repented and been converted and have become the children of God.

5:8 And there are three that bear witness in earth, the Spirit [God's Spirit dwelling in us], and the water [baptism], and the blood [the sacrifice of Christ applied to us]: and these three agree in one.

These three agree in one, simply means that they agree together in full unity bearing witness of our conversion.

The water of our baptismal commitment, the application of the blood sacrifice of Jesus Christ and the presence of the Holy Spirit of God dwelling in us bears witness - are the proofs - that we are the children of God.

The Spirit of God is not a unique personal being; it is the mind, the life, the presence and the power of God, some of which can be given to every person.

Just as there is one spirit of man, some of which is given to every human being; there is one Spirit of God, some of which can be given to every human being in varying quantities as God so wills.

The Holy Spirit is not an independent being, it is the very nature, the mind, the life, the intellect, the presence and the power of God; for it is written that God is Spirit and God is also Holy. Therefore the presence of the Holy Spirit is the presence of some of the nature of God, given to dwell wherever God wills.

Throughout the scriptures air [breath] or wind, fire, pure olive oil and water are used to illustrate the nature of the Holy Spirit. These different symbols are instructional allegories to teach us about the different aspects of the Holy Spirit.

At the very beginning the spirit in man is pictured by the breathing of God into the man and after his resurrection and ascension to the God the Father to be accepted by Him Jesus gave the Holy Spirit to some of his disciples like this:

John 20:22 And when he had said this, he breathed on them, and saith unto them, Receive ye the Holy Ghost.

The sounding of the trumpets in the Tabernacle/Temple was a resounding proclamation of the presence of God through God's Spirit, via the air blasting through the trumpets making a great sound.

Jesus himself describes God's Spirit as a wind which has power but cannot be seen.

John 3:5 Jesus answered, Verily, verily, I say unto thee, Except a man be born of water and of the Spirit, he cannot enter into the kingdom of God. **3:6** That which is born of the flesh is flesh; and that which is born of the Spirit is spirit. **3:7** Marvel not that I said unto thee, Ye must be born again.

3:8 The wind bloweth where it listeth, and thou hearest the sound thereof, but canst not tell whence it cometh, and whither it goeth: so is every one that is born [resurrected to spirit] of the Spirit.

The Holy Spirit or Shekinah represented by fire fell on the Tabernacle on its dedication to indicate the presence of God in the Tabernacle.

Leviticus 9:24 And there came a fire out from before the Lord, and consumed upon the altar the burnt offering and the fat: which when all the people saw, they shouted, and fell on their faces.

The Holy Spirit or Shekinah represented by fire also fell on the Temple at its dedication to indicate the presence of God in the Temple.

2 Chronicles 7:1 Now when Solomon had made an end of praying, the fire came down from heaven, and consumed the burnt offering and the sacrifices; and the glory of the Lord filled the house. **7:2** And the priests could not enter into the house of the Lord, because the glory of the Lord had filled the Lord's house. **7:3** And when all the children of Israel saw how the fire came down, and the glory of the Lord upon the house, they bowed themselves with their faces to the ground upon the pavement, and worshipped, and praised the Lord, saying, For he is good; for his mercy endureth for ever

The Holy Spirit or Shekinah represented by fire also fell on the converted brethren at the Feast of Pentecost to indicate the presence of God in the spiritual Temple of God's spiritual people.

Acts 2:3 And there appeared unto them cloven tongues like as of fire, and it sat upon each of them.

Fire purifies destroying all uncleanness, just as God's Holy Spirit - if used and followed - will destroy all sin and uncleanness out of God's people leaving behind the pure refined gold of godly character.

The priests were anointed with the Holy Oil which is symbolic of the Holy Spirit and the presence of godliness.

The two lampstands burned the holy oil giving light in the tabernacle; were an allegory that the Holy Spirit in us causes the light of our godly example to shine brightly; if we make use of and follow it to live by every Word of God.

The Waters of Salvation and the Woman at the Well

John 4:7 There cometh a woman of Samaria to draw water [from a well in Samaria]:, and Jesus said to her, Give me a drink. **4:8** (For His disciples had gone away [and He was just sitting there alone]. **4:9** Then said the woman of Samaria to Him, How is it that thou, being a Jew, asks water of me which am a woman of Samaria? for the Jews have no dealings with the Samaritans. **4:10** Jesus answered her and said, If you knew the gift of God, and who is it that says to you, Give me to drink; you would have asked of Him [that He give drink to you], t**hat He would give to you living water.**

4:11 The woman said unto Him, Sir, thou has nothing to draw up water with, and the well is very deep: from whence, then, hast thou this living water? 4:12 Art thou greater than our father Jacob, who gave us the well, and drank thereof himself, and his children, and his cattle? 4:13 Jesus answered and said unto her, Whosoever drinks of this water shall thirst again.

Whoever drinks physical water is going to get thirsty again. Drink of physical water and after a while we get thirsty again; and we drink again, and we get thirsty again and so on.

4:14 But whosoever drinks of the water that I shall give him shall never thirst; for the water that I shall give him shall be in him a well of water, springing up into everlasting life.

The water that Jesus Christ gives is the Word of God and the Holy Spirit, which leads us into eternal life. And that water of the Spirit is in us and growing in us and flowing in us and was poured out on us, because we were called by God the Father and have sincerely repented, committing to go and sin no more; to keep all of the ways of God and to follow God's Spirit.

We took the gift of God's Holy Spirit represented by the living water into ourselves when we sincerely repented and committed to follow and be cleanses by the Water of the Word of God.

He who has imbibed the living water, has taken into himself the whole Word of God and with it the Holy Spirit. The person who is zealous for the Word of God and thirsts after the living water of Salvation; has eternal life dwelling in him, unless he later rejects God's Spirit and quenches it, but as long as he is faithful, he has eternal life living in him.

John 7:37

On the occasion of the seventh or last day of the Feast of Tabernacles - on the last Feast of Tabernacles that Jesus observed before He was crucified the next spring - was used by Christ to teach that He was the Messiah, the source of salvation, the source of the Living Water of Salvation for all Israel and for all mankind.

We can understand this from the event in John 7:37 that the sixth day of the Feast of Tabernacles was drawing to a close and toward the seventh day of the Feast of Tabernacles which was the Last Great Day of the Feast of Tabernacles, not because it was a holy convocation, but because it was the "Day of the Great Hosanna".

It was on this day, at the time when the priests had come from Siloam with the golden pitcher, and poured its contents to the base of the altar, and the psalms have been sung to the sound of the flute, the people responding and worshiping and rejoicing as the priest three times sounded three full blasts upon the two silver trumpets that Jesus cried out loudly in the temple to all the people.

As all of this was happening, suddenly, from the midst of the congregation came a loud, strong, clear voice; from a man, just as Psalm 118 had been completed.

> **Psalm 118:14,** The LORD is my strength and my song, and is become my salvation. **118:15** The voice of rejoicing and salvation is in the tabernacles of the righteous: the right hand of the LORD doeth valiantly [for His people]. **118:16** The right hand of the LORD is exalted: the right hand of the LORD has done valiantly.
>
> **118:17,** I shall not die, but live, and declare the works of the LORD. **118:18** The LORD hath chastened me sore: but He hath not given me over to death. **118:19** Open to me the gates of righteousness [which is commandment-keeping]: I will go into them [through the gates of righteousness], and I will praise God: **118:20** This gate of the LORD, into which the righteous shall enter.
>
> When we are called and we repent of sin we, then enter into the gates of righteousness which is [righteousness is to live by every Word of God] the salvation of God.
>
> **118:21** I will praise thee: for thou hast heard me, and become my salvation.

Christ cried out; **John 7:37…'If any man thirst, let him come unto me and drink.'** With those words, He was clearly telling all the people: I am your salvation, I am Messiah, I am the Christ. It is through Me that you receive salvation! and that impressed the people and it shocked the leaders.

Now when Jesus said this, He said if any MAN thirst. He did not say if any Jew or any Israelite thirsts, He said ANY MAN, thereby revealing that salvation was being opened up to ALL humanity, and that the Feast of Tabernacles refers to the main harvest of humanity.

And He cried out in the midst of the seventh day of the Feast of Tabernacles, not on the Eighth Day as some wrongly suppose, because they misunderstand the term Great Day of the Feast.

John 7:37, In the last day, that Great Day of the Feast [of Tabernacles], **Jesus stood and cried out, saying, If any man thirst, let him come unto Me and drink. 7:38 He that believeth on Me, as the scriptures hath said, out of his belly shall flow rivers of living water.**

That is, God pours His Spirit out on the sincerely repentant who are His; those who zealously work to live by every Word of God will filled with the Holy Spirit, the spiritual Water of eternal life.

Then as the Spirit of God fills the people, they are enabled to follow God and to live by every Word of God.

. . . (But of this spake he of the Spirit [This is a direct quote; revealing that this Living Water represents the Holy Spirit.]**, 7:39 But this spake He of the Spirit, which they that believe on Him should receive: for the Holy Spirit was not yet poured out or not yet given; because that Jesus was not yet glorified.)**

He had not yet been sacrificed and raised up. **7:40** Many of the people [many of them], when they heard this saying, [they] said, **Of a truth this is that Prophet.**

The term 'that prophet' is a reference to Jesus by Moses, who said 'behold the day will come when a prophet will arise like unto myself, him you shall follow, him you shall obey.'

And they remembered the words of Moses and they said, 'of a truth, this is that prophet that Moses spake of.' And that prophet was Jesus Christ. That Prophet did not any other man, but Jesus the Christ ONLY! **'This spake He of the spirit which they that believe on Him should receive.'** This is clearly explaining the water as representing the Holy Spirit; and revealing Jesus the Christ as "That Prophet".

We can go back to the first verse again, '**In the last day, that Great Day of the Feast** [The seventh day of Tabernacles], **Jesus stood and cried and said if any man thirst, let him come unto Me and drink, and he that believes on Me as the scripture hath said, out of his belly shall flow rivers of living water.**'

The more zealously we study and learn and keep the whole Word of God, the more of God's Spirit and the more understanding we will be given.

The less we study and the less we zealously keep the Word of God, and the more we compromise, the more the Spirit will be held back from us, and we will be quenching that Spirit, and over time will have less and less.

As Christ said, 'whosoever who believeth in me', which is **anyone, everyone that believes in Christ, not just believes but acts on that belief having the works of faith, because faith without works is dead.** Anyone who believes on Christ and starts to keep His commandments, seeks to learn His ways, diligently works to zealously obey Him, to become like Him, to try and please Him; is going to have the living waters of salvation poured out upon them.

We need to realize how much we need God, because we cannot save ourselves. It is impossible. And no other man can save us either.

Salvation is a direct personal responsibility. We as individuals have to respond to the call and go directly to Christ and to God the Father and to the Word of God. Focus on that. Do not focus on anyone just because he says he is somebody; but take those words and test them by the Word of God and always the Word of God MUST come first.

Jesus Christ is the Fountain of the Living Waters of Salvation:

Jeremiah 17:13 O Lord, the hope of Israel, all that forsake thee shall be ashamed, and they that depart from me shall be written in the earth, because they have forsaken **the Lord, the fountain of living waters** [the Living Waters being God's Holy Spirit].

The Spirit of Power and Eternal Life

When we sincerely repent of all PAST sin and we commit ourselves through baptism to STOP sinning and to live by every Word of God; we are reconciled to God the Father by the application of the atoning redeeming sacrifice of Jesus Christ; and at that point God will give us a portion of the Holy Spirit - a portion of the very nature and power of God - to dwell within us

Romans 8:11 But if the Spirit of him that raised up Jesus from the dead dwell in you, he that raised up Christ from the dead shall also quicken your mortal bodies by his Spirit that dwelleth in you.

Roman 8:14 For as many as are led by the Spirit of God, they are the sons of God.

The gift from God of his Holy Spirit enables us to become like God because the Holy Spirit is the essence and nature of God.

The Holy Spirit is the very nature and mind of God which is in God the Father and Jesus Christ the Son, and God can give a portion his Holy Spirit - his nature and mind - to dwell in us together with our spirit; empowering us to learn, internalize, retain and to live by every Word of God; growing spiritually and ultimately becoming holy as God is holy.

Paul writes **Romans 7:12** Wherefore the law is holy, and the commandment holy, and just, and good.

Godly love is about how we live and act; and to love God is to do as He says and docs. Words of love and emotional feelings, without the actions of loving God by keeping His Word, are false and deceitful and are not godly love at all. Many have been deceived into proclaiming words of love without the actions of loving God as God commands us to love Him and others.

1 John 3:18 My little children, let us not love in word, neither in tongue; but **in deed and in truth**.

John 4:24 **God is a Spirit**: and they that worship him must worship him in spirit and in truth.

Leviticus 11:45 For I am the Lord that bringeth you up out of the land of Egypt, to be your God: ye shall therefore be holy, for **I am holy**.

1 Peter 1:16 Because it is written, Be ye holy; for **I am holy.**

The Holy Spirit [the nature of God] is the Spirit of power and of a sound godly mind.

2 Timothy 1:7 For God hath not given us the spirit of fear; but **of power** [self-control], **and of** [godly] **love, and of a sound** [godly] **mind.**

God's Holy Spirit elevates the capacity of the human mind [the spirit in man] from the level of complete incompatibility with God, to the level of a child in godliness, allowing us to grow in godly understanding and conduct, learning to be like God, just as a child learns from its parents.

God's Spirit is the Spirit of Truth and is the very nature of God; God is Truth and the Spirit 0of God is truth. God's Spirit cannot be divided against God or any part of the Word and nature of God; for the Spirit of God is the very nature of God.

From the receipt of the gift of God's Holy Spirit, that Spirit begins to lead us into the truth of God and towards a passionate zeal to be like God - in full unity with God - through living by every Word of God.

Since the Spirit of God is the mind and nature of God; wherever God or godliness is, God's Spirit is also present.

Therefore it is written that God dwells within each of His people through the agency of God's Spirit. That is, when God gives a portion of His Spirit to a person, a small bit of godliness is placed in that person, and from there the person must use [exercise] that Spirit by diligently seeking the truth which the Spirit is leading us into. This is the message of the parables of the pounds and talents (Luk 19:13-26, Mat 25:14-30)

We must follow the Holy Spirit by rejecting our own past errors and sins, and embracing all truth as we learn it. If we reject growth in the truth we are rejecting the lead of God's Spirit and quenching whatever amount of the Holy Spirit which we have been given.

Briefly, true conversions is a process which begins with God the Father calling us and working with us, opening our minds to understand a little truth; then we must respond positively to that call with an eagerness to learn more, to apply what we learn in the conduct of our lives and to sincerely repent of our PAST sins.

Then we are ready to make a baptismal commitment to sin no more, destroying the old sinful person in the water of baptism and rising up a new person committed to live by every Word of God from thenceforth and forever. At this point we are reconciled to God the Father by the application of the sacrifice of the Son and we may ask for the gift of the Holy Spirit.

Our Father will then give us a small amount of the Holy Spirit and if we follow it, continually rejecting error and learning and growing in godliness, internalizing the very nature of God through diligently learning and living by every Word of God; we shall overcome all wickedness. God IS a Holy Spirit; therefore the Holy Spirit is the nature, mind and presence of God. When God places his Holy Spirit somewhere, as in the Temple, or in someone, he is placing a bit of the nature and presence of God in that place or person.

God's Holy Spirit is given ONLY to those who sincerely repent of all past sins and commit to sin no more; through learning obeying and living by every Word of God from henceforth and forever more. We know this because God's Spirit is only given to those who obey God: **Acts 5:32** And we are his witnesses of these things; and so is also **the Holy Ghost, whom God hath given to them that obey him.**

When that repentance and commitment is made, the redeeming sacrifice of Jesus Christ will be applied to pay for our PAST sins now repented of, and we will be reconciled to God the Father who will give the gift of the Holy Spirit, or mind, nature, power and presence of God to dwell within us, which will lead and empower us to keep our commitment to become like God in every way.

> The Holy Spirit does not bring instant no effort personal perfection; it is an enabling power which will give us the ability to grasp spiritual things, but we must use that enablement to diligently seek to learn, understand and properly apply God's Word in our lives.

> We have been cut off from God by our sins and groping blindly in darkness; God's Spirit is like turning on a light so that we can see, but we must still make the effort to see, to learn, to understand and to properly apply the Word of God in our lives!

The presence of the Holy Spirit will manifest itself in certain ways often called the fruits [or indicators, or results] of the presence of the Holy Spirit, which will develop more and more over time, as we overcome more and more and grow in godliness.

We call the end results of anything, its consequences or fruits; the Holy Spirit in us produces these fruits in us.

Galatians 5:22 But the fruit of the Spirit is love, joy, peace, longsuffering, gentleness, goodness, faith, **4:23** Meekness, temperance: against such there is no law.

As we are faithful and progress in our godly development, God may also give us further gifts of the Holy Spirit to enable us to function as a help to others in the Ekklesia.

- For the past 6,000 years God the Father has been calling certain people to be reconciled to him through:
- Sincere repentance,
- A baptismal commitment to STOP sinning and to live by every Word of God,
- The application of the sacrifice of Jesus Christ, the Lamb of God to redeem us from our repented sins,
- The gift of the Holy Spirit and
- If we make a diligent effort to persevere and overcome all sin, and internalize the very nature of God; to become holy as God is holy, through the power of God's Spirit dwelling in us; then we will be changed to spirit and resurrected to eternal life.

The coming of Christ is now at hand; when Christ comes Satan will be removed for 1,000 years and God's Spirit will be poured out on all flesh **Joel 2:28** And it shall come to pass afterward, that I will pour out my spirit upon all flesh;

Then after the millennium Satan will be destroyed and all those who have lived and died in their sins will be resurrected back to physical life and given an opportunity to be called to reconciliation with God.

God's plan for personal salvation is to call out certain people to reconciliation with him, through:

1. Responding positively to God's call by believing, and then
2. Adding to that belief the works of faith, which are sincere repentance from living contrary to the Word of God
3. Making a baptismal commitment to STOP sinning and to live by every Word of God in future, then
4. The atoning sacrifice of Jesus Christ, the Lamb of God; will be applied to us, and we will be reconciled to God the Father through the forgiveness of our sincerely repented PAST sins, and

5. We shall be given the gift of God's Holy Spirit to dwell within us enabling us to learn, retain and live by every Word of God

6. If we then persevere to diligently internalize the very nature of God through serious study, learning and by passionately applying the Word of God to our lives.

7. We shall be at peace with God and we will receive the gift of the resurrection to eternal life.

In God's own timing ALL humanity will receive the same opportunity and the vast majority of mankind will be brought into the Family of God, which is what the Biblical Festivals are all about!

This book is about the process of Personal Salvation, for studies into the overall plan pictured by God's Biblical Harvest Festivals please see the Spring and Fall Festivals books.

The entirety of the New Testament is an explanation of the New Covenant. Please see our Commentary/Studies through the Gospels and Epistles or visit our website.

Visit Our Website

theshininglight.info

www.ingramcontent.com/pod-product-compliance
Lightning Source LLC
Chambersburg PA
CBHW081147230426
43664CB00018B/2837